MENNONITES IN THE GLOBAL VILLAGE

Leo Driedger

Before the 1940s, 90 per cent of Mennonites in North America lived on farms. Fifty years later, fewer than 10 per cent of Mennonites continue to farm, and more than a quarter of the population – the largest demographic block – are professionals. Mennonite teenagers are forced to contend with a broader definition of community, as parochial education systems are restructured to compete in a new marketplace. Women are adopting leadership roles alongside men. Many Mennonites have embraced modernity.

Leo Driedger explores the impact of professionalism and individualism on Mennonite communities, cultures, families, and religion, particularly in light of the scholarly work of futurists Alvin and Heidi Tofler, which has described the shift from a homogeneous industrial society to a diversified electronic society. Driedger contends that Mennonites are in a unique position in meeting the electronic challenge, having entered modern society relatively recently. He traces trends in Mennonite life by reviewing such issues as the shift from farming to professionalism, the role of mass media, and increased social interaction. Mennonites face many of the challenges that other religious minorities in North America encounter in the move to modernity, and this study provides in-depth insights into this transition.

LEO DRIEDGER is Professor of Sociology at the University of Manitoba.

LEO DRIEDGER

Mennonites in the Global Village

UNIVERSITY OF TORONTO PRESS
Toronto Buffalo London

© University of Toronto Press Incorporated 2000
Toronto Buffalo London
Printed in Canada

ISBN 0-8020-4181-7 (cloth)
ISBN 0-8020-8044-8 (paper)

Printed on acid-free paper

Canadian Cataloguing in Publication Data

Driedger, Leo, 1928–
Mennonites in the global village

Includes bibliographical references and index.
ISBN 0-8020-4181-7 (bound)   ISBN 0-8020-8044-8 (pbk.)

1. Mennonites – Canada – Social conditions.   2. Mennonites – United
States – Social conditions.   3. Mennonites – Cultural assimilation –
Canada.   4. Mennonites – Cultural assimilation – United States.   5. Infor-
mation society – Canada.   6. Information society – United States.   I. Title.

BX8118.5.D74 1999   305.6′87071   C99-932100-5

The University of Toronto Press acknowledges the financial assistance to its
publishing program of the Canada Council for the Arts and the Ontario
Arts Council.

This book has been published with the help of a grant from the Humanities
and Social Sciences Federation of Canada, using funds provided by the
Social Sciences and Humanities Research Council of Canada.

University of Toronto Press acknowledges the financial support for its publishing activities of the Government of Canada through the Book Publishing
Industry Development Program (BPIDP).

Canadä

To my four grandparents, whom I never met

Contents

Figures and Tables

Figures

Tables

Preface

I am writing this preface, sitting on a century-old chair that belonged to my grandmother, who could not have dreamed that her grandson, who still speaks her dialect and shares her Anabaptist beliefs, would be writing this on a computer. Dressed in centuries-old fashions, she bore silently the excommunication of her husband from the Old Colony Mennonite Church because he owned a store and car. She would have been pleased to know that this grandson, who went to school four times as long as she, lived in the big city most of his life, and taught at the university for thirty-five years, would still be an active Mennonite. In terms of our Mennonite identities, she and I represent the premodern, modern, and postmodern range, and in that we are very different in many ways. In this volume, I wish to show those differences, that process, that range.

In the 1990s, Mennonite historians in North America completed two historical series tracing the Mennonite experience from its beginnings through to 1970. A four-volume work on the Mennonite experience in the United States was published between 1985 and 1996, and a three-volume set on Mennonites in Canada was published between 1974 and 1996. The last volume in each series devoted a considerable amount of space to the effects of modernization, but historians are reluctant to treat current events, so they stopped at 1970.

Sociologists are less reluctant to work with the latest social trends, so this is a chance to trace Mennonite life and thought through the last thirty years into the 1990s, just before we enter a new millennium. We begin with the world premodern, modern, and postmodern settings, and then explore changing identities in North America, where the largest Mennonite continental concentration is located. To what extent have American and Canadian Mennonites left their local rural villages for the global information village? How have they fared in these modern and postmodern arenas?

Special thanks are due Darlene Driedger, without whose help this work would not have been possible.

Leo Driedger
Winnipeg, October 1998

MENNONITES IN THE GLOBAL VILLAGE

1

The Global Challenge

In the summer of 1998, two hundred Mennonites met in Bluffton, Ohio, to discuss 'Anabaptists and Postmodernity.' We also discussed the electronic information revolution, and how computers, e-mail, and the Internet were changing communication, human interaction, and communities. Theologians debated whether Mennonites should still seek to articulate universally recognizable truths, and historians argued about the viability of tracing linear patterns. Poets, novelists, and short-story writers called for more individual subjective examinations of the Mennonite psyche, while others were more determined than ever to take vows of stability in increasingly diverse hyper-modern multi-ethnic, multi-religious worlds. Fifty years after the Second World War, many Mennonites have moved from the safe rural village reserves to the urban global village. What better example could you find through which to explore what happens when a traditional religious group hits the wall of electronic information?

The Premodern, Modern, and Postmodern Revolutions

Peter Berger (1977:2) has suggested that 'the forces of modernization have descended like a gigantic steel hammer upon all the old communal institutions – clan, village, tribe, and region – distorting or greatly weakening them, if not destroying them altogether.' What happens when this hammer of modernity strikes a traditional religious group? How have North American Mennonites, who trace their roots to sixteenth-century Anabaptism, survived the encounter with modern forces?

There is a general restlessness among many scholars, including sociologists, that we are in the midst of a revolution, and business-as-usual will no longer do (Abbott 1997). This was apparent in 1996, when the journal *Contemporary Sociology* featured more than a dozen reviews of new books in the sociology of the postmodern revolution. Lawrence Cahoone's (1996) seven-hundred-page anthology, featuring forty-two contributors, is a good attempt at going back to premodern times to trace the rise of modernization into the present postmodern era. Cahoone organizes his *From Modernism to Postmodernism* volume by focusing on modern civilization and its critics, and suggests that we have problems with the meaning of 'postmodernism,' because we do not adequately understand what is 'modern.'

The Electronic Revolution

The new electronic information revolution crept upon us via the telegraph, telephone, radio, television, and computer, blossoming forth at the end of the twentieth century in fax, e-mail, the Internet, and more. At the end of the 1980s, the sociology department where I work changed from typewriters to computers. Five years ago, only one member in our department was on e-mail; by the end of the 1990s, those who don't have it are embarrassed to be without it. A majority now have 'voice mail' at home; cellular telephones are almost ubiquitous; and more and more people are going on-line with a home page, as computers become almost as common as telephones. While I am writing this, Kenneth's Starr's report to the American Congress is on the Internet for the whole world to see.

Demassified production – short runs of highly customized products – is the new cutting edge of manufacture (Tapscott 1998, 2–3). Labour unions in the mass-manufacturing sector are shrinking, and giant television networks shrivelling as new channels proliferate. The family system is also becoming 'demassified' as the extended family is almost gone. In modern times, the standard nuclear family is giving way to 'demassified' versions: single-parent households, live-alones, childless couples, and remarried couples are the new norm. The entire social structure changes as the homogeneity of modern society is replaced by the heterogeneity of the postmodern age.

The complexity of the new social system requires more and more information exchange among its units – companies, government agencies, hospitals, associations, institutions, even individuals. This creates a ravenous need for computers, digital telecommunications networks, and media (Tapscott 1998, 16). These fast-moving changes threaten to slash many of the existing economic links between rich economies and poor, and, within countries, between those who try to keep up and those who can't.

Nationalism is the ideology of the nation-state, which is the product of the Industrial Revolution. Agrarian societies wish to begin competition in the industrialization process, and soon demand independence and nationhood. Republics of the former Soviet Union, new countries of the dissolved Yugoslavia, the Czech and Slovak republics, which have emerged out of Czechoslovakia, Palestine and Israel, Quebec in Canada – all demand yesterday's emblems, including flags, armies, currencies, that define nation-state freedoms in the industrial Second Wave. However, postmodern economies are well on their way to puncturing national 'sovereignties,' which again must be changed to compete in the borderless world that McLuhan (1964) called 'the global village.' Change extends to reorganizing production and distribution of knowledge and communication, interrelating data in more ways, and assembling information and knowledge into larger symbols and models. The massive smokestack factory is being replaced with the borderless electronic information demassification of smaller units. Knowledge versus capital is a revolutionary change indeed. Knowledge-based technologies are reducing the need for massive inventories as instant information takes the place of high-cost inventory, thereby reducing taxes, insurance, and the costs of inventory management (Tapscott 1998, 38–40).

'Shakedown' in the Economy

Angus Reid's *Shakedown* (1996) is a rather frightening wake-up call to what is happening in the new digital economy. He charts the demise of the 'Spend-and-Share Era,' a term he uses to describe the period of national prosperity and optimism that characterized North America from the 1960s to the 1980s. Reid shows that we have entered a scary new era of corporate downsizing, declining government services, budget-cutting, and shrinking incomes. Technology and globalization seem to be killing more jobs than they are creating, while the top 20 per cent gets richer and the bottom 80 per cent poorer.

Reid (1996, 14–41) outlines how institutions such as governments, professions, and large corporations, which were beacons of safety and security during the past fifty years, are no longer making our lives as predictable in an age of discontinuity. He also outlines ten myths we must face: big is safe; growth is good for everyone; science and technology will save us; a good education means a good job; loyalty is all; location matters less; time is linear; events are predictable; culture is a sacred trust; and the public interest still counts. What could be more threatening to traditional security than to say that spatial patterns are obsolete, and that our familiar means of orientation – maps, calendars, and clocks – can no longer be depended upon? Empirical forms such as photographs, newspapers, and magazines are being replaced by fleeting electronic screens of the Internet, where images and messages are changed at will, with little time to think or ponder. Information is becoming a storm of particles: no single item remains long, and the whole is a confusion of vague impressions that stream past, but are not registered by, our consciousness.

In the 1960s the birth-control pill freed women to enter an era of experimentation with sex, unhampered by the fear of unwanted pregnancy. During this time, church attendance in Quebec dropped from 80 to 20 per cent, and the province's birth rate plunged from one of the highest to one of the lowest in the developed world. By 1968, Canadian households with a gas or electric stove had increased to 94 per cent, from 48 per cent in 1948 (Reid 1996, 46–7). During this period, persons in Canada offered safe haven to draft dodgers, the Catholic Church abandoned the Latin mass, astronauts walked in space, nuclear generating plants spewed out power, new plastics created disposable packaging, and downtowns began to decline as shoppers headed for the new suburban malls. There was an air of optimism: television became a new focus, the credit card was gaining popularity, manufacturing was pumping away at almost full capacity, inflation was below 3 per cent, and wages were growing at twice that rate; meanwhile, governments were spending on terrestrial space, bilingualism, multiculturalism, and the 1967 Montreal World's Fair (Reid 1996, 45–50).

'In 1969, Canada had no debt ... in 1996, the country was crippled with more than a $500-billion debt still reeling from the aftershock of the latest Quebec referendum' (Reid 1996, 70). How times have changed! The post-1960s Spend-and-Share era resulted in massive labour-force growth, voracious patterns of consumption, a burgeoning public sector, and the transition to an economy based on services rather than on resources or industry (Reid 1996, 71). However, a new era is taking shape, one in which television is fuelling consumerism and computers are multiplying our capacity to store and communicate information. Microsoft's Bill Gates is raising the ante and broadening our understanding of what this electronic technology can do. But few ask how we got here, or where we are going. E-mail and the Internet have opened a path to globalization; as a result, pressure is mounting for lower trade barriers, increasing use of global money lenders, the globalization of culture and world opinion. Capitalism has become supreme. In the meantime, technological societies are ageing, with increased longevity and declining fertility, facing the inevitability of baby boomers retiring and swamping society's capacity to support them.

Mennonites in the Global Village

The multidimensional complexity of change that characterizes the 1990s electronic information revolution has extended to all aspects of North American life, including to that of the Mennonites. Mennonites have survived for almost five hundred years, since the Protestant Reformation. While the Anabaptists, ancestors of the Mennonites, were very much in the thick of changes in the sixteenth century in continental Europe, many were persecuted and forced into the margins of their societies, where they became more conservative. In general, Mennonites resorted to agriculture as a safer means of making a living. However, after the Second World War, Mennonites in Canada and the United States (the countries having the largest concentration of Mennonites in the world today) re-entered the cities. This shift has resulted in enormous changes, linked to the three stages of modernization – namely, premodern, modern, and postmodern. To examine these changes as they affect Mennonites in North America, we need to consider the demographics of where Mennonites emerged, how they scattered into many countries of the world, and how they diversified in response to modernization.

Global Mennonite Membership

To get some sense of the dynamics of intertwined premodern, modern, and postmodern forces, let us trace some of the shifts in Mennonite demographics. In table 1.1 we see that, in 1984, almost half (46 per cent) of all world Mennonites lived in two countries – the United States and Canada.[1] Fifteen per cent lived in each of Africa and Asia, and about 12 per cent in each of Europe and Latin America. In 1998, a short

TABLE 1.1
World Mennonite Membership, 1984 and 1998

	% of world Mennonites		Number of countries		Mennonite membership		% Member increase (1984–98)	Organ- ized bodies 1998
	1984	1998	1984	1998	1984	1998		
North America	46.1	39.2	2	2	333,704	415,978	+25	31
Africa	14.8	30.4	11	12	107,221	322,708	+202	21
Asia and Pacific	15.7	14.8	8	9	113,504	157,059	+40	23
Latin America	10.7	9.7	23	24	76,698	102,050	+33	98
Europe	12.8	5.8	13	13	92,368	61,866	−32	19
Total	100	100	57	60	723,474	1,059,661	+46	192

Source: Mennonite World Conference 1984, 1998

generation later, important demographic shifts had taken place: the North American Mennonite population had dropped to 39 per cent; the African population had doubled, to 30 per cent; and the Mennonites in Europe (their place of origin) had dropped from 13 to only 6 per cent of the world Mennonite population. The number of countries in which Mennonites lived remained roughly the same (57 in 1984 and 60 in 1998).

The world Mennonite population grew from almost three-quarters of a million in 1984 to just over one million in 1998, which represented a 46 per cent increase in a short generation. This change varied greatly by continents. The Mennonite population in Europe, which dates back to 1525, as part of the Protestant Reformation, actually declined, from 92,368 in 1984 to 61,866 in 1998. African Mennonites, however, tripled, from 107,221 in 1984 to 322,708 in 1998. Asian membership growth, at 40 per cent, was closest to the world average, while Latin American (33 per cent) and North American (25 per cent) growth was below the average. While the U.S. and Canadian combined membership at one time represented over half of all world Mennonites, by 1998 their concentration, although still the largest, had dwindled to just over one-third.

It is quite obvious that Mennonite membership growth and decline vary enormously in the world. Thus, we need to examine the more detailed demographics in order to understand and explain the social dynamics. To what extent are demographic factors of births, deaths, and migration significant, and to what extent are modernization factors of education, urbanization, and industrialization important in explaining such enormous divergent change?

Historical Demographic Rise and Fall

To gain some sense of where Mennonites began, and where they still flourish, we begin by examining the European record (see table 1.2). The Anabaptists, who were the Mennonite forebears, began in Switzerland in 1525. In the wake of severe persecution and emigration, only 2,750 remained in 1984, a figure that had declined slightly, to 2,500 in 1998. A few years after the Swiss group was established, a branch formed in the Netherlands. This group is the source of the name Mennonite, after an early leader, Menno Simons. They were urbanized, having settled in Amsterdam especially, and there were still over 20,000 left in the Netherlands in 1984. However, by 1998 their numbers had declined, to under 14,000, apparently as a result of assimilation. After the early 1500s, persecution drove them eastward, to Poland, Czechoslovakia, and Ukraine, but none remained there after the two world wars. Even though large numbers left Ukraine for North America in significant migrations in the 1870s, 1920s, and 1940s/1950s, many still remained in the USSR, with an estimated 55,000 having survived the Russian Revolution, two world wars, and communism. In 1984, that group represented more than half of the 92,000 Mennonites in Europe. However, by 1998 there were barely 3,000 left. During this period, a dozen republics became independent of the Soviet Union to become the newly created Commonwealth of Independent States (CIS). Greater freedoms allowed most of the Mennonites to leave the CIS, and most of them went to Germany, a relocation that increased the German Mennonite population from 11,932 (West and East combined) in 1984 to 39,610 in 1998. Others came to the Americas as well.

As early as the 1600s some Swiss and German Mennonites came to the United States and Canada, but the largest migrations came to North America in the 1870s, 1920s, and 1940s/1950s. In 1984, the United States and Canada ranked first, with 46 per cent of all world Mennonites; however, this proportion had declined to 39 per cent by 1998, even though their numbers increased by 25 per cent, from 1984 to 1998. It is these children of the original European Mennonites who have modernized greatly that we wish to examine in much more detail in this book.

European Mennonites began mission work in the 1800s in Asia, as is

TABLE 1.2
Mennonite Population, 1984 and 1998

		Mennonite Membership	
	Country	1984	1998
Europe	USSR/CIS	55,000	3,350
	Netherlands	20,200	13,500
	Germany	11,932	39,610
	Switzerland	2,750	2,500
	France	2,000	2,000
	Austria	185	360
	Luxembourg	105	100
	Belgium	73	39
	Italy	66	189
	Spain	33	120
	England	15	88
	Ireland	9	10
		92,368	61,866
North America	U.S.A.	232,192	287,345
	Canada	101,512	128,633
		333,704	415,978
Asia and Pacific	Indonesia	62,911	87,466
	India	43,998	62,823
	Japan	2,710	3,450
	Philippines	2,500	1,576
	Taiwan	1,200	1,494
	Vietnam	150	115
	Hong Kong	35	–
	Australia	12	45
	China	–	90
		113,516	157,059
Latin America	Mexico	31,161	20,689
	Paraguay	13,939	25,009
	Bolivia	6,203	6,714
	Brazil	4,750	6,690
	Honduras	2,850	10,245
	Colombia	2,633	2,515
	Belize	2,591	3,131
	Nicaragua	2,412	6,600
	Dominican Republic	1,800	2,902
	Guatemala	1,789	5,972
	Argentina	1,576	3,070

Table 1.2 Mennonite Population, 1984 and 1998 (*concluded*)

	Country	Mennonite Membership 1984	Mennonite Membership 1998
	Uruguay	971	924
	Puerto Rico	909	750
	Haiti	900	924
	Costa Rica	850	2,025
	Chile	400	–
	Panama	400	700
	Jamaica	385	557
	Venezuela	85	591
	El Salvador	75	462
	Trinidad	44	160
	Ecuador	15	325
	Barbados	–	725
	Guyana	–	300
	Cuba	–	70
		76,698	102,050
Africa	Zaire/Congo	66,408	175,837
	Tanzania	13,614	32,100
	Ethiopia	7,000	57,011
	Zambia	6,000	12,026
	Zimbabwe	5,184	20,606
	Nigeria	5,000	7,268
	Kenya	2,653	11,646
	Ghana	854	3,022
	Angola	395	2,600
	Somalia	100	–
	Upper Volta	13	–
	South Africa	–	283
	Malawi	–	229
	Burkina Faso	–	80
		107,221	322,708
Totals		723,507	1,059,661

Source: Mennonite World Conference 1984, 1998

evident in the more than 60,000 Mennonites residing in Indonesia in 1984. By 1998, the Indonesian group had increased to 87,466 and was still the largest concentration of Mennonites in Asia. The second-largest Mennonite concentration in Asia began when missionaries from North America started work in India. By 1998 there were 62,823 Mennonites in India. Asian Mennonites increased by 40 per cent in a generation, between 1984 and 1998, about the world growth-rate average, representing about 15 per cent of all world Mennonites. These Mennonites were the first of non-European origin, of another race, living in very different cultures in which Christians are a tiny minority.

In the 1920s, some of the most conservative Canadian Mennonites tried to escape the pressures of assimilation by migrating to less-industrialized Mexico. In 1984, that group was still the largest in Latin America, but by 1998 they had declined by a third. Migration was again a factor. Although they had fled Canadian industrialization seventy years earlier and tried to maintain very conservative villages in block settlements in Mexico, where only horses, not tractors, were allowed, by 1998 large numbers were returning to Canada and many others had assimilated into Spanish/Mexican culture. The second-largest group in Latin America, 13,939 in Paraguay in 1984, were refugees of the two world wars in Europe. They flourished, so that by 1998 they had almost doubled to 25,009, becoming the largest Mennonite group in Latin America.

The largest demographic changes have occurred in Africa. Again, owing to mission work, there were over 66,000 Mennonite members in the Congo (formerly Zaire) in 1984, by far the largest group in Africa, and the third-largest in the world. Only 16 years later, that membership had tripled, to 175,837, the Congo's concentration passing Canada's to become the second-largest in the world. Indeed, Africa has experienced an explosion of Mennonite population growth: by 1998, there were 57,011 members in Ethiopia (eight times as many as in 1984), 32,100 in Tanzania (almost three times that of 1984), and 20,606 in Zimbabwe (four times as many as in 1984). Most of these Mennonites are Black; many come from animistic religious backgrounds; most live in preindustrial rural villages; their incomes, education, and occupations are at very low levels; their fertility rate is very high, which escalates population growth. These world modernization factors require further examiniation.

Changing Influences of Modernization

In order to trace the influences of modernization on Mennonites around the world, we have selected some of the countries in which the largest number of Mennonites are located (see table 1.3). In this table

TABLE 1.3
Regional Modernization and Mennonite Membership Growth

	Modernization factors			Membership growth		
	Percentage urban	Life expectancy 1998 (years)	Fertility 1998	Membership 1984	1998	% Member increase 1984–98
Europe	75+	70+	1.5+			−32
Germany	86	70	1.5+	11,932	39,610	
Netherlands	88	75	1.5	20,200	13,500	
Switzerland	60	74	1.5	2,750	2,500	
USSR/CIS	73	69	1.2	55,000	3,350	
North America	75+	75+	1.5+			+25
Canada	77	78	1.6	101,512	128,633	
U.S.A.	75	76	2.0	232,192	287,345	
Latin America	60+	60+	3.0+			+33
Mexico	74	72	3.1	31,161	20,689	
Paraguay	45	65	4.8	13,939	25,009	
Asia	25+	50+	3.0+			+40
Indonesia	30	63	3.2	62,911	87,466	
India	26	59	3.4	43,998	62,823	
Africa	20+	40+	5.0+			+202
Zaire/Congo	30	44	6.5	66,408	175,837	
Tanzania	20	50	5.0	13,614	32,100	
Ethiopia	15	40	6.5	7,000	57,011	

Source: Data on modernizations are from National Geographic Society 1998, 194:4

we have ranked the geographic regions, not historically as in table 1.2, but according to degree of modernization, beginning with Europe and ending with Africa. To measure modernization, we use three indicators: degree of urbanization, life expectancy, and fertility.

In table 1.3, we have listed the European countries in which the Mennonites originated, and we see that these countries are also the most modern (highly urban, with a long life expectancy and low fertility). The Netherlands is the most urban country. The life expectancy of its citizens is 75+ years, and their fertility rate is 1.5 children per woman of childbearing age. Looking at Mennonite membership in all countries of Europe in 1984 and 1998, we see a 32 per cent decline, which is especially evident in the USSR/CIS and the Netherlands. As pointed out earlier, emigration out of the CIS was the major factor, and that is why Germany's 1998 membership figures are up. The decline in the Netherlands seems to be the result of assimilation. Membership decline is certainly greatest in these original, and most modern, countries.

In contrast, the three countries in Africa where the largest numbers of Mennonites are located are definitely the least modern, and many of the residents live in villages characterized by premodern conditions. These countries are roughly 30 per cent urban; the life expectancy there is only between 40 and 50 years, and the fertility rates average over 5 children per childbearing woman, which is four times the rate for European Mennonites. It is clear, using these three indicators, that Africans are more premodern. Are their membership numbers also different? The combined membership growth for these three African countries from 1984 to 1998 was 200 per cent, which is also reflected in the growth rates in the Congo and in Tanzania. The membership in Ethiopia, the least modern of the three, grew by eight times from 1984 to 1998.

Mennonite membership growth is highest in premodern African countries, and lowest in the most modern European countries, which suggests that demographic factors tend to enhance membership growth, and modernization tends to depress it. What about growth in North America, Latin America, and Asia? We see from table 1.3 that North America is about as modern as Europe, although urbanization rates are not as high as in the Netherlands, and fertility in the United States is a bit higher. We also see that membership growth in North America between 1984 and 1998 is 25 per cent. Latin American urbanization and life expectancy are lower, and birth rates are about twice as high as in Europe, while overall membership growth in Latin America is 33 per cent. Asian modernization indicators are somewhat higher than those of Africa. Roughly 25 per cent live in cities, the life expectancy is up to 50 years or more, and the fertility rates are over 3. Asian membership increase over a short generation is the second-highest, at 40 per cent, as assimilationists would expect in countries that rank second-last in terms of modernization. There is a striking correlation between increased modernization and membership decline.

From these demographic findings, it is clear that, depending on where we look, we will find Mennonites in sixty countries of the world who are premodern, modern, or postmodern. We will find more premodern Mennonites in Africa, but even there the premodern-to-postmodern range exists. In this work we plan to look much more thoroughly at Mennonites in North America, where the modernization process is much more advanced. Before we do that, however, we need to examine the range of outcomes that can occur when modernization is introduced – from complete loss of Mennonite identity to complete retention of identity – by exploring some of the well-known theories.

Changing Social Mosaics and Nets

Armand Mauss (1994), in his *The Angel and the Beehive*, begins by saying that, 'in the center of Salt Lake City, on either side of Main Street, two important traditional Mormon symbols confront each other; the angel on the temple spire and the beehive atop the roof of the Hotel Utah.' He continues: 'the angel represents the other-worldly heritage of Mormonism, the spiritual and prophetic elements, the enduring ideals and remarkable doctrines revealed ... The beehive, on the other hand, is a symbol of worldly enterprise ... and all aspects of ... involvement with the world, cultural as well as economic ... the aesthetics of the world, and more generally the sense of accommodation and comfort with the ways of the world that one enjoys ...' (Mauss 1994, 3). Is this polarity also evident among Mennonites?

Accommodation versus Assimilation

Theorists of assimilation suggest that all humans, of whatever culture, language, or belief, will be drawn into the industrial fray by the promise of improvements in the well-being of all. The arrival of immigrants to the shores of North America provided the opportunity for a new beginning; it offered new freedoms to experiment and let the human spirit be creative. The immigrants did not wish to be dominated by a majority group, as many had been in Europe, so they were wary of the powerful. According to the melting-pot theory, many immigrants no longer wish to continue the traditions of the restricted Old World, but opt for the opportunities of the New. Openness to abandoning the restrictive past for future opportunities is common in the assimilation theory of ethnic change.

Americans often refer to their country as a melting pot, in which all groups contribute to the American dream. The United States is viewed as a new nation, a new culture, a new continent to which all might contribute. Assimilation theory suggests that immigrant groups will be synthesized into a new group. This evolutionary process creates a new whole that differs from its constituent parts and different from the original.

A chief advocate of this process was Robert Park. He suggested that immigrants came into contact with the new society and took either the route of least resistance (contact, accommodation, and fusion) or a more circuitous route (Shore 1987). Whereas the latter route could take longer and could entail considerable resistance to change on the part of the immigrant, the end result would be the same – the loss of a distinctive ethnic or religious identity.

The theory of assimilation was, and is, attractive because it is dynamic. It takes into account the enormous technological change that dominates North American societies. Furthermore, numerous studies show that many north European groups, such as the Dutch, the Scandinavians, and the Germans, fairly quickly lose many of their distinctive cultural traits, such as ethnic language use (Driedger 1996). However, in the eyes of some, melting-pot assimilation is too deterministic. It may be useful in explaining a general process that some groups undergo, but it does not take into account the many dimensions of cultural change. Not all of these forces may be changing in the same direction; as well, the targets of change may be quite different.

Herberg (1955) suggested that in the United States the many ethnic groups have remained in larger religious categories, such as Protestant, Catholic, and Jew. Certainly the French in Quebec have remained largely Catholic as a bulwark against assimilation, and 'prophesied' synthesis is not happening in Canada. The racial component, well represented by Blacks, aboriginals, and Asians, is not 'melting' very noticeably. To what extent other ethnic groups, such as the Chinese and Italians, are 'melting' is a subject requiring more research. Many religious groups, such as the Jews, Hutterites, and Mennonites, are not assimilating, although they are changing a great deal.

Modified Pluralism

Gordon (1964) suggests that assimilation is not a single social process, but a number of subprocesses which he classifies under the headings 'cultural' and 'structural.' 'Cultural assimilation' includes the incoming group's acceptance of the modes of dress, language, and other cultural characteristics of the host society. 'Structural assimilation' concerns the degree to which immigrants enter the social institutions of the society (e.g., political, educational, religious, social) and the degree to which they are accepted into these institutions by the majority. Gordon suggests that assimilation may occur more readily in economic, political, and educational institutions than in the areas of religion, family, and recreation. As Newman (1973, 85) points out, however, 'Gordon contends [that] once structural assimilation is far advanced, all other types of assimilation will naturally follow.'

Gordon's multivariate approach forced scholars out of their unilinear rut. The seven stages or types of assimilation he established included cultural, structural, marital, identificational, civic, attitudinal, and behaviour-receptional forms of change. Gordon's major contribution is his complex multilinear, multidimensional view of the change process. It has been seen as a considerable improvement on Park's assimilation cycle. Although Gordon was concerned with assimilation, he did not negate pluralist expressions in religion, the family, and recreation. An examination of any group – including the Mennonites – shows that there are enormous ranges of differences.

Glazer and Moynihan (1963) distinguish four major events in New York's history that they think structured a series of ethnic patterns reflecting modified pluralism rather than modified assimilation in that city. The first was the shaping of the Jewish community under the impact of the Nazi persecution of Jews in Europe and the establishment of the state of Israel. The second was a parallel, if less marked, shaping of a Catholic community by the re-emergence of the Catholic school controversy. The third was the migration of Southern Blacks to New York following the First World War and continuing after the 1950s. The fourth was the influx of Puerto Ricans following the Second World War (Driedger 1996).

Glazer and Moynihan (1963) claim that the melting pot did not neatly function in New York in a deterministic way. They further claim that, throughout U.S. history, the various streams of population, separated from one another by origin, religion, and outlook, seemed always to be on the verge of merging, but that the anticipated commingling was always deferred. While all groups change, those that are able to shift focus from traditional cultural identities to new interests may maintain their distinctive identities. This formation recognizes change and maintains that identification can be shifted. It also suggests that some groups may change more than others and implies that the outcome may be a pluralist mixture differing from the Anglo-conformist target. Indeed, Glazer and Moynihan contend that traumatic conflict experiences may encourage a sense of identity in so far as they lead to fighting for shared values and differences.

Multicultural Pluralism and Conflict

Whereas proponents of the melting pot assume that minorities will assimilate and lose their separate identities, scholars of pluralism and conflict focus on the alternative options of solidarity and identity that are available to minorities (Berry and Laponce 1994, 3–16). Like Max Weber, advocates of these theories assume that there are alternatives to losing oneself in the industrial arena, and that many individuals and groups have the creativity and resources to fight modern alienation, by maintaining their ethnic *Gemeinschaft*. In particular, Durkheim studied questions of social cohesion and solidarity, which many scholars of ethnicity have also explored (Berry and Laponce 1994; Driedger 1996).

Ideal cultural pluralism may be represented by different distinct groups who live side by side in relatively harmonious coexistence. 'The author of this view of pluralism was a Harvard-educated philosopher of Jewish immigrant stock named Horace Kallen,' who espoused pluralism for three main reasons (Newman 1973, 67). He argued that there are many kinds of social relationships and identities that can be chosen voluntarily, but that no one may choose his or her ancestry. Further, each of the minority groups has something of value to contribute to a country, and that the U.S. constitution carried with it an implicit assumption that all people were created equal, even though there might be many distinct differences.

Whereas the preceding discussion of assimilation tends to emphasize the overwhelming influence of technology and urbanization, sweeping away all forms of religious and ethnic differentiation before it, cultural pluralism tends to focus on countervailing ideological forces such as democracy and human justice which presuppose that all people are of equal worth and all should have the freedom to choose their distinct quality of life. In fact, the trend towards permissive differentiation seems to be set. In North America we have accepted pluralist religious expressions, which were hardly tolerated in Reformation Europe. The same is now true of the political scene, where a diversity of political parties and ideologies exists and is accepted by society. Multiculturalism in Canada is now also recognized federally, albeit ambiguously and not without some resistance.

The theories of modified assimilation and modified pluralism allow for a greater measure of inherent conflict in the social system. Gordon's modified assimilation allows for it to occur at different rates, which can bring about disjuncture and stress; Glazer and Moynihan's modified pluralism suggests that the minority becomes very much a part of the industrial urban process of change, which involves conflict and turmoil, as new forms of identity emerge. The counterculture in pluralism becomes a subcultural antithesis to the larger society. Simmel (1955) contended that both conflict and consensus are ever-present in society, and Coser (1956), Dahrendorf (1959), Mauss (1994), and Driedger (1996) follow this view. In general, these theorists assume that all social phenomena reflect a combination of opposed tendencies.

Our discussion of the assimilationist–pluralist range of options suggests that the two opposite ideal poles are seldom if ever present in reality. The majority of activity occurs between these two extremes and shows varying degrees of conformity to the majority or separation into a distinctive identity. In the middle we find considerable conflict between the two tendencies; as a result we have a range of outcomes that depend on which pole is stronger and more influential. Examples of the entire range of ethnic identity, or the lack of it, can be found among Mennonites.

Local and Global Mennonite Diversity

In chapters 2 and 3 we develop professionalism and individualism as important change factors in today's information revolution. In many ways, as Peter Berger suggested, these are powerful change factors that assault the traditional rural Mennonite village. Not to obscure what is meant by the local numinous village where face-to-face relations were maintained in a *Gemeinschaft* community setting, we focus on the sacred village in chapter 4. It is here that a distinct religion; culture; set of values, beliefs, attitudes; foods; and architecture were nourished in the past.

Chapters 5 and 6 show how the media influenced a shift of values away from the local traditional village to the larger arena of the 'global village.' In some ways 'global village' is a misnomer, because face-to-face spatial relations change: even though fax, e-mail, and the Internet can continue to keep people in touch as quickly, the quality of the interaction changes. It is these changes of space, symbols, and structures that need to be explored to better understand the nature of the change from the traditional rural village to an electronic information world referred to as the 'global village.'

The four-volume Mennonite encyclopedia published in the 1960s, and updated by a fifth volume in 1990, illustrates both local diversity in each of the sixty countries in which Mennonites live and the global historical, linguistic, cultural, racial, and theological diversity of Mennonites in the 1990s. The four-volume 'Mennonite Experience in America' series published between 1985 and 1996 by Richard MacMaster (1985), Theron Schlabach (1989), James Juhnke (1989), and Paul Toews (1996) illustrates well the historical complexity of the largest concentration of American Mennonites. A three-volume series published between 1974 and 1996 by Frank Epp (1974, 1982), and Ted Regehr (1996), shows a similar historical diversity in Canada. Two volumes published by sociologists J. Howard Kauffman, Leland Harder, and Leo Driedger, in 1975 and 1991, show the enormous sociological diversity of Mennonites in the United States and Canada, which is a Mennonite mosaic, a kaleidoscope of ferment and change.

Two Mennonite world organizations have kept premodern, modern, and postmodern Mennonites in touch with one another and with their diversity through the Mennonite Central Committee (MCC) and the Mennonite World Conference (MWC). The MCC was begun in 1920 by North American Mennonites to help their suffering Mennonite kin with material relief after the First World War. The MCC has since developed into an agency of 1,000 workers distributing material aid and rehabilitation in fifty countries. Young people volunteer for one or more years of service, are exposed to many in the world who live in premodern villages, and come back home to share what they have heard and experienced first-hand. Thus, modern and postmodern North American Mennonites work with premodern Mennonites and many others, which results in much cross-fertilization, understanding, and sharing at the poverty levels in which these people find themselves.

The Mennonite World Conference (MWC) first met in Basel, Switzerland, in 1925, and has met roughly every six years since. In 1996, it met in Calcutta, India. Mennonite delegates from sixty countries, who were premodern, modern, and postmodern, gathered in a theological, social, cultural, and emotional interchange and celebrated for a week. Such opportunities provide the context to recognize unity amid much diversity.

In this work, we focus on Mennonites in the United States and Canada. In Part I, we review the extent of the information revolution, and how professionalization and individualism have shaped Mennonite life in North America. In Part II, we examine symbolic extensions of cultural change, media shifts, and changes from extended to nuclear and lone-parent families. In Part III, we show how, in the midst of post-modern diversity, considerable reconstruction is taking place, where teens are growing both roots and wings, schools are changing from monasteries to serving the marketplace, women are increasingly finding equal opportunities for leadership, and central beliefs in love and peace have turned from passive non-resistance to active peacemaking.

PART I

THE INFORMATION REVOLUTION

2

Emerging Mennonite Urban Professionals

Donald Kraybill and Phyllis Pellman Good are uneasy about the change from martyrs who died for their faith in the past to today's Mennonite urban professionals in chic suits (Kraybill and Good 1982). It represents a clash between the old and the new, the familiar and the strange, resulting in tensions that call on first-generation urban-professional Mennonites to engage in critical reflection. Mennonites have shown an ambivalence towards the professions, because their ancestors were primarily craftspeople and, later, agriculturalists who worked with their hands. Missionaries, ministers, teachers, nurses, and doctors were among the first accepted service professionals. However, many fear that some professionals may not be as serving as they appear, and could easily become masters in disguise, a role that runs counter to that envisioned by Anabaptists. Professionals are often members of teams playing games with in-group rules and arcane hierarchies that strive towards goals – including power where respect, status, prescriptions, supervision, control, autonomy, knowledge, titles, and publicity – which seem hard to integrate with past virtues of humility and 'Gelassenheit.' These values are uncharted territory for Mennonites.

These new 'professionals' Emerson Lesher has unceremoniously labelled 'Muppies,' and in his 'manual' he pierces the sacred façade of professionalization (Lesher, 1985).[1] 'Muppie' sounds so ordinary, so sacrilegious – rather flippant, in fact. In contrast to the Anabaptist martyrs who found their way into the *Martyrs Mirror* (a published volume of martyr reports), Muppies seem so secular, so profane. Whereas the Mennonite ancestors lived and died in revolutions, and worked their hands to the bone as immigrant pioneers in strange and unwelcoming lands, Muppies need vacations, because doctors, teachers, nurses, social workers, city planners, and lawyers burn out and need to recoup. Thus, the sacred 'martyr aura' is now changing to a new 'professional aura,' which Lesher gently ridicules. Are Mennonites becoming mere Muppies? If so, what happens to the greater causes for which their forebears died?

More than half of North American Mennonites are now urban. We have been tracing the extent of urbanization of Mennonites for twenty-five years, noting an increase since the end of the Second World War (Driedger and Kauffman 1982). In 1989 four times as many Mennonites were in the professions (28 per cent) as working the land (7 per cent). This profound change is reshaping their future. The pace of change is amazing when we consider that almost all were rural fifty years ago, before the outbreak of the Second World War. As late as 1972, only one in three lived in cities with populations of 2,500 or more (Kauffman and Harder 1975).

Ten years ago we explored Mennonite urban trends in the 1970s, comparing Canadian and American differences, and found that Dutch Mennonites were more prone to urbanize than were Swiss Mennonites (Driedger and Kauffman 1982). We also found that life in the city did not affect theology and religious participation very much. On the other hand, we found that many attitudes towards moral issues and social concerns changed considerably.

It is time to update the consideration of the effects of urbanization on Mennonites: to (1) plot changes since 1972; (2) compare differences in the various regions; (3) explore the impact of urbanization on attitudes and activity; (4) assess the affect of professionalization; and (5) make some observations on what the future holds. But, first, let us briefly examine the background: where Mennonites came from.

Mennonites of the Anabaptist Past

The sixteenth-century Anabaptists were part of a larger religious refor-mation which followed the invention of the printing press, during the European feudal age. They trace their origins to 1525, as part of a set of larger religious movements that emerged in response to the political, economic, and social ferment of the time in Switzerland, Holland, and Germany. It was a time of massive deconstruction that resulted in much diversity and pluralism, where religious Catholic metanarratives were reformed, economic feudalism was challenged, and the dominant hierarchical Holy Roman Empire crumbled into multiple European nation-states (Snyder 1995). The Anabaptists were seen as radicals, and persecuted by both Catholics and Protestants, who felt threatened by the Anabaptist faith and lifestyle. Too much change in volatile situations causes those who want to retain order and stability to resist. Persecution drove many Anabaptists from the urban commercial fray, where they began, into centuries of 'quiet in the land,' a life lived on the periphery of societies as tillers of the soil (Kauffman and Driedger 1991, 28).

Sixteenth-Century Urban Anabaptists

Cornelius Krahn (1980, 6) reports that 'the Anabaptist Mennonite Movement started primarily in larger cities such as Zurich, Bern, Strasbourg, Emden, Amsterdam, Leeuwarden, Groningen, Leyden, Rotterdam, Antwerp, Brussels, Münster, and Cologne. In the Swiss, South-German, and Austrian cities, the Anabaptist movement was crushed and survived only in remote areas. It was different in the Netherlands.' Of the thirteen cities Krahn lists, only two are Swiss. The majority are North European trading ports of the commercial Hanseatic League, which flourished in the Baltic sea for centuries. While Anabaptists in Central Europe fled the cities, in the northern cities they survived, first, as an underground movement; later, as a tolerated minority; and, finally, as a recognized religious group (Krahn 1981, 92; Snyder 1995, 143–58).

Urbanism among Mennonites of the Low Countries is as old as Mennonitism itself. Today there are more than 1,000 Mennonites in Amsterdam, and a number of other cities (Krahn 1980, 6). Amsterdam and Rotterdam were part of the Hanseatic League, whose ships plied the North and Baltic seas between the various ports of Bergen, Oslo, Stockholm, Copenhagen, Danzig, Amsterdam, Rotterdam, and London. While Menno Simons himself emerged out of rural Friesland, he nevertheless served Mennonites in many urban centres of the sixteenth century.

W.L.C. Coenen (1920, 1–90) made a study of the Anabaptist martyrs in the Netherlands and found that not one of the 161 martyrs was a farmer. Among the fifty-nine occupations identified were twenty-seven weavers, seventeen tailors, thirteen shoemakers, six sailors, five carpenters, five goldsmiths, five hatmakers, four bricklayers, three bakers, three leather dealers, three teachers, three saddlers, and three potters (Krahn 1980, 8). Most of them, as craftspeople, industrial workers, and businessmen, were part of a more urban commercial society. There were also Mennonites in rural areas in North Holland, Friesland, and Groningen. Persecution drove some eastward into Prussia, mostly into the countryside but also to the suburbs of cities such as Altona, Hamburg, Danzig, Marienburg, Elbing, and Kongisberg (Penner 1978). Many became middle-class citizens.

Paul Peachey's (1954, 102–27) study of the social origins of the Swiss Anabaptists lists 762 Swiss individuals who were connected with the Anabaptist movement in Central Europe; 150 of these were urban (20 per cent). There were 612 villagers and peasants (80 per cent), whom he classified as rural. The peasants made up about three-fifths of the total number of persons listed, or about 460. Of the 150 who were urban, 20 had been clergy (14 priests and 6 monks), 20 were urban lay intellectuals (including Grebel, Manz, Denck, and Hugwald), 10 came from the nobility, and 100 were citizens and urban craftspeople. Among those who were in the crafts, tailors and bakers were most common.

Most of the urban leaders of clerical, intellectual, and noble background within two years (1525–7) were martyred or died early natural deaths, recanted, were exiled, or succumbed to some unknown destiny (Moore 1984). Thus, the Swiss Anabaptist movement was only one-fifth urban to begin with, and almost completely rural two years later and thereafter (Snyder 1995, 1–23). Severe persecution made an urban foothold impossible. The early Anabaptists were more urban in northern than in southern Europe, and these differences can also be found in North America, as we will see.

The Rural, Agricultural Retreat

The persecuted Anabaptists in Switzerland, Austria, and South Germany were indeed much safer as they fled up the mountainsides and into the valleys of the rugged Alpine regions (Snyder 1995, 51–64). Mountains tended to serve as barriers to social interaction when transportation was undeveloped; even today the various segregated valleys have some distinctive customs. In Switzerland four official languages (German, French, Italian, Romansch) still survive. The terrain supports residential segregation, tranquil rural life, and parochial ethnocentrism.

These conditions prompted the Swiss Anabaptists to develop a stronger separatist doctrine than that observed by their Dutch counterparts. The Swiss experience contributed to the development of a 'two-kingdom' ethic, emphasizing the separation of Church and State. The Swiss Anabaptists believed that the followers of Christ are 'called out' from 'the world' to lives of holiness as members of the Kingdom of God. While acknowledging the legitimacy of government over the 'affairs of the world,' the Anabaptists asserted the primacy of the claims of God over the claims of government. This separation was later expressed in the United States in the form of a general avoidance of participation in the political process; the separatists viewed the rural environment as retreat from involvement with the secular and morally compromising world of commerce, industry, politics, and entertainment typical of the city (Driedger and Kauffman 1982, 270–5).

Central Europe was the heart of the non-commercial, non-industrial feudal age. The commercial activities of the Roman Empire in the Mediterranean filtered only slowly from the seaports of Venice and Genoa northward across the Alps into Central Europe. Likewise, as the new commercial centre shifted to the Baltic Sea and North Europe in the fifteenth and sixteenth centuries, urbanization penetrated the European heartland much more slowly (Moore 1984).

The South German Anabaptists in the cities were crushed and fled up the mountainsides and into the rural valleys. The mountainous terrain promoted segregation and slowed communication and social interaction. The urban industrial complexes of first the Roman age in the Mediterranean, and later of the sixteenth-century commerce and industry of northern Europe, never did influence this central part of continental Europe as deeply as they did other areas. It was out of this setting that the Swiss Mennonites, with a separatist, two-kingdom ethic, came, largely to the United States, but also to Canada.

The Hanseatic League was established in the thirteenth century to do commerce in northern Europe, in the area around the North and Baltic seas. By the fourteenth and fifteenth centuries, there were seventy member Hanseatic city-states. They stretched from London in the west to Novograd (in western Russia) in the east, from the northern city of Bergen, Norway, south to Leipzig, Germany, and Cracow, Poland (Breasted and Huth 1961, 38). The silk- and linen-making crafts spread into France and the Netherlands as an important part of this North European trade. The Anabaptists emerged, during the preindustrial age (1500–1785), as craftspeople in this commercial region of northern Europe.

With the invention of the steam engine in 1790, the revolution of modern technology began. Machine power increasingly replaced animal and human muscle power. Industry moved from small *'Gemeinschaft*-like' (face-to-face) settings into larger factories. Because its coalfields, the source of energy, gave England an enormous advantage, it began to dominate industrial technology. By this time the Anabaptists had moved eastward into the Danzig (Gdansk) area, in what is now Poland (Klassen 1989). Nationalism also grew with industrialization. The pressures of the Prussian state, of which Danzig was then a part, forced large numbers of Mennonites to move farther eastward into Ukraine. Mennonites first moved to Russia in 1789, just before the steam engine was invented. Many Mennonites, however, stayed in the Netherlands and the Danzig area.

Northern Europe, especially the Vistula Delta, was the area from which most Russian Mennonites came. They began to leave Prussia in 1789 and 1803 to form the Chortitza and Molotschna settlements in Ukraine. Here they became largely farmers on the interior steppes, but their commercial and industrial skills led them also to develop business and commerce related to agriculture (Toews 1981). Some left Russia less than a hundred years later, emigrating to Canada and the United States in 1874. Others followed in the 1920s. Still others emigrated to Canada in the late 1940s and early 1950s. Their early Dutch urban proclivities lasted through the Russian agrarian period, making them more prone to urbanization in Canada (Urry 1989).

Of the two major Mennonite branches that emerged in Europe – the Swiss and South German farmers, and the North European entrepreneurs – we would expect the North European Mennonites to move into cities in North America (Driedger and Kauffman 1982). This early basic dualism is only one variation of the pluralist Anabaptist movement of the past that has continued into the present.

The Urban Revolution

The Effects of Modernization

Mennonites remained agricultural and rural much longer than the national U.S. and Canadian averages, by isolating themselves in ethnic enclaves before the Second World War. Since the 1940s, however, modernization has increasingly affected them as well; enormous changes are taking place, as is demonstrated by Kauffman and Driedger (1991). Urbanization, increased education, occupational change, a rise in

TABLE 2.1
Demographic Variations, by Residence, 1989

Variables	Residence			
	Rural farm	Rural non-farm	Small city	Large city
Socio-economic status				
Percent college graduates	18	29	38	46
Percent professional occupation	14	25	31	40
Median household income	$28,333	29,672	30,279	36,111
Mobility				
Percent living in community less than five years	6	12	16	16
Percent non-resident members	4	6	7	10

income and mobility – are all indicators of modernization shown in table 2.1.[2]

In the past Mennonites were largely content to read and write. By 1989, however, the mean educational level had risen from high school in 1972 to an average of first-year college. While only one in six Mennonite farmers were college graduates in 1989, almost half of those residing in large cities had attained this educational level.

Increased education also provided more opportunities for a variety of occupations. By 1989 only 7 per cent of the males farmed, while four times as many (both genders) were in the professions (28 per cent). This enormous change in fifty years varied by residence, with only 14 per cent of these professionals living on farms, as compared with 40 per cent who worked in large cities. With greater urbanization and professionalization, incomes also rose, from $28,333 per farm household annually in 1989 to $36,111 for those in large cities. Modern urban trends towards higher education, occupational status, and income contributed to a general rise in socio-economic status.

Mennonite urban professionals (Muppies) are also more mobile. Table 2.1 shows that, on the average, more than twice as many large-city as farm Mennonites lived in their respective communities less than five years. The same was true for residency, with more than twice as many large-city Mennonites being non-resident members. Clearly, the indicators of modernization, such as urbanization, socio-economic

TABLE 2.2.
Percentage Urban, Five Denominations, 1972 and 1989

	Percentage Urban	
Denominations	1972 $N = 3,591$	1989 $N = 3,083$
Mennonite Brethren (MB)	56	73
General Conference Mennonite (GC)	40	53
Evangelical Mennonite (EM)	39	47
Mennonite Church (MC)	26	37
Brethren in Christ (BIC)	30	32
Five denominations	35	48

status, and mobility, combine to push in the direction of change. However, these changes vary by denomination and region.

Denominational Urbanism

To plot changes in urbanization, we surveyed five Mennonite denominations in 1972 and 1989, who represented three-quarters of the Mennonites in North America, and found great differences and changes (Kauffman and Driedger 1991). In 1972, one-third in Canada and the United States lived in cities of 2,500 population or more; by 1989, this proportion had increased to one-half. More than half of the Mennonite Brethren (MBs) were urban in 1972, and, by 1989, three out of four lived in the city. General Conference Mennonites (GCs), the other denomination that was of largely Dutch-Prussian origin, changed from 40 to 53 per cent urban during the seventeen-year span.

The three denominations who are mostly of Swiss-Mennonite origin ranged from one-quarter to less than half urban. Almost half of the members of the Evangelical Mennonite Church (EMCs) had become urban in 1989, but the Brethren in Christ (BICs) had hardly changed, remaining two-thirds rural. From 1972 to 1989, the proportion of rural Mennonite Church (MC) respondents dropped from three-quarters to two-thirds, the greatest change among Swiss Mennonites. Two-thirds of the Dutch Mennonites (MBs and GCs) were urban, while roughly one-third of the Swiss Mennonites (EMCs, MCs and BICs) were urban in 1989 (Kauffman and Driedger 1991). These changes require further examination.

Regional Urban Trends

Mennonites in North America vary greatly as to how urban they are. Only one in five Mennonites in the American East lived in cities of 2,500 or more in 1972; this proportion had changed to one-third by 1989. (The percentage of Mennonites living in urban areas in 1972 and 1989 can be seen in figure 8.1, on page 167.) Mennonites in the American East have always been mostly rural, although by 1989 they had caught up to the Midwest and the Prairies, where very little change occurred between 1972 and 1989.

On the other hand, American Mennonites on the Pacific coast were the most urban in both 1972 and 1989. By 1989 almost all lived in cities. Dutch-origin Mennonite Brethren are dominant on the West Coast, centred around their Pacific college and seminary located in metropolitan Fresno.

The greatest surprise, however, is the widespread relocation to the city on the Canadian prairies. While less than half (42 and 44 per cent) of Mennonites were urban in the most westerly four Canadian provinces in 1972 (seen in figure 2.1), 75 and 77 per cent lived in cities by 1989. Again, the Mennonite Brethren in the Fraser valley and Vancouver, in British Columbia, had the highest percentage of city dwellers, similar to the U.S. Pacific coast Mennonite Brethren.

On the Canadian prairies, where three out of four Mennonites lived in the city in 1989, more than half were still rural in 1972. This great change in the Canadian prairie population is very unlike the lack of change on the U.S. plains. Since Mennonites on the prairies are largely of Dutch-Prussian origin, why did this change happen in Canada and not in the United States? Winnipeg, Saskatoon, and Calgary drew rural Mennonites by the thousands, while Wichita and Kansas City in the United States did not. How can we explain these enormous differences?

The least change occurred down the centre of North America. Two-thirds of the Mennonites in the American Midwest and plains remained rural over a generation. Ontario Mennonites are closer to half urban, but they, too, changed very little after 1972. Schools and institutions in small urban areas like Goshen–Elkhart and Bluffton in the Midwest, and Newton–Hesston–Hillsboro, with their three colleges, in the U.S. plains states, boosted small-town communities. Kitchener–Waterloo, bolstered by Conrad Grebel College, anchored Ontario Mennonite urbanism.

TABLE 2.3
Percentage of Rural–Urban Residence, United States and Canada, 1989

Residence	United States				Canada			
	East (%)	Midwest (%)	Plains (%)	Pacific (%)	East (%)	Prairies (%)	Pacific (%)	Total N = 3,006
Rural farm	21	27	32	9	29	16	8	23
Rural non-farm	34	23	9	6	8	3	9	17
Village (under 2,500)	12	15	24	2	16	6	6	13
Small city (2,500–25,000)	24	22	21	18	9	22	18	21
Medium city (25,000–250,000)	6	10	6	25	32	20	43	15
Metropolis (250,000 plus)	3	3	8	40	7	33	16	12
Total	100	100	100	100	100	100	100	100

Diverse Urban Types of Change

These two national and regional variations deserve attention in terms of more specific characteristics on a continuum from rural-farm to metropolis; these subtler variations are shown in table 2.3.

The East: The Most Rurban

The American East Coast is the most densely populated urban area in North America, with its strip city reaching from Boston to Washington. The Mennonites and Amish live only a few miles from Philadelphia, having clustered around Lancaster, Pennsylvania, and Harrisonburg, Virginia, where Mennonite schools, colleges, and a seminary are located. This urban development, with its fast highways and media, tends to dominate rural areas. The countryside feels 'rurban,' or half urban, especially where Amish farms remain small, situated close to each other. Table 2.3 shows that most Mennonites in the East lived in rural non-farm settings (34 per cent), in small towns (12 per cent) or villages. It is a rurban lifestyle, where farm smells and sounds are mixed with village sprawl, and *gemütlichkeit*, where small businesses flourish.

Midwest: The Least Change

The American Midwest, with Goshen College, together with the Associated Mennonite Biblical Seminary in Elkhart (the largest), at the centre, represents early Mennonite commitment to small towns in Indiana. Bluffton College in Ohio adds institutional strength to the Midwest, where in 1989 two-thirds of Mennonites were rural. Roughly one-quarter, lived on the farm, another quarter on non-farm plots, and yet another quarter in the small cities, with very little urban change since 1972. All three of our Swiss-background denominations (MC, BIC, EMC) are well represented here, interspersed among populations of Amish, who maintain the rural-farm tradition. A hundred years ago, Mennonites began city mission work in Chicago, where struggling churches have increased in number (eighteen in 1989), but not in size (1,000 members all together). In many ways Chicago is still peripheral to small-town Mennonite ways and aspirations in the Midwest.

American Prairies: Most Rural-Farm

Thirty-two per cent of the Mennonites in the U.S. plains states are rural farm; this group represents the largest concentration of rural Mennonite farmers, and more than twice the Mennonite average in 1989. This is a decline since 1972 (39 per cent). Three Mennonite colleges in Kansas (Bethel, Hesston, Tabor) represent three different denominations (GC, MC, and MB, respectively), all located within a few miles of each other. Mennonites on the U.S. plains committed themselves to small towns early (Bethel, established in 1887 in Newton, was the first Mennonite college in the United State; Tabor was established in Hillsboro, and Hesston in Hesston), which has retarded the natural flow to Wichita, only a few miles away. Only six churches have been established in Wichita, despite the vast Mennonite hinterland nearby. This group of Mennonites has the most rural-farm residents in North America – a surprise since they are predominantly of Dutch GC and MB heritage.

The Pacific: Most Metropolitan

By 1972 three out of four Mennonites on the American Pacific coast lived in cities, and this proportion increased to 83 per cent in 1989. The Dutch Mennonite Brethren dominate the area, and are centred in Fresno, California, where Pacific College and the Mennonite Brethren Seminary (now Fresno Pacific University) are located. These metropolitan Mennonites have been the most urban for more than a generation. In light of these findings, a number of interesting questions arise: Why do MBs move to the West Coast in such large numbers? What makes Mennonites in the far west so pro-urban? Why is there such an enormous contrast between the American East and West coasts? The discrepancies between urban east and west must surely differentiate attitudes and styles of life, and thus must be examined also.

Ontario: The Most Balanced

Mennonites in Ontario exhibit the most balanced history in a number of respects. They have changed little in a generation; four of our five groups are located here, with substantial numbers of GCs, MCs, and MBs (GCs and MCs have formed the Eastern Mennonite Conference). Kitchener–Waterloo, where Conrad Grebel College is located, is clearly their dominant centre. The largest of their number (32 per cent) were located in medium-sized urban centres. Those who farmed in 1972 (29 per cent) in the main continued to do so in 1989. Like Mennonites in the American East and Midwest, they shy away from large metropolises with only 2 per cent in 1972 and 7 per cent in 1989 living in centres of 250,000 plus. In many ways Mennonites in Ontario are most balanced demographically.

Canadian Prairies: Most U-Shaped

Mennonites in the three Prairie provinces are unique in that they had their largest two concentrations in 1972 on the farm (42 per cent) and the metropolis (35 per cent) – opposite ends of the rural–urban spectrum – with fewer than one-quarter in categories between. This polarization was less pronounced in 1989, with greater shifts from the farm to smaller cities. The greatest surprise, however, is that by 1989 three out of four (75 per cent) lived in the city, an enormous contrast to their U.S. plains cousins (35 per cent urban). It is difficult to explain why Canadians have moved so strongly into Prairie cities such as Winnipeg (forty-seven churches), Saskatoon (fourteen churches), and Calgary (nine churches), while there were only six churches in Wichita in 1988. Mennonites on the Canadian prairies are almost all of Dutch origin. They include many more recent immigrants from the 1920s and 1950s who stayed in the city, which was not the case on the American plains. Canadian prairie Mennonites have followed the West Coast urban trend.

British Columbia: Greatest Urban Change

In one short generation Mennonites in British Columbia changed from 42 per cent urban in 1972, to 77 per cent in 1989. That is the largest Mennonite urban change in North America in the span of a mere seventeen years. After their Pacific Coast cousins in the United States, they are the second most urban Mennonites in North America. Further, as is the case on the U.S. Pacific coast, Mennonite Brethren predominate, and by far the largest number reside in medium-sized urban areas (between 25,000 and 250,000). This is somewhat misleading since many of these Mennonites live in politically independent suburbs of the greater Vancouver metropolitan area, which has a population of more than 1.3 million. Large numbers of these urban Mennonites came to British Columbia from South America after the Second World War, and almost all of them are of Dutch–Russian origin. Let us now examine to what extent these multiple changes and variations have affected Mennonite values.

Changing Perspectives and Values

Modernization and shifts to the city vary by region, but how do they affect beliefs, morals, and religious practice? Surely the shift from the sufferings of refugees and martyrdom to an urban professional lifestyle has some effect. Are urban Mennonites still committed to Anabaptist visions? Are Muppies less insular and more outreach-oriented, having greater concern for their social settings? Are they more open to the needs of the larger society? How do they find new changed identities, and are they more prone to individualism, secularism, and materialism? These were the fears of traditional Mennonites, and, judging from the many recent publications on 'identity,' these seem to be the new challenges of the modern age (Driedger 1988; Redekop and Steiner 1988; Loewen 1988).

Rural Orthodox and Moral Norms

Basic theological Christian beliefs have been and remain strong in rural areas, with four out of five rural Mennonites scoring high on 'general orthodoxy,' as shown in table 2.4.[3] Basic tenants of the faith, such as belief in God, Jesus as divine, miracles, the resurrection, the existence of Satan, and life after death, remained highly salient among Mennonites, with a slight decline among the city dwellers. However, only one in four scored highly on specific belief systems, such as Fundamentalism and Anabaptism, and again rural Mennonites scored somewhat higher than urbanites. Generally, rural Mennonites supported beliefs more strongly, with some erosion of norms and values among Muppies, who were inclined to be less normative.

The same trend is evident with respect to more personal moral issues. Traditional rural Mennonites scored higher than city Mennonites on moral attitudes, such as being against smoking, drinking, attending movies, use of drugs, premarital sex, homosexuals, masturbation, gambling, and dancing.[4] The same was true for actual moral behaviour, where rural Mennonites abstained more from drinking, smoking, and dancing. One-third of the rural Mennonites were against or abstained from these practices, while only half as many large-city Mennonites held rigorously to the same moral norms. Roughly three-

TABLE 2.4
Variations of Norms and Values, by Residence

Subject High rating on**	Percentage by residence			
	Rural farm	Rural non-farm	Small city	Large city
Beliefs				
General orthodoxy	79	80	73	65
Fundamentalist orthodoxy	27	28	23	18
Anabaptism	27	23	26	19
Moral issues				
Moral attitudes	37	34	30	16
Moral behaviour	34	34	29	19
Religious practice				
Church participation	30	31	32	23
Devotionalism*	21	22	20	18
In-group identity				
Ethnicity	21	27	24	21
Communalism	24	24	21	19
Separatism*	16	17	20	15
Concomitants of modernization				
Secularism*	19	18	21	20
Individualism	19	16	15	18
Materialism*	18	19	15	17
Church outreach				
Evangelism	13	19	22	20
MCC support	18	17	22	24
Social concerns				
Pacifism	16	13	25	26
Welfare attitudes	13	12	22	26
Race relations	23	23	35	42
Role of women	20	25	36	43
Openness to the larger society				
Political participation	18	19	20	30
Ecumenism	21	23	30	37
Political action	34	36	41	51

*Percentage variations are not statistically significant.
**Highest percentages are boxed.

quarters of the sample were selective and did not hold to these norms as exclusively.

One-third were highly involved in the church, attending worship regularly, participating in Sunday school and youth meetings, serving the congregation, and holding leadership positions; this declined slightly, to one-quarter, in large cities. Only one in five scored high on devotionalism, including reading the Bible regularly, saying mealtime grace, and engaging in family devotions, and this did not vary by place of residence. In summary, rural Mennonites were somewhat more orthodox theologically and held to individual moral norms more strongly than did big-city Mennonites.

Urban Openness, Outreach, Social Concerns

We expect that Mennonites who have entered the city to follow their professions, business, and the like, will be more open to interaction with others. In contrast to rural Mennonites, who exhibited normative concerns for orthodoxy and morals, urban Mennonites are indeed more open and more socially concerned, and reach out more, as shown in table 2.4.[5] Half of the metropolitan Mennonites scored high on political action, encouraging study of political issues, and endorsing candidates in their churches, a tendency shared by only one out of three rural Mennonites. Big-city Muppies also encouraged voting in elections, holding political office, more than those on rural farms, although the numbers were lower. It seems logical, then, that twice as many big-city as rural Mennonites would also favour ecumenism and greater cooperation with other Christians. Muppies were generally more open to the larger society and willing to participate more.

Muppie openness to the larger society was also evident in the high scores in pacifism (one in four) for urban Mennonites. Twice as many Muppies also strongly endorsed a greater role for women in the work of the Church, expressed concern for racial equality, and had more sympathy for helping the poor. Exposure to the larger society tends to expand the world-view, decreasing the preoccupation with in-group preservation, and encouraging concern for the plight of others. Urban Mennonites work more freely with both genders, and they have more opportunities to learn and empathize with all. Furthermore, contact with a diversity of faiths, races, and ideologies also makes them more tolerant. They also recognized a more-stratified society, including its poor, and were more willing to help.

This urban openness also carried over into willingness to reach out more. In contact with many others, city Mennonites have more opportunity for evangelism, although only one in five scored high on that measure. The same was true for support of the Mennonite Central Committee and its relief and development efforts. Thus, city Mennonites acted upon opportunities to meet others, thus becoming more involved politically and ecumenically; developing more concern for equality of women, races, the poor, and peace; and became more involved in outreach evangelism and MCC work. Clearly, rural and urban Mennonites have different perspectives and values.

Converging Values and Ideals

While there were distinct rural and urban differences, there were also similar values. Roughly one in four or five scored high on ethnicity, communalism, and separatism. We might have expected rural Mennonites to score higher on all three. Ethnicity, as manifest in preservation of an ethnic language, and choice of in-group friends, schools, and organizations, was not highly salient to most, and it did not vary by residence. Communalism, as in linkage to in-group friends, church, and conferences, did not vary by extent of urbanism either. The same was true for separatism.

Older traditional Mennonites have often expressed the fear that, as modernization increases, Mennonites will become more individualistic, secular, and materialistic. This was not the case. Roughly four out of five did not score high on each of these three modern concomitants, and that finding did not vary by residence. The strong Mennonite commitment to theology, friends, and Church seem to have counterbalanced the ravages of individualism, secularism, and materialism. Traditional fears about modernization were not realized in 1989.

The Professional Revolution

It is clear that Mennonites have become more urban and that this change has implications for norms and values. But what about the greater change from the dominance of farm life among Mennonites before the 1940s to a mere 7 per cent who were still farming in 1989? One in four is now a professional (28 per cent), the largest Mennonite occupational group. Forty per cent of big-city Mennonites are in the professions. This profound occupational shift tends to change Mennonite norms and values in ways that are very similar to the effects of urbanization, but with some important variations. It is these changes that Kraybill and Good (1982) are worried about, because the degree is so drastic, and the consequences largely unstudied.

General Characteristics of Professionals

Of the 28 per cent who are professionals, twice as many are male as are female (21 per cent). Four out of ten (42 per cent) are over fifty, and those numbers are heavily concentrated in the ministry. More than a third are middle-aged, between thirty and forty-nine, and one in five is in his or her twenties. Professionals are the most educated (more than half have graduate degrees), and 25 per cent earned $50,000 or more (only business people earned more). Only students are more mobile and non-resident than professionals. Muppies are on the move, used to change, and open to new experiences. Three out of four are also involved in Mennonite church leadership.

There is little difference between denominations, with Mennonite Brethren (31 per cent) slightly more professional than Mennonite Church members (26 per cent). The Swiss–Dutch factor is not important (28 to 29 per cent), and national U.S.–Canadian differences are also minor (25 to 29 per cent). Regional differences in Canada are insignificant, but they are much more important in the United States, ranging from 24 per cent professional in the East to 37 per cent on the Pacific coast. American Mennonite Brethren are considerably more urban and professional than Mennonite Church adherents in the American East.

Farm versus Professional Norms

Since Mennonite professionals come out of a strong farm past, it is logical that we compare the two at opposite poles, as shown in table 2.5. We expect that urban and professional norms and values correlate highly, and that is the case. Mennonite orthodoxy is highest among farmers who are considerably more orthodox (86 per cent) theologically than professionals (67 per cent). Only students are less orthodox. One-third of the farmers score high on fundamentalist theology, while fundamentalism appeals to very few professionals (12 per cent).

Farmers are also strong on moral attitudes, an area in which professionals do not score high, regardless of urban differences. This is illustrated by attitudes towards drinking, with more than twice as many

TABLE 2.5
Comparison of Farm and Professional Values and Norms

	Occupations						
Subject High scores on:	Farmer %	Housewife %	Blue collar %	Business %	Student %	Professional %	Total %
Orthodox theology	86	84	75	72	58	67	74
Fundamentalist beliefs	31	36	28	23	9	12	24
Moral attitudes	38	43	36	25	14	16	29
Abstain from drinking	88	88	79	68	79	71	79
Traditional husband/wife roles	45	29	34	27	8	20	27
Secularism	26	15	27	21	32	13	19
Individualism	18	17	17	20	30	11	17

professionals (29 per cent) drinking occasionally compared with 12 per cent of the farmers. One-third of the business Mennonites are in contact with those who drink, which seems to account for their highest scores. Presumably housewives are more isolated at home, having less contact with others, so they score highest on moral attitudes and are among those who drink the least.

Almost half of the farmers prefer traditional segmented roles for husbands and wives in the family, where the women are responsible for domestic matters and the man goes out to work. Less than half as many professionals (20 per cent) prefer traditional family roles, and almost none of the younger students (8 per cent) do. As Mennonites urbanize and become increasingly more professional, family roles also change extensively. As women follow careers and join the workforce, this attitude, too, is changing, even among housewives.

Few Mennonites score high on individualism. Differences in individualism and secularism may surprise some readers, however. Farmers are more individualistic, usually responsible for their own property and work, scoring twice as highly as professionals, who usually have to work with others. More farmers (26 per cent) score high on secularism, presumably because they are capitalists tending to their private property, more than professionals (13 per cent), who are involved in ministerial, educational, medical, and social services. This empirical evidence contradicts past traditional myths that the rural farm best conserves religious values. These indicators in table 2.5 are but a few probes that reveal farm and professional differences.

Unique Professional Values

Professional and urban openness to the larger society correlate highly. Muppies favour more outreach and are more concerned with social issues than are rural farm Mennonites. They are intensely in contact with the larger society, and table 2.6 shows that three out of four feel more conflict between faith and society than do the others. We have too little information on economic attitudes, but over half in our sample favoured joining labour unions, with almost twice as many professionals in favour (65 per cent) as farmers (37 per cent). Almost as many business and blue-collar workers favoured joining unions.

Professional openness shows especially in politics, where two-thirds voted in most elections, with three out of four professionals doing so. Professionals are more liberal politically. In Canada twice as many Mup-

TABLE 2.6
Comparison of Farm and Professional Outreach and Openness to Society

	Occupations						
Subject	Farmer %	Housewife %	Blue collar %	Business %	Student %	Professional %	Total %
Feel faith/society conflict	45	58	48	56	63	72	59
Favour joining unions	37	40	58	61	51	65	54
POLITICAL VALUES							
Favour political action	34	34	38	44	50	46	41
Favour political participation	17	18	15	25	*	32	22
Favour Liberal/NDP	16	26	26	31	31	44	32
Voted Turner/Broadbent	20	20	22	29	*	36	27
Favour Democratic	9	14	16	19	21	33	19
Voted Dukakis	11	12	11	17	*	34	19
SOCIAL CONCERNS							
Favour women leadership	22	20	23	38	43	53	35
Equal role for women	19	21	21	31	35	49	31
Fair race relations	11	23	20	22	53	49	31
Pacifism	11	16	12	15	24	30	20
Pro–welfare help	8	13	13	16	29	27	18
OPEN TO OUTREACH							
Serving others	25	37	20	23	9	40	30
MCC support	19	17	14	17	17	29	20
Favour ecumenism	18	19	27	25	31	39	28
Doing evangelism	19	17	14	17	17	29	20

*Most were too young to vote.

pies voted for left-of-centre Liberal or New Democratic parties and their leadership candidates, John Turner and Ed Broadbent, respectively. Although not as many American Mennonites voted for left-of-centre Democrats, the division of farm-versus-professional preferences was much greater in the U.S. sample. Four times as many professionals (33 per cent) voted Democratic, compared with only 9 per cent of the farmers; preferences for candidate Dukakis were similar. Pastors, social workers, teachers, and medical personnel tend to be more concerned with the poor, because they see these needs in their work daily. Mennonite farmers are more isolated and less aware of these needs.

Greater social concern among professionals is also reflected in more openness to women leaders in the Church. Half of the professionals favour more equal roles for women in the family, and half of them also extend this sense of equality to other races as well. Farmers are much less open (22 and 19 per cent, respectively). Professionals also score high on pacifism and providing more extensive help to those in need of welfare. Greater exposure to outgroup needs tends to make professionals more empathetic to the needs of the world.

This professional openness also extends to Church outreach. Orientation to serve others was strongest among professionals, wanting to treat others fairly, using resources for others, volunteering in Church and service agencies, and visiting sick non-relatives and shut-ins. Twice as many professionals also favoured ecumenism, wanting to cooperate with other denominations, actually engaging in such work, and being open to uniting with others. Professionals supported the work of the Mennonite Central Committee more, being satisfied with its general program, and of the Mennonite Disaster Service and the capital offices in Washington and Ottawa. The social concern and openness to service may not surprise some, since professionals have more contact with people and their needs, but this also extends to evangelism, where twice as many professionals as farmers invited non-Christians to Church and attempted to lead others to Christ. The total outreach of professionals is higher than any of the other occupations, suggesting that Muppies have more opportunities for service, and they also follow up on these opportunities more.

Conclusions

The ancestors of the Mennonites, the sixteenth-century Anabaptists, emerged after the invention of the printing press, when laypersons could more freely read. This new technology was followed by major changes, such as the Protestant Reformation, the Peasants' Revolt, and the beginnings of capitalism. The Anabaptists emerged out of this European caldron of ferment, emerging in many diverse forms, in what is Switzerland, Germany, and the Netherlands. Their leaders were craftpersons, mobile for their times, in touch with the laity in cities and rural areas alike. They developed a theology of the individual priesthood of every believer, a voluntary believers' church, separation of Church and State, and radical love, renouncing all forms of violence, including war. They hammered out new theologies in their changing times, thereby attracting many as they progressed from preindustrial, premodern times to modernity.

Since then, Mennonites have become more urban and professional. There are signs of both opportunity and potential problems lurking in the background. These we have not been able to explore in depth. As Gordon Kaufman suggests, 'for too long we Mennonites have allowed the modern world simply to overtake us, and have not attempted carefully and intelligently to assess what was happening ... So our urban churches have been, as far as possible, simply transplanted rural Mennonite churches in character and quality ... The question of how the Mennonite interpretation of Christian faith can be relevant to modern urban and professional life has seldom been faced directly' (Kaufman 1982 5:9). Even here psychological, social, and theological research is needed.

Don Kraybill and Phyllis Pellman Good (1982) sense the perils of professionalism that Muppies increasingly face. Our data show that Muppies more than others sense conflict between their Christian values and society. Serving the profession can subvert genuine service. Professions often pose as humanitarian when many feed into greedy economic systems. Professionals tend to create mythologies that they are more holistic than others, a premise that needs testing. Specialization creates distance between client and professional. This tends to fragment, breaking up the whole. Language creates a mysterious shroud over professional rituals, which often fail to deliver. Guarding these secrets and manufacturing need are common by-products. Professors and physicians can easily forget the agony of those who want to learn and need to heal, often resisting review. Professions can become surrogate churches, posing as substitute reservoirs of values, friends, and meaning. All this adds up to professional power to define need, prescribe treatment, conduct therapy, and evaluate work (Kraybill and Good 1982). These subtle trends have not been adequately researched.

3

Individualism Shaping Community

The emphasis on normative theology and cohesive community in the 'voluntary' believers' church has been so strong in Anabaptist writings that the values of individualism, which has increasingly come to shape postmodern society, have been neglected (Holland 1995).[1] Indeed, in many conservative Mennonite traditions, individualism has been viewed as suspect, and as a result it has been suppressed to a great extent, interfering with the process of creative change. We wish to examine the strengths and liabilities of individualism, and to show that it is an essential ingredient of strong leadership. First, let us cast the concept of individualism in a theoretical context, and then examine the empirical evidence.

Sorting Individual Types

Alexis de Tocqueville coined the term 'individualism.' In his *Democracy in America*, he claimed that it is the 'chaotic but creative moment of transition from aristocracy to democracy that makes the best form of society possible' (Tocqueville 1969; Bellah et al. 1985, 3). 'At that moment the repressive and conservative features of the old society are broken through so that new ideas can come forth, but there is still enough social solidarity left that initiative from popular leaders can mobilize support for significant reform' (Bellah et al. 1985, 3).

We cannot assume that there is complete commensurability between such larger societal changes and churches/denominations or groups such as the Mennonites changing within a society. However, Tocqueville's idea that tradition can still play a positive role of purpose and focus when individuals enter the larger societal arena, is provocative.

When traditional hierarchies are strong, there is little room for experimentation, but when social structures are changed, through immigration, mobility, and revolution, there is again room for individual initiative. Mennonites, especially, have migrated so often that they have often experienced new situations that called for new creative powers. In old structures, bureaucrats put their energies into maintaining their own power, a focus that is not conducive to new initiatives. Democracy, Tocqueville suggested, is the way to cultivate and prolong creative voluntary periods of excitement and growth. It is like the surfer who rides the crest between the old receding and the newly forming waves, who is at the peak of creativity and requires all the individual resources of freedom, independence, balance, judgment, anticipation, selection, and finesse to survive.

The Puritans, Quakers, Amish, Mennonites, and others left the old feudal states and ecclesiastical structures to find new freedoms in North America, creating homesteads on virgin soil, unleashing the pent-up creative energies smouldering in the hearts of the oppressed. Thrown together, using many languages, cultures, and religions, they, with the Native people who welcomed them, nurtured their freedom, while creating new communities, churches, cultures, and societies. The persecutions, migrations, and mixed pioneer settlements helped to create individualism, in the context of the *Gemeinschaft*.

Changing Personality Types

Tocqueville's thesis requires further analysis. Newcomers (which often included Mennonites who moved every several generations) are faced with alternatives, such as (1) segregating and isolating themselves again, or (2) assimilating into the host society and losing their identity, or (3) some modified version of being a stranger or middle person, like a broker seeking to balance the pulls and pushes of both in-group and host cultures, which is more postmodern.

In *The Lonely Crowd*, David Reisman (1950) developed tradition-directed, inner-directed, and other-directed types. The tradition-directed person is typical in non-industrial non-urban societies where birth and death rates are high and where spatial and social mobility is low. As these people are introduced to the industrial environment, they move through an inner-directed phase in which they become conscious of their traditional state and begin to become aware of other non-traditional options. Their rising awareness creates much evaluation and inner turmoil. Reisman's other-directed type is one who has become urbanized, lives in an industrial environment, and is oriented towards secondary others who have entered his or her social arena and influenced his or her values (Driedger 1996).

In the case of the tradition-directed, the in-group culture controls behaviour minutely: there is intensive socialization, and a careful and fairly rigid etiquette. Little energy is directed towards finding new solutions for age-old problems or towards developing new agricultural techniques or the like. Usually the tradition-directed ethnic is found in a rural, agricultural, or food-gathering society, although these values are also brought to the city by ethnic villagers (Gans 1962).

A broker or middle person is one who enters the urban, industrial fray seeking to remain an integral part of both worlds. Pierre Van den Berghe (1981, 137) claims that every country has its middle persons: 'Turkey has Armenians and Greeks; West Africa has Lebanese; East Africa has Indians and Pakstanis; Egypt has Copts; Indonesia, the Philippines, Malaysia, Vietnam and Thailand have the "Chinese".' These are minorities who compete well and are also fairly well-to-do socio-economically. When they compete in the melting pot economically, they seem to be able to separate their economic and social lives, and retain their separate ethnic identity. Van den Berghe (1981, 138) suggests that there exists a cluster of characteristics of 'middlemen' minorities (MM) that are remarkably uniform from society to society. MMs usually maintain strong extended families, perpetuate endogamy, and try to perpetuate their own cultural, institutional, and spatial identity so that they acculturate more slowly than most other groups. Van den Berghe (1981, 138) classified MMs as an urban *petit bourgeois* social class, better off than the majority of the population but often far from wealthy. This better-than-average socio-economic status often provides them with many advantages in competition with their neighbours. MMs often hold ethnic values such as thrift, frugality, lack of ostentation, and postponement of gratification. Jews, Chinese, Japanese, East Indians, and Mennonites come readily to mind.

Georg Simmel's 'the stranger' is similar to the middle person. The concept of 'the stranger' unifies the two characteristics of fixity and transience (Simmel 1950, 402). Simmel thought that the stranger could retain a separate identity by controlling his behaviour with others, often by being physically near them to perform economic functions, for example, but distant with respect to their values. On the other hand, the stranger could often be far away from his reference in-group when performing his duties in urban society, but could still retain a symbolic feeling of nearness and belonging to his in-group. We would expect that when the stranger or middle person enters the strange environment of others, he or she is secure only if the person is grounded in a reference group, or socially and psychologically motivated by the norms and networks of such a group.

For many migrants, however, retaining a stable secure base is difficult. Robert Park's (1950, 348) ideal marginal person, however, is typical of another type to which many Blacks from the rural American tenant farms of the South belong when they move into northern cities. This change of residence, typical of new migrants, and the concomitant breaking of home ties with the traditional rural values and norms, resulted in great cultural upheavals that led to change and sometimes to disorganization and conflict.

Park thinks of the marginal person as a racial or cultural hybrid: one who lives in two worlds, but is more or less a stranger in both; one who aspires to, but is excluded from, full membership in a new group. The marginal person is between two cultures, and not fully a part of either. 'Park's excluded marginal man was depicted as suffering from spiritual instabililty, intensified self-consciousness, restlessness, and in a state of malaise' (Levine, Carter, and Gorman 1976, 830). He thought of him as a person who could not cope in the new situation, a potential deviant who might look for outlets of expression in unacceptable ways. This type is becoming more evident as Mennonites increasingly seek to survive in the city for several generations. Anabaptists began as surfers seeking to live between two waves (worlds), but soon opted for more tranquil shores, where they lost their surfing skills. Today, new Anabaptists enter cities like a surfer who mounts an emerging wave, but surfing skills are quite undeveloped. However, individual aptitudes, armoured by traditional *Gemeinschaft* security, can go a long way towards learning to survive and compete.

Bellah's Four Individual Types

'In 1985, Robert Bellah and his coauthors (Richard Madsen, William Sullivan, Ann Swidler and Steven Tipton) published their best-selling book *Habits of the Heart* and, almost overnight, restored the interest of sociologists in the concept of individualism' (Ainlay 1990, 135). They define individualism as 'a belief in the inherent dignity and ... sacredness of the human person,' and 'a belief that the individual is a pri-

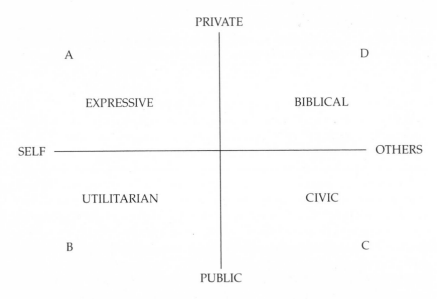

Figure 3.1   Model Based on Bellah et al.'s (1985) Four Types of Individualism

mary reality whereas society is a second-order, derived or artificial construct ...' (Bellah et al. 1985, 334). They devote their entire book (1985), and a subsequent reader (1987), to constructing four types of individualism (biblical, civic, utiliarian, expressive). They claim that 'individualism lies at the very core of American culture,' and this sacredness of the individual involves the 'right to think for ourselves, judge ourselves, make our own decisions, and live lives as we see fit' (Bellah et al. 1985, 143). The same could be said for Anabaptists and their ancestors. All four types of individualism assume these rights, but our deepest problems are also linked to individualism.

To sort some of the dimensions of individualism, we have plotted the four individual types in figure 3.1, along polarities of commitment and local or public arenas. 'Expressive individualism holds that each person has a unique core of feeling and intuition that should unfold or be expressed if individuality is to be realized' (Bellah et al. 1985, 334). Expressive individualism is related to the phenomenon of romanticism in eighteenth- and nineteenth-century European and American culture. Today it may be expressed most clearly by the artistic communities in creative writing and the arts (painting, sculpturing, etc.). In figure 3.1 we suggest that the self is the primary focus of commitment in a 'local village' arena. The downside of expressive individualism is that it can be too focused on self and its limited locale, while the opportunities lie in expressing most deeply individual psychological and creative feelings, motives, and desires.

Utilitarian individualism is usually traced to John Locke, who held that the individual was prior to society, and that the individual's self-interest should be maximized. For Hobbes, the desire for power over others, and the fear that others wish you ill, was clearly present, suggesting that the individual needs to be wary of social commitments. Bellah et al. (1985, 145) suggest that 'America is also the inventor of the most mythic individual hero, the cowboy, who again and again saves a society he can never completely fit into, because he can shoot straighter and faster than others.' The other American hero is the hard-boiled detective, a loner, whose marginality is his strength. Society in each case is corrupt to the core. In the case of Locke and Hobbes and their utilitarian individualism, we ask: can such individualism, where the self has become the main focus of reality, be sustained? In the case of the cowboy and detective, we ask: are such individuals indeed real and plausible? We have plotted the utilitarian as the self-contained individual who may express individualism in a more public arena. It is a contract individuals enter into with society in order to advance their self-interest. Both the expressive and utilitarian forms of individualism are considered impoverished vehicles because they focus on immediate payoff, rather than the traditions which have formed us, or the larger problems and needs of society (Bellah et al. 1987, 4). Television and the mass media, they claim, are largely utilitarian and expressive forms, playing to emotions, wants, and desires of the self.

In contrast to the private expressive and public utilitarian individuals who focused on the self, the biblical and civic forms of individualism are private and public expressions and action directed towards others. Bellah and colleagues' (1985, 335) Republican tradition, which Ainlay (1990) has renamed 'civic individualism,' originated in classical Greece and Roman traditions, expressed later in civic humanism of the late medieval and early modern Europe, and contributed to the formation of modern Western democracies. It presupposes that citizens are motivated by civic virtue as well as self-interest, for moral purposes such as justice and the public good. In the United States the civic and biblical forms of individualism seem to have agreed on common purposes of justice.

The tradition that originates in biblical religion, widely diffused in American and Canadian culture, is carried primarily by Jewish and Christian religious communities (Bellah et al. 1985). Numerous versions, including Puritan and Protestant sects who promoted voluntarism, were refugees from European state church regions, who sought religious freedom from the establishment and were willing to live with religious diversity. These groups inspired a notion of government based on the voluntary participation of individuals. The biblical record is laced with – indeed is dominated by – individuals, so we should not be surprised when individualism and Christianity highly correlate, as Max Weber already suggested in his *Protestant Ethic and the Spirit of Capitalism*. What was more individual than Abraham leaving the first great urban civilization, mesopotamia, to start a new religion in the wilderness; Jacob stealing a blessing from Esau; and his grandson Joseph becoming a major minister in Pharaoh's cabinet in charge of famine relief in the second great urban civilization of Eygpt? Moses learned independence in Pharaoh's court, and eventually challenged Pharaoh himself, leading the children of Israel into the desert, while Joshua set out to conquer Palestine. The prophets receive ample attention for their independence, as in the courage of Jeremiah, the commitment of Ruth the immigrant, Esther the leader, Hosea the deviant, Jonah the coward, and Amos the shepherd railing at the city folks. The New Testament is dominated by two individuals, Jesus, who defied traditions all around him, and Paul, who travelled all over the urban Mediterranean world, from Jerusalem to Rome, challenging entrepreneurs, religious and political leaders, where he could find them. Mennonites especially, after they retreated into agricultural villages, have a community tradition that has obscured the importance of individualism, subsuming individual leadership drive under the will of God. When new Mennonite leaders foment another schism, setting themselves apart in the name of Christ, we are often surprised and puzzled. We should not be, because the Anabaptist *Martyrs Mirror* shows clearly that Mennonites have a history of individualism. Recently Mennonites have been reluctant to acknowledge current individualism, although C.J. Dyck's *Twelve Becoming* (1973), for example, celebrates individualism.

Although religious groups vary, both civic and biblical individualism see the person in the context of a larger whole, a community and a tradition capable of sustaining genuine individuality and nurturing both private and public life (Bellah et al. 1985, 143). However, modern expressive and utilitarian forms of individualism today seem to be growing at the expense of biblical and civic traditions of individualism. Biblical and civic individualism are committed to others in their major focus; it is doubtful that expressive and utilitarian forms of individualism, focused on the self, can be sustained for long. While we have plotted biblical individualism in the private–other cell, such individualism also involves important public commitments to action. However, Mennonite biblical individualism has been formed largely in the context of the private local village community, and only for some have their religious sights begun to include the larger arenas of the public global village, to which we turn next.

Exploring Creative Alternatives

To get some sense of whether this conceptual and theoretical discussion has some confirmation in fact, let us consider some contemporary historical examples of how individualism has played an important role in leadership training, especially in times of transition, as Tocqueville predicted, and then examine the 1989 Church Membership Profile (CMP II) data to see whether the four individual types developed by Bellah and colleagues can be documented.

Alternative Service as Individualism

While examples of Mennonite individualism are numerous, we need to turn to larger historical phenomena that have shaped modern Anabaptist individualism. Involuntary alternative service during the Second World War provided an opportunity for young Mennonites to leave their traditional rural communities and learn new work in new cultures outside their ethnic enclaves. These men who resisted military service and entered alternative service, working in forestry projects, mental hospitals, and the like, were forced out of their enclavic rural communities (Klippenstein 1979; Driedger and Kraybill 1994). Out of this tragic blessing emerged leaders forged through trial by fire who are just now moving out of the leadership core of the Mennonite Church. A recent photo in *Mennonite Life* showing Kansas men who served included four who became college presidents, major editors of Church papers, several presidents of the General Conference Mennonite Church, the Mennonite Church, published writers, including theologians, and many pastors who were the driving force behind the Board of Christian Service and the MCC in the 1950s and 1960s. In Canada the pattern was the same, conscientious objectors likewise becoming stalwarts in Mennonite schools, churches, and institutions, which illustrates well the connection between individual courage and commitment to alternative service, which developed leaders for the church.

The Second World War, and the opportunity it created for alternative service, sparked the ferment that pushed Mennonite youth into the world, showing them opportunities for service in the larger society, and it also provided much needed experience and practice for them in surfing the tide between their traditional community and the newly forming waves outside it. As Tocqueville predicted, this creative newfound individualism, still anchored in social in-group solidarity, changed and launched a new phase in the Mennonite Central Committee, formed in 1920. The MCC was founded to help Russian Mennonites, and it remained a relief agency, serving in-group needs largely for its first twenty-five years. However, during and after the war, the creative forces of Mennonite alternative service released hundreds of the most able, committed Mennonite youth to help serve the needs of those outside their Mennonite enclaves (Kreider and Goossen 1988).

These Mennonite conscientious objectors would be good examples of Bellah and colleagues' (1985) biblical individualism. They were individually committed to the biblical understanding of their historical opposition to taking part in war. Their families and communities had for generations, and centuries, been tested with respect to these beliefs. Their significant others cheered them on in their years of doing alternative service with others, by supporting them financially, socially, and morally. Many met other like-minded Mennonites, Quakers, Brethren, Catholics, and others in their work camps, where they made enough of a sacrifice in time and income that they had to rethink and evaluate their actions. Many adjustments were made, as Tocqueville (1969) predicted, and energies were channelled towards helping others rather than bemoaning their lonely fate away from family and friends. For a time they were 'strangers' working out the meaning of it all, living between their longed-for home community and their alternative calling, in a strange cold world where they were often misunderstood.

MCC Outreach and Individual Leadership

The Mennonite Central Committee originated in 1920, when Mennonites in North America came to the rescue of Mennonites in the Soviet Union after the First World War. During the war, Ukrainian Mennonites were caught in the crossfire of the Red and White armies' struggle for power, especially in the south, where they lived. During this Communist revolution, when the Reds and Lenin came to power in 1917, many Mennonite villages were pillaged, most of their lands were lost, and horses had been confiscated so they could no longer farm their land. When severe hunger and famine hit the country, Mennonites in North America came to the rescue with food, clothes, tractors, and relief to help their kin and people.

When the Second World War began, in 1939/41, Mennonites in Canada and the United States were again faced with conscription. A majority of Mennonite young men and a few women chose alternative service, working in forestry camps, mental hospitals, and the like. After service as conscientious objectors, young Mennonites returned to their home communities, but many applied what they had learned and used it to create forms of what Bellah et al. (1985) called 'civic individual service,' focused not on their own people, but on service to others. This clearly falls into cell C of figure 3.1, as civic public service.

Similar to what Tocqueville saw in the new American democracy, Mennonite youth were jettisoned out of their traditional segregated environment, and encountered new ideas; they returned to launch a variety of MCC service programs of voluntary service, PAX, relief work, the Mennonite Disaster Service, and Mutual Aid, which during the past fifty years has evolved into an other-directed MCC, with 1,000 workers in more than 50 countries, supported by an annual budget of $30 million. Alternative service forced youth into the larger arena; as a result, the old traditional in-group structures and old patterns of leadership gave way to refresh ideas stemming from youth and their experiences. For fifty years, the MCC has been able to extend these renewed democratic forms of leadership training, which are now widely recognized in North America generally. However, there are signs that bureaucracy is becoming entrenched in the MCC, that inertia is growing, that funds and personnel are being deployed locally and access to them has become restricted.

The MCC has been especially successful in sending out what Simmel would call 'strangers,' those whose roots are deeply lodged in the sending churches, who are clearly focused and directed by a committed agency – youth who are able to surf successfully on the crest between the new challenges and their traditional in-group values and the communities from which they come. Such biblical individualists, with MCC experience, return home with new leadership potential.

Entrepreneurs in the Professions and Business

The Anabaptists in the sixteenth century were heavily engaged in the craft industry, which provided them more mobility than was available to those who worked the land as serfs. As Mennonites increasingly urbanize and change their occupations from farmers to professionals and business people, the Muppies and entrepreneurs are again forced to surf, this time on the waves of urbanism and professionalism, and new enterprise. While, before 1940, most Mennonites farmed, by 1989 only 7 per cent did, and larger numbers were engaged in the professions (28 per cent), business (9 per cent), and sales/clerical jobs (11 per cent) (Driedger 1993). Mennonites no longer are segregated spatially, nor are their patterns of making a living segmented. This entrepreneurial revolution, where half who are now urban are surfing the metropolitan crest, will require all the individual resources of balance, judgment, anticipation, selection, and finesse that they can muster. There are both hopeful and discouraging signs.

Urbanization has again launched Mennonites into the cities, where more ready-made natural individual opportunities for influence and service exist. By 1989 half had at least some college education, and one in five had at least a year of graduate school, as was the case in the general population, and this level of education gave them the resources to engage in independent competition for jobs and income. Mennonite socio-economic status has increased considerably since 1972, and they have become more independent, self-reliant, and free to make their own decisions than ever before (Kauffman and Driedger 1991, 37–40). Opportunities, for Muppies especially, to engage in all forms of Bellah and colleagues' (1985) civic individualism, are amply available to many. As teachers, doctors, nurses, social workers, lawyers, and clergy, Mennonites find opportunities for civic public service ready-made in the form of serving others, but there are also utilitarian opportunities to practise individualism that can enrich the self and, at the same time, serve the public. Keeping the professions focused on civic rather than utilitarian needs is the challenge.

In business and sales, entrepreneurial opportunities tend to drift towards serving the public for private profit, part of the capitalist enterprise. While farmers also work the land for private profit, farming has always involved an element of 'working God's soil to feed others,' which has a civic, or even biblical tone; nonethless, it often became quite utilitarian for many Mennonites. Thus, being a business person, with explicit entrepreneurial goals linked to working in public to make money, has been a hard sell among Mennonites in the past. One of the complaints of many Mennonite business people has been that the Church gladly takes their donations but is reluctant to grant them full membership on par with that bestowed on church workers (Redekop, Ainlay, and Siemens 1995).

Hornaday (1982, 25) defines entrepreneurs as exhibiting 'a cluster of traits, including self-confidence, perseverance or determination, energy or diligence, resourcefulness, and ability to take calculated risks, a need to achieve, creativity, initiative, flexibility, a positive response to challenge, foresight, and dynamism or leadership.' That is a rather heady list, hard to reconcile with humility and being the 'quiet in the land,' traits that conservative Mennonites value. So it is clear that with one in ten Mennonites in business, times are changing, as is also evident from cases that show that the conservative group 'did not want business people in the church,' and that some thought 'a businessman was a crook' (Redekop, Ainlay, and Siemens (1995, 48). Many Mennonite entrepreneurs felt trapped between the cultural expectations of the Mennonite and non-Mennonite worlds. Thus, long-standing Mennonite suspicion of, or even hostility towards, business and profit persists (Redekop, Ainlay, and Siemens 1995, 78). Service for others is valued, and potentially competitive self-aggrandizing is often taboo.

Redekop et al. (1995, 94) found that sons who followed their fathers in business promoted those who showed creativity (69 and 37 per cent), while fathers promoted family members (36 to 18 per cent). A majority of Mennonite business people felt a sense of achievement (58 per cent), and they said they had entered business to bring security to the family (72 per cent). Many found pleasure in risk-taking, and were happy in the Mennonite drive for work. Many thought it was helpful to be a Mennonite in business because Mennonites are honest, have integrity and a good reputation, work hard, are dependable, offer quality products and are helpful. Some business people tended to overconform and be religiously conservative to prove their loyalty, with the result that entrepreneurs are more orthodox.

Individualism in the Creative Arts

The creative arts, such as music, writing, and printing, seem to be the new frontier for Mennonites to express individualism today. The musical tradition began early, in Amsterdam, carried eastward into Russia and North America, where choirs were well integrated into church practice and institutions of the community. In Canada this tradition was continued especially by Russian Mennonites, who came as immigrants in the 1920s, such as K.H. Neufeld, H. Neufeld, John Konrad, and Ben Horsch in Manitoba, and David Paetkau in Saskatchewan. These choral leaders constantly extended the traditional choral boundaries into classical arenas, but not without meeting considerable   resistance. Institutions such as Mennonite schools became favourable grounds in which to further the musical cause. A second cycle of musical creativity was spearheaded by George and Esther Wiebe, at Canadian Mennonite Bible College (CMBC); William and Irmgard Baerg and John Martens, at Mennonite Brethren Bible College (MBBC); Helen Martens, at Conrad Grebel College; and Henry Engebrecht, at the University of Manitoba. It extended individual creativity into the outside worlds of concert halls, universities, television, and the media. Hundreds of choir directors, soloists, and instrumentalists were able to extend their expressive individualism, largely within and with the blessing of their churches.

Creative writers had a much harder time, as Arnold Dyck, of Steinbach, and later Winnipeg, could well attest. Trained in Europe, Dyck found limited interest in his plays, novels, pamphlets, and art, until more recently, when urban Mennonites such as Al Reimer, Harry Loewen, Victor Doerksen, and Elizabeth Peters resurrected his works in a four-volume publication (Doerksen et al. 1985–90). Rudy Wiebe, a Mennonite college graduate, also experienced a rude jolt when his first of many novels, *Peace Shall Destroy Many*, got him into trouble in his Mennonite Brethren community, and he was let go from his editorship of the *Mennonite Brethren Herald*. Fortunately, he found a welcome hearing at the University of Alberta, where his many novels and creative works have continued to win national prizes.

While Arnold Dyck and Rudy Wiebe were marginalized individuals, still related to the Mennonite Church, most younger Mennonite creative writers have voluntarily left the Church. Winnipeg especially is a hotbed of largely 1870s-heritage Mennonite writers who began writing about their frustrations in the traditional family and community. Scores of books have been written by Mennonites from Winnipeg alone during the past twenty years, including by Patrick Friesen, Di Brandt, Sandra Birdsell, Armin Wiebe, Sarah Klassen, Audrey Poetker-Thiessen, David Waltner-Toews, Diane Driedger, and John Weier.[2] Some of these expressive individual younger writers began by examining their local traditional past; others turned to the larger scene for their inspiration.

Many of the older immigrant Mennonite creative writers, such as Arnold Dyck, first wrote about their experiences in the Ukraine, whence they had emigrated in the 1920s, and used Low German characters, such as Koop and Bua, to illustrate the humour in Canadian Mennonite village life, but many conservatives did not appreciate such exposure. Armin Wiebe used such Low German writing in his well-known *The Salvation of Jasch Siemens* (1984), illustrating the very different village context in which agricultural Mennonites of the past found themselves. Many of these creative writers, however, feel marginalized in their own community, finding it hard to identify with the Mennonite Church.

Others, such as Di Brandt, found Mennonite family and village upbringing oppressive. Brandt tried to relate to more liberal versions of the Mennonite Church when she moved to Winnipeg, but finally gave up on it. *Questions I Asked My Mother* (1987) illustrates the pain and anger she went through, in the change from premodern village life to new modern and postmodern life as a stranger in search of freedom. Patrick Friesen could also be put into the category of angry Mennonite writer, well illustrated especially in his novel *The Shunning* (1980), which was also turned into a play, where the agony of living in an oppressive village community leads to a cry for release. His latest book of poems, *A Broken Bowl* (1997), examines the burden of history, heaped atrocities, moral decay, and unimaginable sufferings. It is an angry lament, a summoning of fragments in an exhausted world, which uses many of the postmodern symbols of deconstruction, and the failure of religious metanarrative, leaving the scattered pieces of a broken bowl. These recent younger writers clearly fit into Bellah and colleagues' expressive type of individualism, whereby the very private emotions of the deep inner self are given a voice.

While the visual artistic Mennonite community is not nearly as expanded and developed, it, too, is characterized by a creative expressive individual influence, as is evident in the works that are increasingly being exhibited in both Mennonite schools and elsewhere. Here *Fraktur* traditional art, well developed in the Swiss Mennonite branch, grew out of accepted community patterns, as did music. It is well accepted because it uses visual forms of birds, animals, plants close to, and dear to, the more conservative rural Mennonite past. Les Brandt, Dale Boldt, Margaret Doell, Aganetha Dyck, Helene Dyck, Leonard Giesbrecht, Lois Klassen, Ernie Kroeger, Grace Nickel, Susan Shantz, Jean Smallwood, Al Toews, and Erma Martin Yost are but a few who

TABLE 3.1
Indicators of Mennonite Personal Independence and Expressive Individualism
(N = 3,083)

Values that guide life and thought	Not important (%)	Not very important (%)	Somewhat important (%)	Important (%)	Very important (%)
Being able to make *own decision*	0	2	16	56	26
Being *self-reliant*	0	3	20	51	27
Taking care of own needs – being *independent*	1	5	29	49	16
Being *free* to do what I want to do	2	19	45	27	7

were recently presented in *The Mennonite Artist: Insider or Outsider*. As the title of the book suggests, they too feel like 'strangers,' riding the crest between their traditional and newly expanded worlds (Reimer 1990).

We do not have the space here to examine in detail these musical, creative writing, and visual artistic forms of expressive and civic individualism. Nor do we have the time to explore more utilitarian forms of individual expressions found in the expanding long- and well-developed business community, which Calvin Redekop (1995) has begun to examine. The professional Muppie worlds could not be examined either, nor the emerging world of the Mennonite media and Mennonites in the provincial and national media, which some have begun to explore (Driedger and Redekop 1998). Indeed, in Winnipeg, where 22,000 Mennonites live, Mennonite names appear daily in the media, and in the daily newspapers everywhere.

Finding Bellah's Individual Types

Following the figure 3.1 model, which plots the four individual types posited by Bellah et al. (1985), let us also use Kauffman and Driedger's (1991) four personal independence indicators to measure expressive individualism. In table 3.1 we see that a majority of the sample of more than 3,000 North American Mennonites and Brethren in Christ thought

that making your own decisions, and being self-reliant, being independent, and being free to do what you want were important. Four out of
five wanted to make their own decisions and be self-reliant, and one-
quarter thought this was very important. Two out of three wanted to
take care of their own needs, and one-third thought it important to be
free to do what you want. It is quite clear that Mennonites are strongly
independent.

These four indicators have not been linked to any utilitarian, civic, or
biblical commitments, so we have a measure of independent expressive individualism. These individual expressions of self-reliance, independence, and freedom can be used for selfish ends as well as for
service to others.

While expressive individualism represents private values of the self,
utilitarian individualism represents values that guide the individual in
public life and thought, which we have measured by using six indicators: security, getting ahead, saving, earning, and aspirations towards
fashions and home furnishings. Six of ten respondents thought it
important to earn enough money so as to be secure in old age, so they
would not be dependent on others. One-third thought it important to
work hard to get ahead financially, while one-quarter did not consider
this important. So we are beginning to have a range of values, with
almost half of respondents favouring those in the middle. The profile
for saving as much money as possible is very similar to getting ahead;
respondents seem to be torn between getting ahead for themselves and
caring about other values. Once earning as much money as possible is
the goal, the numbers begin to skew towards less importance. When
the emphasis is clearly on stylish dressing and home furnishings,
almost two-thirds no longer think it important, and very few admit to
personal dress and home comfort as being important. Mennonites
seem to favour utilitarian individualism for the purpose of security
and caring for oneself, but when the focus turns to money, dress, and
home comfort, very few give it high priority.

While expressive and utilitarian individualism focus on the private
and public self, civic and biblical individualism focus on other traits.
Using five indicators for civic individualism, table 3.3 shows us that all
Mennonites in our sample wish to be at peace with others and treat
others properly, and four out of five also want to use their resources for
the good of others. These Mennonites are strongly motivated towards
the welfare of others, and we also see that three-quarters actually volunteered to work for church and community agencies, and visited

TABLE 3.2
Indicators of Utilitarian Individalism and Values that Guide Mennonite Life and Thought
(*N* = 3,083)

Values that guide life and thought	Not important (%)	Not very important (%)	Somewhat important (%)	Important (%)	Very important (%)
Earning enough money to be *secure* in old age	1	6	33	47	13
Working hard so as to *get ahead* financially	3	19	45	29	5
Saving as much money as possible	3	22	48	23	4
Earning as much money as possible	4	33	44	17	2
Being *dressed* in the latest styles and fashions	14	49	29	7	1
Getting the nicest *home* and furnishings I can afford	10	49	33	7	1

non-relatives when they were sick or shut-in. The strong independence found in Mennonite expressive individualism does not seem to be a deterent to helping others. This seems to confirm the findings in table 3.2, that while Mennonites want to be secure, get ahead, save, and earn, they do not wish to do so exclusively for their own ends, but for the welfare of others also.

Biblical individualism illustrates the tension between the self and others as well as the private–public dilemma. As table 3.4 indicates, three out of four Mennonites agree that church membership means that the individual should be willing both to give admonition and to receive it. This involves the courage to restrict the individualism of others, and also to be restricted by others for the sake of the Church. One-half think of their religion as being a more personal choice, while one-third lean towards accepting direction from church doctrine, which illustrates the self–other dilemma. When faith is pushed as a private matter, one-third agree, but well over half then opt for less pri-

TABLE 3.3
Indicators of Mennonite Civic Individualism

Values that guide life and thought (actually were active)	No importance (%)	Not very (never) (%)	Somewhat (few times) (%)	Important (occasionally) (%)	Very important (frequently) (%)
Being at *peace* with other persons	0	0	2	28	70
Making sure I *treat* others properly	0	1	1	37	61
Using my *resources* for good of others	0	2	18	57	23
Volunteered work for church or community agencies	0	5	18	43	34
Visited a non-relative who was sick, shut-in	0	4	24	48	24

TABLE 3.4
Indicators of Mennonite Biblical Individualism

Values that guide life and thought	Strongly disagree (%)	Disagree (%)	Uncertain (%)	Agree (%)	Strongly agree (%)
Church membership means to give and receive mutual *admonition*	1	9	15	65	10
Religion should be a more *personal choice* than church-doctrine–directed	5	29	14	40	12
Faith is a *private* matter for each to decide and practise	8	47	11	29	5
Not business of church to be directly involved in my *personal affairs*	7	52	17	22	2

TABLE 3.5
Correlations between Expressive, Utilitarian, Biblical, and Civic Individualism (Pearson's rs)

	Expressive individualism (independence)	Utilitarian individualism (materialism)	Biblical individualism (individualism)	Civic individualism (self/others)
Independence	–	.49	.33	−.01
Materialism	.49	–	.28	−.18
Individualism	.33	.28	–	−.31
Civic, self/others	−.01	.18	.31	–
Secularism	.20	.23	.54	−.35
Media use	.11	.15	.17	−.11
Political participation	.10	.05	−.02	.10
Age	.08	.01	−.02	.22
Role of women	.06	.01	−.06	.02
Memberships	.06	.08	−.06	.02
Ethnicity	.01	.02	−.10	.13
Communalism	−.02	.00	−.13	.15
Socio-economic status	−.02	−.04	−.17	.16
Fundamentalism	−.04	.06	−.14	.07
Welfare attitudes	−.05	−.08	−.21	.20
Education	−.06	−.13	−.21	.14
Pacifism	−.08	−.27	−.15	.17
Race relations	−.08	−.17	−.23	.14
General orthodoxy	−.10	−.04	−.23	.07
Evangelism	−.11	−.18	−.31	.43
Charity	−.12	−.08	−.15	.16
Charismatics	−.12	−.12	−.18	.20
Moral behaviour	−.13	−.07	−.19	.15
Moral attitudes	−.14	−.10	−.29	.21
Separatism	−.14	−.16	−.31	.24
Stewardship attitudes	−.16	−.07	−.33	.22
Devotionalism	−.16	−.18	−.38	.45
Religious life	−.17	−.21	−.43	.51
Anabaptism	−.19	−.23	−.42	.29
Aspirationalism	−.24	−.21	−.47	.42

vacy in their decisions and practice. The strongest statement, saying that it is not the business of the Church to be directly involved in personal affairs, is too much individual privacy for six out of ten, and only one in four agree with the statement. It is clear that the largest majority feel most at ease with admonition, which involves restrictions of give-and-take, and a strong majority agree that the Church does have a right to be involved in personal affairs.

In table 3.5, we show the correlations between the four individualism scales we have presented. The first three – expressive, utilitarian, and biblical – were designed to focus on the independence of the individual, and we see that they all correlated negatively with outreach to others, especially associationalism, Anabaptism, religious life, stewardship, and the like. These associations clearly show that focus on the self is an independent phenomenon, quite different from a focus on others, as suggested in our model in figure 3.1. The civic individualism scale shows that, when items are designed to show outreach to others, these correlations are all positive. Correlations of expressive individualism and utilitarian individualism are somewhat lower than the biblical and civic ones. The intercorrelations between the expressive, utilitarian, biblical, and civic scales of individualism are also strong, which suggests that they all measure a similar phenomenon. These findings show the basic differences between focus on the self and concern for others, also which act as a dialectic in religious faith and action.

Conclusions

Alexis de Tocqueville, in studying American society, concluded that creative changes in society occur at special revolutionary times like waves, where new ideas can be introduced when the old society structures are weakened or broken down, and popular leaders can then initiate and mobilize significant reform. We have suggested that the Reformation, when the Anabaptists emerged, was such a time, and that Mennonites are again in such a postmodern revolutionary time, when urbanization, professionalization, modernization, and individualism, enhanced by the electronic media, are shaping Mennonite identity.

We focused especially on individualism and types such as Reisman's tradition-directed, inner-directed, and other-directed personality types. Simmel's 'stranger' and van den Berghe's 'brokers' acted as positive individual leaders in such times, bridging the old and the new, while Park's 'marginal' person was an example of negative breakdown of identity. We explored empirical evidence of these types. Alternative service during the Second World War resulted in renewed leadership, MCC outreach acted as a training ground for leadership, and Muppies and creative artists are two good examples of postmodern 1990s forms of individualism at work. These forms of individualism are strongly shaping Mennonites today, as more and more Mennonite individuals are surfing the crest between tradition and renewal.

Bellah and associates introduced four types of individualism, two of which focused on the self and two on others, which we plotted as a model. We empirically demonstrated that all four forms of individualism are very much present among Mennonites today. Expressive individualism, in the private–self corner, emphasizing self-reliance, independence, free expression, freedom, and making your own decisions, was very strong among most Mennonites. Utilitarian individualism, representing the public–self contrast, was strong on security, getting ahead, and saving, but was less supported when the focus was on personal dress and a comfortable home. Civic individualism, in the public–others corner, which involves being at peace with others and treating others well, using resources for others, volunteer work, and visiting others, was also well supported. Biblical individualism, representing acceptance and giving of mutual admonition, was strong, but there was a considerable range in the extent to which faith should be a private matter, the extent to which the Church could direct individuals, and the extent to which the Church should be involved in personal affairs. We conclude that individualism has been, and still is, strong among Mennonites, and that they use such initiative and assertiveness extensively for the service of others.

PART II

SYMBOLIC EXTENSIONS AND CHALLENGES

4

Cultural Changes in the Sacred Village

When the Mennonites first came to Western Canada from Ukraine in the 1870s, they basically transferred their agricultural villages by pitching their immigrant tents on the untamed prairies. They were faced with reordering old experiences into a new, meaningful order (*nomos*) that would shield them from the terrors which lay ahead (Berger 1967, 19). This new construction of reality was like a 'sacred canopy' – a tent-like roof used by the Jews as protection from the elements in their wilderness wanderings. This canopy, symbolized by a blanket with poles at each corner to hold it up, provided a protective roof so struggling pioneers could begin to feel a sense of togetherness, of wholeness, of being at home. These strangers in a new land turned to familiar elements such as religion, community, culture, institutions, and land to use as poles to stake their Mennonite claim. Humans tend to attribute the sacred to structures that provide protection, hence the 'canopy' that provides a mysterious sense of safety in a reconstructed familiar.

Communal Separation of the Sacred and Profane

To make some sense of what such a sacred canopy or Mennonite traditional village in the 1870s felt like, let us, in typical postmodern story style, sketch the early life of the author's grandfather, who arrived in Manitoba from Ukraine as a fifteen-year-old boy in 1875. It is the experience of an 'individual' within one family and community, using Erik Erikson's (1977) model of ritualization to demonstrate the dynamics of a quest for individual freedom within a traditional rural Old Colony Mennonite community that seeks to control.[1]

The Numinous Village: Trust and Recognition

The cohesive Mennonite community (the village) is designed to care for its members. There is mutuality of recognition; regular and mutual affirmation and certification. The Old Colony Mennonite village becomes a hallowed place. Even the names of villages (Blumenfeld, Reinland, Gruenthal), first used 500 years ago in Holland, have been faithfully transplanted to Prussia, Ukraine, Canada, Mexico, British Honduras, Bolivia. The house–barn architectural combinations begun in Holland were brought to Canada, as were their outer and inner structures and the furnishings of the buildings. The church and German school take their appointed places in typical row villages. The village settlement, the church services, the voluntary organizations are all part of the numinous ritual of Old Colony Mennonite village life (Redekop 1969; Sawatsky 1971; Driedger 1982).

Johann Driedger was born into such a Mennonite village in Chortitza, Ukraine, in 1859, one of hundreds of similar villages. His well-written letters attest that he received a solid six years of German education in Ukraine, before he came with his family to Manitoba. They helped form the village of Blumenfeld (field of flowers), one of about 100 villages established in a solid block reserve settlement in southern Manitoba (Francis 1955). Johann Driedger lived in Blumenfeld for twenty-nine years, until the age of forty-four. Although very little is known about his early life, we do know that he served as village *Schultze* (mayor), an elected office, which suggests that he was in good standing with the community. There was a numinous trust relationship, filled with a mysterious sense of a presence of the sacred. Indeed, the 'Gemeinde,' as they called their total church fellowship and community membership, could be viewed as a sacred canopy (Berger 1967).

Individualism was suspect in such a community. There were very clear cultural mores, customs, and boundaries (Driedger 1992). The women dressed in the fashions of the sixteenth century, with long dark blue or black dresses, large shawls, black headdresses, hair parted in the middle. The men wore shirts without collars, and dark suits, and no ties. Adornments such as watches, rings and other jewellery, and makeup were taboo. Figure 4.1, a photograph of the Johann Driedger family taken in 1906, just after they left their Manitoba village, shows the typical dress. Houses and churches alike were very plain. From the 1906 photograph, we see that Johann Driedger and his family were traditional members of the very traditional Old Colony Mennonite

Figure 4.1   The traditional Driedger family: A product of the numinous village

church, involved in the numinous rituals of trust and separation, prone to ritual excesses of cultural and religious idolism.

The Judicious Stage: Autonomy versus Legalism

Signs of individual autonomy and innovation were already evident when Driedger was still in the Blumenfeld village in Manitoba. He began a small store in the back of his village farmhouse. Johann's eldest son, Peter, left for Saskatchewan (then part of the North-West Territories) in 1902, and Johann and his family soon followed in 1904. Whether there were push factors in Manitoba, we do not know. Perhaps the less structured opportunities in what was the North West Territories in 1904 beckoned irresistibly. The Driedgers settled at Clarks Crossing, on the edge of another solid Mennonite block reserve settlement (Driedger and Church 1974). They did not settle in a Mennonite village, but Johann built a store in the open country on the railway line (on the margin of the community spatially separated). While he farmed some, he now became a businessman and a postmaster, both non-traditional Mennonite occupations. Living some ten miles north of the city of Saskatoon, where he bought his supplies, and some ten miles south of the nearest Mennonite church, he later purchased an automobile to replace the much slower horse.

Signs of innovation are also evident in the photograph (figure 4.1), which was taken in 1906, after they had been in Saskatchewan two years. Johann has a white handkerchief in his pocket, and he is wearing a striped shirt with a collar, both interpreted traditionally as a sign of arrogance. Indeed, photographs were frowned upon, so having a family photo was itself a form of innovation.

There is much evidence that Johann was testing his individual wings to see what was considered right or wrong; he was experimenting with the boundaries of approval and disapproval (Driedger 1982). The Old Colony norms did not condone photo-taking, living outside a Mennonite village, non-farm occupations, and dress innovations. Driedger was testing his self-reliance in his play with what was permissible. He found pleasure in exerting his will, feeling capable and justified in using it (Erikson 1977, 93).

Dramatic Initiative: Village versus Town

The dramatic initiative of Johann Driedger began in early 1907, when he purchased a store in Osler, a small hamlet of several hundred residents three miles from the nearest Mennonite village. Driedger had just transferred his goods from Clarks Crossing to the Osler store when, on 19 February, four businesses (Heinrichs, Kalbfleisch, Fowler, and Driedger) burned to the ground (Warman Commission of Inquiry 1908). The Heinrichs' store, next to Driedger's, caught fire first, and Driedger accused Heinrichs (both were Old Colony Mennonite members) of arson with the intent to eliminate Driedger as a competitor. Driedger had taken out Old Colony Mennonite fire insurance on his Clarks Crossing store, but it was not clear whether the insurance covered the newly transferred goods to the store in Osler. Heinrichs had insured his business with a more liberal Minnesota Mennonite insurance company and expected ample recompense for his losses.

The Mennonite church elders were placed in a dilemma: How much opening up to new trends could they afford? Should they allow their members to insure businesses (which was taboo) under the Mennonite insurance plan? Now that Mennonite stores were even located in a hamlet (also taboo), should they also support coverage? What about one church member (Driedger) accusing another (Heinrichs) of arson? Driedger had been slowly getting out of line in the past as it was. In fact, while they were deliberating over what to do, Driedger was building a new modern house in Osler, presumably to move into town and start another store. The situation seemed to be getting out of hand. The church leaders demanded that Driedger be reconciled with Heinrichs and refused to pay any insurance on Driedger's losses. Driedger was outraged.

Within a year, in the spring of 1908, the frequent visits and discussions (arguments?) led to the excommunication of Driedger. Thus unexpected disaster highlighted community-control problems and pushed the Mennonite leaders into a more legalistic position. Driedger's individualistic autonomy and egotism would be put to shame, and community pressures would be employed (by the ban, and by business boycott) to bring him under control. By withholding fellowship and assurance of salvation in the believers' community, they sought to raise self-doubt.

Our research shows numerous innovations in such a solid Mennonite rural community. Consciously or inadvertently, some members were searching for self-identity, and probing the boundaries of the permissible (Driedger 1982). There were many excommunications, but the reasons for such drastic actions are not always clear. Increased 'worldliness,' 'lack of humility,' 'bad behaviour,' 'not following the word of God' were some of the reasons given by Bishop Wiens (1908) at the Warman hearings. Often the elders stepped in when they felt they were losing control over their members.

Driedger's residence in the open country, not the village; his store and post office taking precedence over farming; his slight deviations from the traditional dress; and his questions about the biblical source of Mennonite community traditions were not sufficiently blatant to warrant excommunication. Better reasons were needed why a former village mayor, a prominent community member, and an articulate conscientious churchgoer should be excommunicated (Hollander 1960, 365). The fire and insurance problem provided the elders with a clear opportunity for dramatic initiative in the form of excommunication. The autonomy of Driedger had gone too far; he was plotting against the community; he was emulating 'worldly' models, instead of the traditional Mennonite community model.

The Formal Stage: Industry Expanded

Driedger dug in his heels after the excommunication in 1908. The church had exerted its will in formalized action by invoking the ban (ostracism by all), and by boycotting Driedger's businesses. As far as the church was concerned, the process got stuck at the judicious (second) stage; they wished to stop initiative and industry. Driedger fought back by continuing to participate in the church and community, by establishing five businesses in four towns (two in Osler), and by taking formal legal action four times. Such methodical actions by Driedger resulted in an excess of formalism to avoid self-enslavement on the part of Driedger, and to assure self-preservation on the part of the church.

Johann's family tried to continue church attendance in the village of Neuanlage. Dietrich, the youngest son, recalls how the whole family entered the church and sat down. Slowly, all the other members got up and left, leaving only Driedger and his family. On another occasion, in a letter to Bishop Wiens, Driedger complains that, when he came to church, the members inside held the door shut so he could not enter.[2]

Johann's persistance became such a problem that the church elders had a non-Mennonite by the name of Fisher sworn in to act as a constable to keep Driedger away, five years after he was excommunicated. Mennonite boycotts of Driedger's businesses were as effective as the ban on church attendance. After the ban in 1908, Mennonites no longer did business with Driedger in his store in Clarks Crossing. Since the community was solidly Mennonite, Driedger had to abandon the building (no one bought it from him). In his efforts to continue business, Driedger bought a second store in Osler (the first was burned in 1907). Here, too, the boycott was so effective that the store never did well. J.C. Friesen tells of how Driedger ordered a train carload of flour, most of which he could not sell (Driedger 1982).

The boycott forced Driedger to set up businesses in the surrounding towns outside the block settlement of the Old Colony Mennonites. In 1914 he bought up stock in 'Big 22,' a large hardware store in Saskatoon, and opened a store there briefly. In 1915 he bought a store in the town of Dalmeny, and that same year bought a hotel in Osler. If his store in Osler was boycotted, perhaps something else would work. In 1916 he bought stores in the town of Langham, and in the town of Hague. These attempts at conducting business outside of the Mennonite community were shortlived. In the meantime he tried butchering, cattle sales, farming, and well-drilling in the solidly Mennonite community.

The ban and the boycott drove Driedger to take legal action four times. This was a desperate formalized action, because traditionally court action was most taboo of all. In 1912, at a farm auction, Driedger's highest bid for an item was not honoured by the Mennonite auctioneer, on the grounds that Driedger was not a member in good standing with the Mennonite community. Driedger took the auctioneer to court and won. Buoyed by his success in court with Leoppky, Driedger took three others to court in 1914. Driedger lost his court cases with Houlding (over a business dispute in Saskatoon), and with Guenther (a Mennonite). The fourth court case was against the Mutual Fire Insurance Association of the Old Colony Mennonite Community, where Driedger (seven years after his store burned in Osler in 1907), now sued the Mennonites in an attempt to force them to honour his policy with them, and cover his fire losses.[3] The church tried to collect $1,000 in voluntary contributions, but not much came of it.

This formal stage resulted in much activity. Driedger especially sought to introduce elements of initiative and industry (stages 3 and 4), but the old church dug in its heels at the judicious stage (stage 2), restricting individual autonomy. The church was able to enforce the ban by social ostracism and economic boycott. Driedger replied in kind with legal action and proliferation of business enterprises. Both Driedger and the church were engulfed by ritual excesses of formalism, with a result neither side had hoped for.

Ideology: Tradition versus New Commitments

On 28 and 29 December 1908, about seven months after the excommunication of Driedger, Bishop Wiens, Driedger, and others testified at the hearings of a provincial commission of inquiry into separate Mennonite German schools, held in the hamlet of Warman, in the heartland of the Old Colony Mennonite community. One-fifth of the 100-page proceedings is devoted to questions and answers of Bishop Wiens (Driedger 1982). Wiens answered in an evasive style, and in very general terms: 'the Word of God teaches,' 'the whole community,' 'because he was disobedient,' 'live by the Scriptures.' The examiner is seldom able to nail him down to specifics. Johann Driedger was present at these hearings, and testified against the bishop, the church's forms of excommunication, and the ban. Driedger testified he was not sending his children to public schools even though he was excommunicated, his friends could not have dealings with him, and members boycotted his businesses. Driedger's observance of Wiens's constant referral to the Scriptures at the hearings seemed to drive him to biblical study and the use of the Bible in his letters and disputations shortly thereafter. Johann's youngest son informed us that his father studied the Bible incessantly, especially during the winter months.

Numerous copies of Driedger's letters reveal a conversant knowledge of the Bible. Indeed, his interpretation of the Scriptures seems quite orthodox, but forward-looking. Numerous informants told us that Driedger and the elders of the church, including Bishop Wiens, had frequent long debates on the meaning of the Scriptures with regard to Mennonite behaviour. These disputations often became loud and emotional. Driedger, a practical businessman, seemed to hope that logical discussion would persuade the ministers that his more liberal interpretations were acceptable. However, these disputations on biblical grounds were frustrated by the elders' vague and general open-ended answers, versus Driedger's drive for specifics. Specifics were not forthcoming, and the power of the elders prevailed.

Having lost the support in the local Mennonite community, Driedger sought support elsewhere through correspondence. His chief confidant was his uncle Peter Elias, of Hochfeld, Manitoba, a minister in the Old Colony Church, who was more open. The ten letters we have, written by Elias between 1908 (shortly after Driedger's excommunication) and 1916, are often long epistles of quotations from Scripture which encourage Johann to continue to seek reconciliation.[4] Some of these scriptural references and a spirit of reconciliation find their way later into Johann's letters to the elders. In a 23 February 1912 letter to the Old Colony minister, John Leoppky, Driedger writes: 'I cannot begin to express how sorry I am that I cannot come to a reconciliation with Bishop J. Wiens. Indeed the more we discuss together the farther apart we seem to become. I often remember how on July 19 you, Wall of Hochfeld, and Wall of Neuanlage were able to talk together in a spirit of love and the longing we seemed to have for reconciliation.'[5] Many letters suggest that Driedger missed a close Christian fellowship very much. He continued to try to get that fellowship in his old church. Many would have formed a new fellowship, but it seemed that this was not yet possible in his lifetime. His study of the Scriptures pointed to a new ideology. He was eager to commit himself to a new community that would integrate Christianity with the changing times. And although his convictions were solidifying in a new direction, he could not persuade the old church to change, nor find individuals wishing to build a new fellowship.

Nomos-Building: Integrity versus Authority

On 26 February 1919, Johann Driedger sent a letter to the church, saying 'Enclosed find $1,000 to cover the grief which I have caused during the past eleven years. I have hurt you deeply, and I am sorry that because of me you have had so many expenses, worry and work. Please forgive me for hurting you during all these years.' In a later letter also addressed to the church he wrote, 'So I ask all of you for forgiveness ... stretch forth your brotherly hand to me poor sinner ... let us all together be reconciled.'[6]

Driedger died a year later, in 1920. The church elders performed the funeral service, and he was buried in the Reinland village cemetery, later joined by his wife. One of the pallbearers, his nephew Cornelius Driedger, reported that his body (in the July heat) smelled so bad that the horses did not want to enter the yard. Perhaps this was a symbol of the whole affair! Driedger was brought to his knees: two years later the bishop and the staunchly conservative Mennonties left *en masse* for Mexico.

A comparison of the photos in figures 4.1 and 4.2 shows the enormous cultural change that had taken place in the Driedger family between 1906 and 1919. Figure 4.1 represented the Old Colony leadership ideal; figure 4.2 represents the modern cultural ideal of Johann

Figure 4.2   Culture change. Johann Driedger and his sons in 1919

Driedger. The two are incompatible. They symbolize conflicting norms of what it means to be a Mennonite in modern Saskatchewan.

Had Driedger lived only two years longer he would have seen Bishop Wiens and the orthodox Old Colony Mennonites leave the area for Mexico, because of the pressures of the Saskatchewan government to set up public schools in their villages. The solid village patterns were changed, and the ban would have been broken. Had he lived only eight years longer, he would have seen a more liberal General Conference Mennonite church built in Osler in 1928 (two blocks from his store). Abram, his second son, was on the building committee, and Cornelius, his fifth son, was the first secretary of the Church council. Four of Johann's ten children joined this church, and dozens of his grandchildren and great-grandchildren are today youth leaders, choir directors, ministers, conference workers, and service and missions workers in the church. His two youngest children (aged eight and six when he was excommunicated) never joined, nor attended, any church at all. In the process of working out his ideology, during the ritual excesses of Old Colony totalism, these last two children may have been victims of identity confusion.

Driedger did not have the opportunity to see the new *nomos* which would certify a new modern numinous community for his kin. Authoritarianism had its day in his lifetime.

The Sacred Village and Its Deconstruction

In 1955 the author made an intensive study of the Hague–Osler Old Colony Mennonites community in Saskatchewan.[7] In 1977 he restudied this settlement and found that many changes had taken place. The purpose of the study was to show how the village structures of the Old Colony had changed, and to isolate some of the processes which contributed to this change. It was a longitudinal study of Mennonites between 1955 and 1977, similar to classical studies done by Robert and Helen Lynd (1929 and 1937) of Middletown, and Robert Redfield's (1956) study of Tepoztlan, restudied by Oscar Lewis (1960) later.

Old Colony Village Organization

Most of the fifteen Old Colony Mennonite villages established in the Hague–Osler area beginning in 1895 were still in existence in the 1955 study. Neuanlage (established in 1895), Neuhorst (1898), Reinland

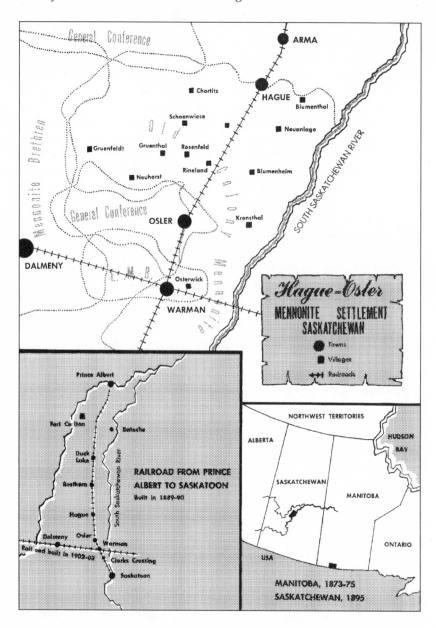

Figure 4.3   The Hague–Osler Mennonite settlement in Saskatchewan

(1898), Blumenthal (1898), Gruenfeldt (1899), Gruenthal (1899), and Blumenheim (1900) were flourishing (Driedger 1955). Chortitz (1898) and Rosenfeld (1905) were declining. Osterwick (1899), Hochstadt (1902), Kronsthal (1902), and Schoenwiese (1902) had declined to a few farmers only (Driedger 1955).

By 1977 many changes had taken place. Neuanlage (forty resident families), and Neuhorst (forty family residents) were still the largest villages, but populations in Blumenthal (fifteen families), Gruenthal (twelve families), Blumenheim (ten families), Reinland (seven families), Gruenfeldt (seven families), and Chortitz (six families) had declined considerably. The villages of Rosenfeldt (four families), Hochstadt (four families), Hochfeldt (three families), Kronsthal (two families), Osterwick (one family), and Schoenwiese (none) were no longer in existence, except for a few farmers who lived on or near the original village sites (Driedger 1977b).

Originally all of these villages were organized along the Russian Mennonite village pattern, which included a wide village street; a row of homes and farmyards on each side of the street, totalling 20–50 families; usually a German school, and often a church and graveyard, located at one end; a common pasture for all the cattle; house–barn combinations with a distinct architecture; and a village *Schultze* (mayor) and his elected committee. In addition to a section or a half-section of land on which the village and pasture were located, and which was held in common by the villagers and its committee, each family took a homestead of one quarter-section of land surrounding the village (Driedger 1955). This basic village pattern existed for about twenty-five years; large numbers of the more conservative villagers moved to Mexico in the 1920s, when the solidarity of the pattern was disturbed.

In 1955, most of the village organizational structure was still intact. The larger villages such as Neuanlage and Neuhorst had changed, as the children attended the government school outside the village. A small store, and a few small entrepreneurs such as a blacksmith or a cobbler, had been added, but basically the villages were intact. A few empty lots left by emigrants could be seen here and there. To a lesser extent the organizational pattern for most of the other villages was also in operation, although some villages had begun to disband, in part because they were never as large, or as well organized in the beginning. Many of the other villages in 1955, although not as large, or as robust, as Neuanlage and Neuhorst, still continued the original organizational pattern.

Figure 4.4   Comparison of a house–barn combination, Neuanlage, 1955 (top)
with a modern dwelling, Neuanlage, 1977 (bottom)

By 1977 all except one (Gruenfeldt) of the fifteen villages had abandoned their common village titles and common village pastures. Neuanlage and Rheinland surveyed their land in 1976, and the common
village title was subdivided among the various residents. About half of
the villages still elected a *Schultze*, and many had an elected village
committee. The role of the *Schultze*, however, had declined, from the
leader of all village matters in the early days, to the party responsible
for a few matters such as collecting church dues, calling meetings to
discuss village concerns, and maintenance of the village street. Half the
villages no longer had a village leader and committee. The village
architecture had changed drastically. While in 1955 there were still
some house–barn combinations in most of the villages, by 1977 few of

these structures could be found. Whereas buildings were never painted in the early days, and many were still unpainted in 1955, most of the houses, barns, and churches were painted in 1977. The styles of houses had changed, from wide structures with two small, narrow windows in the gable and two larger windows widely spaced on the first floor, to modern-style architecture. A few renovated old homes still conveyed a hint of the original structure, but they had been changed in many respects. Hip-roofed barns, red barns, long white dairy barns, silos, and a variety of modern styles had replaced most of the original wide, unpainted, wood-shingled, small-windowed (row on top) barns with attached granary-machine sheds.

Religion and Churches

From the very beginning, the Old Colony Mennonites were a religious community holding their village land in common. The village organization, the farm occupations, and their church and religious institutions were perceived as sacred forms of social organization. Churches were not located in all of the villages, but in the early days some held services in the German schools in winter. Churches were always sufficiently near, even in horse-and-buggy days, so all could attend worship services.

Church forms were also important. The church building remained unpainted (a sign of humility); the shutters of the church were painted grey-blue; the architecture had a Russian Mennonite look. The inside of the building was austere. The blue-grey benches had no backs; there were nails above the seats to hang hats; the stage was on the side of the church; the pulpit was identical to the one from which Menno Simons preached; the four *Vorsaenger* (song leaders) sat on the left, and the minister on the right; and a small room was designated for the ministers. The original form of worship included two or more hours of worship, very slow 'olle wies' (old verse) singing from the traditional *Ausband* (early traditional collection of hymns), which contained scores of stanzas; the *Vorsaenger* (song leaders) led the singing, and part singing was not allowed; several sermons copied from those passed on for decades were read; and short Low German 'vermanungen' (teachings) touched on issues of the day. With very few modifications, most of the old practices were still common in the Old Colony churches in 1955.

In 1977 the basic structure of the buildings and services were similar,

Figure 4.5   (Top) Original Old Colony Church (1955); (middle) renovated church, Neuanlage, 1977; and (bottom) Gospel Mennonite Chapel, Osler, 1977

but there were also some changes. The church buildings were painted, and Sunday school rooms had been added, in an adjoining building, in an attached building, or in the basement. The inside was renovated to include electric lights, backs were added to the benches, hatracks had been removed, a room for women with small children had been added, and the pulpit and platform had been moved from the side to the end. The worship service was two hours long; the singing was somewhat faster, but in unison; and the remainder of the service was much like the original. At a typical Sunday morning worship service in Neuhorst, there were forty worshippers present. About half of the worshippers were male, about twenty were above fifty years of age, and about ten were young people (Driedger 1977b).

During the depression there was a move to modernize the 'olle wies' in the church services to a somewhat faster pace of singing, but there was considerable resistance, and a group called 'Bergthaler Mennonites' separated from the Old Colony church in protest. In 1977 the Bergthaler attended churches in three villages, but differences were minimal. A second split from the Old Colony church occurred during the 1940s, when the Rudnerweider (Evangelical Mennonite Mission Conference) left the Old Colony because they wished greater evangelical emphasis. A third loss occurred when many Old Colony young people joined more liberal General Conference churches in the nearby towns of Osler, Hague, and Neuanlage, and this continued into the 1990s.

The two most recent moves away from the Old Colony church have been the Pentecostal church in Gruenthal, and the Mission Chapel in the town of Osler. These two represent the greatest change between 1955 and 1977. The Pentecostal church in Gruenthal, founded in 1955, by 1977 had 300 members, and they had built a new church and held their services only in English.

The newest church, located in Osler, was attractive to many Old Colony and Bergthaler young couples. A young Old Colony minister, who wanted a more evangelical emphasis, found the resistance too great, so he founded a new Chortitzer Mennonite Church (named the Osler Mission Chapel). About 140 attended the new church; most of them were young couples, young people, and children; the service was enthusiastic, vibrant, with a restrained evangelical emphasis. Most of the participants were of Old Colony background. The services and Sunday school were in English, and the format was very similar to an evangelical Protestant church service.

Education and Schools

In the early days most of the villages held German schools based on a curriculum consisting mostly of reading, writing, and arithmetic. The six grades were usually taught by a member of the village, who often did not have very much education. By the 1920s the Saskatchewan government insisted that provincial schools must be established, that teaching must be in English, and that a provincial curriculum be established, designed for eight grades. The Old Colony Mennonites vehemently resisted this intrusion by keeping their children out of these schools, for which they had to pay heavy fines. This contributed to the emigration of hundreds of Mennonites to Mexico in the 1920s. The government was forced to build schools outside the villages, staffed by teachers they hired.

By 1955, all Old Colony Mennonite children in the villages attended these government schools, usually located half a mile outside the village, and few if any German Mennonite schools remained. Sunday schools for children were organized by this time; some German was taught there, but it was limited. Whereas no Old Colony Mennonites attended university in 1955, and very few went on to high school, this had changed somewhat later, and more acquired these higher forms of education.

Whereas in 1955, one- or two-room schools near the villages were the norm, by 1977 all elementary and high schools were consolidated. All the one-room schools had been abandoned, and children were bused to the elementary schools in the towns of Osler, Hague, Warman, and Martensville, and the high school students attended in Warman and Hague. Since the settlement was largely Mennonite, most of the students in these schools were Mennonite, although a large number of the children were of more liberal Mennonite origin. Many of the teachers were Mennonite, from a range of backgrounds.

The Mennonite Family

The Old Colony family, too, had changed. Many families had ten children or more, some as many as fifteen. Although the average family size in 1977 was still above the national average, many families had between two and six children. Since a small percentage of family heads were no longer in agriculture, children were less of an asset, and even farm families were much smaller by 1977. Mennonite endogamy was still high – most married other Mennonites. A lot of dating took place within the villages, although the automobile, and the consolidated school system, provided many more contacts with others, so that dating was much more diversified – mostly among Mennonites. Before 1955, divorce and separation was almost unheard of; by 1977, a few cases of divorce were found, but this has changed since.

By 1955 an interesting change in naming children occurred. Earlier, boys were given standard biblical names: John, Jacob, Peter, Henry, Abram, Frank, Isaac; and girls were named Mary, Tina, Helen, Susie, Margaret, and the like. By 1977 a variety of other names were used. Elementary school records and tombstones in graveyards revealed that the change from biblical names to modern names occurred after the Second World War, so that by 1977 the change was almost complete.

Customs and Culture

Before 1955, Low German was spoken in all of the Old Colony homes, while High German was used in church, with some Low German comments. By 1955 the children were beginning to speak English to each other at home, especially since English was the language of the school. A great deal of Low German was still spoken in the homes by 1977, and most of the children still understand and usually could speak Low German. Many younger families, however, were beginning to use English at home, because they attended English schools and were speaking English at work. Whereas most of the business transactions in the villages and towns were in Low German, by 1977 English was used increasingly. However, most of the storekeepers, post-office, service-station, and business personnel spoke Low German freely when older Mennonite customers preferred to do so.

Whereas Old Colony men never wore ties earlier, some did so occasionally by 1977, although never in church. Suits worn at church services in 1977 were dark; no ties were worn, although some of the men and boys were beginning to wear lighter-coloured shirts. In church, the older women wore black or dark blue embroidered kerchiefs, long dark solid-colour dresses and shawls, while the younger girls wore flowered dresses without shawls, and many did not wear kerchiefs. During the work week, older women tended to wear traditional dresses, while younger women followed the fashion trends increasingly. Women never wore slacks to church, and older women never did so at work either. Dress was changing, although Old Colony Mennonites could usually still be spotted, even in an Eaton's department store in Saskatoon (Anderson 1972).

Perhaps food and eating habits changed the slowest. All of the Mennonite dishes – *plume mous, verenicke, borscht*, farmers' sausage, smoked ham, and various kinds of baked goods – were still the favourites, but some other foods began to appear as well.

Informal Associations

Visiting relatives and friends, and cracking sunflower seeds, were favourite pastimes on Sundays and holidays. This was still very common in 1977 in the villages, especially among the older people. The younger people, however, in 1955 already supplemented such activities with softball (including tournaments) and hockey. By 1977, improvements in transportation made movies, bowling, professional spectator sports, and other activities popular as well. The older Mennonites, however, frowned on too much sports, movies, and entertainment. For many, television was still taboo, although radios could be found everywhere by 1977 – at home, in cars, in the cabs of tractors, and in dairy barns.

Gathering for hog slaughtering was standard practice in 1955; by 1977 this had diminished, almost disappeared. Earlier, barn raisings were common; by 1977, this practice, too, had largely disappeared. Farmers still banded together to seed a neighbour's fields if he had suffered prolonged illness or an accident. Auction sales still took place occasionally, but they were not as popular as they used to be. Mennonite mutual aid, in the form of fire, health, accident, hail, and life insurance, was replaced by reliance on commerical insurance agencies.

Processes of Change

Numerous processes, such as migration, transportation, industrialization, and liberalization, contributed to changes in the Old Colony Mennonite village.

Mennonite Migrations

Mennonites have always migrated frequently, but the Old Colony Mennonites especially developed a form of survival migration so that, when industrialization and modernization crept up on them, a traditional remnant left for more isolated regions (Driedger 1973). The first migration from Saskatchewan took place in the early 1920s, when hundreds of families left the villages for Mexico because of the school question. The Saskatchewan government enacted a law requiring that the major language of instruction in school be English, and that the provincial school curriculum be taught. Up to this time the Mennonites had taught their children in the German schools in their villages, using their own curriculum. This exodus resulted in the disruption of the village structure, the religious and school programs, family networks, and general community organization. The conservatives departed, leaving behind those who were less well to do, or more prone to acculturation.

At the same time, in the 1920s, when many Old Colony conservatives left for Mexico, a large group of Russian Mennonite immigrants arrived. Some of these new immigrants bought the land of those who left and settled within or near the villages. These were more liberal Mennonites: they used more modern technology; established other Mennonite churches, often in towns or cities, creating more liberal religious influences and different economic systems; and drove many people away from the traditional village life.

Additional migration leakages took place in the 1930s, when scores of Old Colony families moved to a more isolated region at Fort Vermilion, Alberta. In the 1950s and 1960s, the drain continued to a new more isolated northern settlement in Fort St John, British Columbia (Driedger 1973).

A fourth migration included the creation of the rurban town of Martensville, halfway between the Mennonite reserve of some twenty-five villages and the city of Saskatoon in the 1950s. Martensville began in 1953 and grew into a town of over 1,000 residents. When the author studied the area in 1955, it was not yet apparent that Martensville, only ten miles from Saskatoon, would become a buffer zone for those who worked in the city. Roads from the villages (20–30 miles) to Saskatoon were very poor. Many of the younger families left the villages to work in Saskatoon, but still wished to live in the less expensive village-like Martensville, where they had Mennonite neighbours.

Some of the Old Colony people moved directly to Saskatoon, where some joined more liberal Mennonite churches, and others did not frequent churches at all, which left behind many of the older people who were less well-to-do to retire in the villages. There was some reverse migration, where some who worked in the city commuted from village to the city.

Transportation and Communication

A second major change since 1955 was the new roads. The railway line between Saskatoon and Prince Albert, which served Hague, Osler, and Warman, was built in 1889–90 (Driedger 1955). When the Mennonites arrived in 1895, they came by rail, and they established their villages so that several were within a mile or two of the tracks. Since the railway stations were in the hamlets of Osler and Hague, and since the trains were confined to their rails, the means of transportation did not threaten early Mennonite isolation and segregation. Only occasionally, a few would take the train to Saskatoon, although later the train was used more frequently.

When the automobile emerged in the 1920s, the church banned those who acquired cars, seeking to restrict mobility, which might make inroads in terms of diminishing isolation and segregation (Driedger 1955). Since the automobile was versatile, more flexible, and within the means of some, it presented a threat. Nevertheless, for those who owned cars, Saskatoon was far away, the roads were unpaved and poor, and during the depression and the Second World War relatively few had the means to travel widely. This was still largely the case in 1955, although there were signs of change. Since 1955, enormous changes in transportation have taken place, with generally improved roads and a big new paved highway cutting through Mennonite country. The big highway brought the villages closer to Saskatoon, so that many became rurban satellite suburbs for Mennonites who worked in the city.

The Influence of Industrialization

The traditional Old Colony Mennonites believed strongly that God wished them to be farmers in the rural setting. In the early days they were all farmers; the church leaders frowned on other occupations, and occasionally used it as cause for excommunication (Driedger 1955). Most of the residents in the villages in 1955 were still farmers. There were a few who were involved in keeping a store, or in working as a blacksmith, or a shoemaker, or a schoolteacher in the village. A few began to work in the city of Saskatoon, but these people usually moved to the city or to Martensville.

By 1977 the economic structure in the villages had changed completely. Most of the villagers were in non-farm occupations, and large numbers worked in the city. To illustrate, of forty residential homes in Neuhorst in 1977, two were farmers; in Neuanlage, six of forty were farmers. The others worked in various occupations in Saskatoon, or in towns and other industry. In the other smaller villages, the ratios were similar: Reinland (2 farmers, 5 non-farmers); Gruenfeldt (2 farmers, 5 non-farmers); Gruenthal (5 farmers, 2 non-farmers); Chortitz (3 farmers, 3 non-farmers); Hochstadt (4 farmers); Hochfeldt (3 farmers). The larger villages maintained their sizes by becoming satellite suburbs for city workers. Villages like Neuhorst and Neuanlage, closer to Saskatoon on the new highway, were able to maintain their population, although the population changed primarily to non-farmers. There was evidence that women also were beginning to work outside the home. Six Neuanlage women and four Neuhorst women were reported working for wages outside the village in 1977 (Driedger 1977b).

The influence of the capitalist free-enterprise system was also evident, along with the changes in occupation. Several of the farmers were located on the outskirts of the villages with very large operations. Tall silos and extensive barns indicated that they were large dairy farmers. Others had many granaries, and large and modern machinery, which showed they were large grain farmers. Large-scale farming was in evidence, and many of these farmers also left the village to build home on the open fields, surrounded by their many acres of land.

Liberalization

Liberalization was a fourth influence that changed the Old Colony in Saskatchewan. When the Mennonites came, they built their German schools in the villages where the schoolteacher, who had limited education, taught six grades. One of the reasons many conservative Old Colony Mennonites left for Mexico in the 1920s was that the government required that all children attend public schools. Many Mennonites paid heavy fines when they sent their children to their German schools, rather than the government schools. By 1955 all of the children in the villages attended these government schools, and these government one- or two-room schools usually had a Mennonite school board, a Mennonite teacher, and a virtually exclusively Mennonite student body. In effect, the schools were in the main Mennonite, teaching the provincial curriculum in English, with a half-hour of German at the end of the day.

By 1977 this had changed drastically by school consolidation. The high schools were consolidated in the towns of Warman and Hague, and the elementary schools were consolidated in Osler, Hague, Warman, Martensville, and other surrounding towns. The schoolchildren were bussed. Since the Hague–Osler–Warman area included mostly Mennonites, these consolidated schools hired many Mennonite teachers, and a majority of the children were of Mennonite origin. However, consolidation had further changed segregation, isolation, and control over the educational process. Many Old Colony Mennonites who continued to move to Fort St John and Fort Vermilion and elsewhere gave encroaching liberalization in education as one of the reasons for emigration. As conservatives continued to trickle away, the liberalization process continued.

Second, the liberalization process continued in religion. As stated earlier, the Old Colony Mennonites had churches only in the villages of Neuanlage, Neuhorst, and Blumenheim. When the villages were first established, there were only Old Colony Mennonites. Slowly this religious solidarity eroded. First, the Bergthaler separated; then, the more liberal Mennonites from Russia came during the 1920s. In addition to the Bergthaler and General Conference Mennonites, the Rudnerweider separated, and finally the Osler Mission Chapel was established, drawing many to Osler and away from the villages.

Rural Cultural Identity in the 1970s

The case of Driedger asserting his individual freedom in a very conservative traditional Mennonite Old Colony community demonstrates the conflict between individual freedom and community control. To what extent was this only an isolated incident, or were there similar changes occurring in the Saskatoon area among other ethno-religious groups as well in the 1970s? Fortunately, Alan Anderson (1972) compared nine rural groups in the area, including Mennonites, and we present his findings here.

Anderson (1972) found that the Hutterites, living in colonies were the most successful in maintaining cultural boundaries. Mennonites, many of whom lived or had lived in a Hague–Osler Mennonite land reserve, were a strong second, almost all still able to speak the in-group Low German, and two-thirds using it at home in the early 1970s. Almost all attended the Mennonite church regularly, three out of four favoured preserving their identity, and two-thirds were opposed to

TABLE 4.1
Cultural Identity of Nine Ethno-Religious Groups in Rural Saskatchewan, and Intermarriage Factors, 1971.[a]

Group	N	Cultural Identity Factors				Family Factors		
		Favour identity preservation (%)	Attend church regularly (%)	Can speak mother tongue (%)	Use mother tongue often (%)	Opposed to religious intermarriage (%)	Opposed to ethnic intermarriage (%)	Extent of intermarriage (%)
Hutterite	(6)	100	100	100	100	100	100	0
Mennonite	(244)	75	86	97	69	69	57	2
Scandinavian	(86)	74	87	89	37	77	52	4
French	(15)	70	91	99	78	81	46	9
German Catholic	(190)	33	94	93	29	70	10	10
Ukrainian Orthodox	(83)	80	70	100	63	43	41	11
Ukrainian Catholic	(154)	82	82	99	69	69	62	13
Polish Catholic	(15)	92	53	100	87	73	40	31
Doukhobor	(20)	85	55	95	70	35	45	40
Total sample	(813)					70	44	9

[a]Data taken from Anderson 1972, by permission.

religious intermarriage (see table 4.1). Almost none had intermarried, and over half were also opposed to ethnic intermarriage.

Other ethnic groups living in the rural areas surrounding Saskatoon also lived in fairly solid rural ethnic communities, and they, too, were able to maintain considerable religious and ethnic solidarity. Except for German Catholics, most favoured identity preservation, most could speak their in-group languages, and except for two groups a large majority also spoke it at home often. A majority attended church regularly, and also opposed religious intermarriages except for the Doukhobor and Ukrainian Orthodox communities. A majority practised endogamy, with very little intermarriage except for the Doukhobors and Polish Catholics. Anderson's 1972 rural prairie study showed solid ethno-religious communities who were maintaining their traditional cultures, although often in modified forms.

Conclusions

The Old Colony Mennonites tried to keep their members in a rural traditional isolated numinous stage, where the leaders could control life in a judicious way. The Church resisted individual initiative and industry, but Johann Driedger persisted in testing the boundaries. Had he lived two or three years longer, he would have seen the Old Colony church retreat *en masse* to rural Mexico. Soon thereafter new modified Mennonite fellowships sprang up, which would have granted him certification. Instead he was forced to recant or remain marginal in a very closed community, to his death.

We have examined the changes that took place in cultural values as modernization began to take hold after the Second World War. Traditional spatial, cultural, economic, and political separation into two world kingdoms gave way to new forms of religious communal identification. Traditional educational, organizational, and social relations were deconstructed, and new forms emerged that were more open to the marketplace. It is these modern and postmodern forces which we need to evaluate and explore in the rest of this volume, to better understand the cultural diversity and the proliferation of values that are increasingly part of Mennonite life in the 1990s.

The author revisited many of these villages again in 1997, and found that they had turned even more into satellite suburbs of Saskatoon. The highway between the big city and the villages had been expanded to four lanes, so commuting was even easier and faster. More new modern houses had been built. Some villages had parks, and commemorative plaques and monuments as some celebrated their centennials. Old churches had modernized, adding sound systems, and two new ultra-modern Mennonite churches had been built in the nearby hamlet of Osler.

5

Media Shifts towards the
Global Village[1]

Mennonites remained rural much longer than most Canadians or Americans, by isolating themselves in ethnic enclaves, at least until the Second World War (Hay and Basran 1992). Since the 1940s, however, modernization has forced Mennonite communities to open up, as demonstrated by Kauffman and Driedger (1991). One important element of modernity is the emergence of the mass media, and their influence in postmodern societies is well documented (Fleras 1994; Hoover 1995; Karim and Sansom 1990). Research evidence on the relationships of Mennonites to the media (Driedger and Kauffman 1991) show that exposure to modern society and to the media has increased. These data provide the opportunity to explore the consequences of media exposure on a people with a rural, pastoral culture and tradition that, until recently, had not had such exposure.

Despite the pervasiveness of the media, there is a lack of research and analysis on the relationship between exposure to the media and ethnic identity in general, and on Mennonites in particular. Research has generally focused on the portrayal of ethnic and minority groups in the mainstream media (Zolf 1989), especially of stereotypes of ethnic and minority groups, and biases in media coverage (Fleras 1994). A second major form of research has focused on the 'ethnic press,' its survival and general influence (Stachniak 1991; Pigades 1991). We will now explore the relationship between media exposure and ethnic identity, beliefs, and values.

Potential Media Influences

Marshall McLuhan is perhaps the best-known proponent of the independent influence of the media (McIlwraith 1994; McLeod 1991). According to McLuhan, the media, and television in particular, bring previously marginal groups out of their local villages, and put them directly in touch with a 'global village' characterized by a heightened awareness and sense of collective responsibility. McLuhan states that, 'as electrically contracted, the globe is no more than a village. Electric speed brings all social and political functions together in a sudden implosion which has heightened human awareness of responsibility to an intense degree. It is this implosive factor that alters the position of the Negro, the teenager, and some other groups. They can no longer be contained, in the political sense of limited association. They are now involved in our lives, as we in theirs, thanks to the electric media' (1964, 5).

This generalization was expressed in McLuhan's *Understanding Media: The Extension of Man* (1964), which quickly established him as the 'oracle' of the new television age. Analysis of the impact of the media also revealed a deep interest in the social-psychological effects of technological change, as noted by Robert McIlwraith (1995), in a recent evaluation of McLuhan and his impact.

McLuhan's views of the independent influence of the media of com-munication were strongly influenced by the work of his mentor, Harold Innis (1951, 1952), who first argued that the media bring with them a bias in social organization and perception (Mowlana 1983). Innis argued that the historical emergence of print technology led to a shift from a time-binding to a space-binding culture. In the realm of community, this meant a shift from orally based communities, histori-cally and geographically rooted, reflecting concerns with religion and ritual, to communities 'not in place, but in space, connected over vast distances by appropriate symbols, forms and interests' (Carey 1989, 160). In these terms, traditional rural agricultural communities very much fit as 'time-bound' cultures: isolated, with an emphasis on oral communication among in-group members expressed at religious ser-vices that had become ritualized over generations, and with a strong sense of connection to the land. Characteristics, attitudes, and values were found among contemporary Mennonites by Kauffman and Driedger (1991), for example, which reflect those of space-bound com-munities, with a vastly heightened awareness of extra-local centres of cultures and social organizations. This involves an orientation to a broader Mennonite community and a greater awareness of centres of culture and power beyond the Mennonite community, combined with a declining concern with history and tradition.

McLuhan extended Innis's ideas to the new electronic media, while also introducing additional elements. McLuhan argued that the relationship between sensory organization and the nature of thought was shaped by a person's direct experience with a medium. He saw television as a high-involvement medium, which leads viewers to crave the same level of involvement in all of their experiences (McIlwraith 1994, 344). This was based on his designation of television as a 'cool' medium, drawing on the distinction between 'hot' jazz, which was highly structured, and 'cool' jazz, which was more unstructured, generating more listener involvement.

In discussing the effects of television, McLuhan also introduced the concept of 'acoustic space,' which sees the world of simultaneous communication to be part of the modern experience. Historically, in preindustrial oral cultures, the individual located him- or herself in the centre of a spherical space. However, in print-based cultures, the individual's experience was seen as being more at the edge of visual space, looking in (McIlwraith 1995, 336). According to McLuhan, the first revolution occurred when the oral tradition was replaced by writing, and the present revolution has occurred as electronic communication has come to replace print. McLuhan argued that these new technologies would return societies to more tribal forms. Television would lead them to see the world from their home space, and interpret their experience from their own spatial and social context, including ethnicity, religion, and community. Levinson (1990), for one, has argued that this analysis of the human experience of space, and its relationship to the organization of thought, is McLuhan's most central contribution. McLuhan also saw television as an 'inner trip' because it was directed towards the viewer, resulting in greater interest in inner experience (McIlwraith 1995, 339).

While Innis did not address the influence of television per se, his general ideas regarding the influence of media can be extended more directly to the newer electronic media by noting that the more immediate effect of these media is to extend communication more rapidly and more efficiently into space. For Innis, access or availability of communication technology transforms the nature of social relations, and hence culture, so that availability is enough to produce changes in culture and society. The extension into space may be seen as equivalent to what McLuhan describes, in more colourful terms, as 'the global village.' Here Innis observed that, with the expansion of the power of the press, 'time has been cut into pieces the length "of a day's newspaper"' (Innis 1954: 72), so we would say that, with television, time has been cut into hours, minutes, or sound bytes. The major difference between McLuhan's and Innis's view has to do with the role of sensory experience of the media, and especially television. For McLuhan, this means that the effects of the media should be related to the individual's personal experience of the media such as the extent of usage. In this chapter we need to find whether Innis's predictions of media *access* or McLuhan's predictions of television *usage* are more salient and important.

McLuhan's views of television as a highly participatory medium are in direct conflict with virtually all current psychological theories. The more popular view sees watching television as a mentally passive experience because more information is provided to the viewer (McIllwraith 1995, 335). According to this view, television is less participatory than radio, because the radio listener must work harder to fill in the missing (visual) information. By the same token, TV is also seen to be less participatory than print, based on the number of sensory modalities that are engaged.

Parallels do emerge, however, between McLuhan's ideas and the views expressed in a variety of disciplines concerning a movement from the modern into a postmodern world. The parallels are to be found in much more interactive formulations of the relationship between the individual and the media, as opposed to the positivist assumptions of the passive subject. As expressed by Stewart Hoover, in a review of the works of Robert Wuthnow, structure is giving way to increasing emphasis on individual valuations based on personal experience. Hoover sees this as central to a 'post positivist approach to media studies.' In contrast with positivist 'effects' research, cultural analysis, and specifically Wuthnow's concept of discourse analysis, sees an interactive process whereby discourse is socially embedded, while the media provide a context in which these symbols and meanings can become embodied and institutionalized. Hoover (1995, 138) calls for an account of 'the contribution of media practices to such things as identity, social solidarity, community, social ordering and moral order.' It is this challenge we wish to pursue in this chapter. Fleras (1994) has made an attempt in this direction, but his work lacks the empirical data to support his ideas. In a recent article, Peter Smith (1992) also tries to link postmodernism with the new social space of ethnic identity, with his call for a return to the 'local' and 'historically particular.'

Our expected findings may be summarized in the following way:

1 Mennonite access and usage of the media will increase over time as they urbanize and become more exposed to the 'global village.'
2 'Local village' characteristics, such as support of in-group religious values, norms, beliefs, and practice, will be negatively correlated with mass-media exposure.
3 As access to and usage of the media increases, participation in McLuhan's 'global village,' in terms of gender equality, political participation, and active concern for peace and welfare, will also increase.
4 As modernization increases in the form of higher education, and increases in income, occupations, and socio-economic status, these will be positively associated with media access. Concomitants such as individualism, materialism, and secularization will also increase with modernization, and be positively associated with media access and use.
5 Innis's media access will be a better predictor of local and global-village values than McLuhan's television usage.

Mennonite Access to and Use of the Media

Survey findings include a substantial amount of information on the quantity and quality of access to and use of the media by contemporary North American Mennonites.

Access to Media Technology

In table 5.1 we observe that in 1989 almost all Mennonites owned a television set. Almost half owned two sets, and one in four owned three or more. Variations among denominations are small. More than one-third had cable TV in 1989, but only 6 per cent subscribed to premium cable-TV services such as HBO, Showtime, or Cinemax, with few reporting that they owned satellite dishes. Exposure to the medium of television also extended to ownership of videocassette recorders by 1989. Almost half of the respondents owned VCRs, and 6 per cent had video cameras.

It is clear that, by 1989, respondents in Mennonite denominations studied (GC, MC, MB, EMC, BIC) had opened themselves up to the modern media. In the 1950s the question of whether one should own a

TABLE 5.1
Mennonite Access to Media Technology in Their Homes, 1989

Access to TV/ technology	Denominations (%)					
	MC	GC	MB	BIC	EMC	Total
TV set	91	98	97	94	99	95
VCR	46	44	44	51	58	47
Cable TV	29	40	50	38	33	38
Computer	19	19	26	18	24	21
Video camera	7	6	7	6	13	7
Premium cable services	6	5	6	5	7	6
Satellite dish	2	2	1	1	1	1

television set was actively debated within the Mennonite constituency. At that time it was by no means clear that almost all would own at least one set forty years later, let alone that many would have expanded into additional services and related technologies.

Trends in Media Use, 1972–1989

Fortunately, we have comparative data shown in table 5.2, revealing changes in the five denominations which have occurred as they were exposed to television. For instance, while 15 per cent of the respondents in 1972 said that they never watched television, the figure decreased to only 7 per cent by 1989. Exposure to other media of communication did not display the same kind of change, however.

Reading of newspapers and books did not increase at all between 1972 and 1989. Listening to recorded music actually declined slightly in 1989. In general, we see a selective increase in media usage by Mennonites over a generation. The influence of television is also enhanced by the emergence of videocassettes as an element of media use in 1989.

Two out of three of our respondents in 1989 watched television at least one hour per day, with small variations among denominations. One out of four watched more than three hours daily. Half of the members of the sample listened to the radio more than one hour or more per day, and one out of four did so three or more hours daily. Just 6 per cent reported that they did not listen to the radio at all.

One out of three respondents read books for at least one hour a day, and the same proportion read newspapers daily. Thirteen per cent never read books, and 4 per cent never read newspapers. One out of

TABLE 5.2
Percentage of Respondents Using the Media, 1972 to 1989

	1972 Hours per day					1989 Hours per day				
	None	1	1.0–2.9	3.0–4.9	5+	None	1	1.0–2.9	3.0–4.9	5+
Watching TV	15	31	38	12	5	7	29	42	16	6
Listening to radio	5	44	30	12	10	6	44	26	12	12
Reading newspapers	3	63	29	3	2	4	64	26	4	2
Reading books	14	51	25	6	5	13	52	25	6	4
Listening to recorded music	19	53	19	5	3	23	55	16	4	2
Watching video-cassettes						62	33	4	1	0

four listened to recorded music for one hour or more daily, while the same proportion never listened to recorded music. At the time of this study, only one in twenty respondents reported viewing video-cassettes.

A composite measure of media use among Mennonites, which classified respondents as high, medium, or low on media consumption, was compiled as well. According to this measure, 14 per cent were identified as high in exposure to the media, 61 per cent as moderately exposed, and the remaining 15 per cent as low in media exposure.

Radio-Program Preferences

Preferences regarding radio programming also reveal that one in four listened to religious programs on the radio and to the news. Radio listening seems to vary considerably by denomination, however. Almost half of the Evangelical Mennonites (EMC) reported that they listened to religious programs, which is significantly higher than of other denominations, and three times higher than for General Conference Mennonites (GC). However, more than one-third of GCs prefer the news. This proportion is twice as high as for Brethren in Christ (BIC) and EMCs.

Listening to music is generally the popular option, where radio is concerned. Over half listed music as their most popular radio preference, with considerable variation in type of music preferred. Popular radio music and easy-listening music were the most common preferences, followed by country and classical music.

Reading Mennonite Newspapers

Thus far the discussion has focused on the involvement of Mennonites with the secular media. However, it must be noted that exposure to Mennonite media is itself quite substantial. Four out of five of the Mennonites in our 1989 sample received the principal Mennonite denomination magazine or newspaper (including the *Mennonite*, the *Mennonite Reporter, Gospel Herald, Evangelical Visitor, EMC Today, Christian Leader,* and the *Mennonite Brethren Herald*). Some variation by denomination was found in this category. Among Mennonite Church (MC) respondents, seven out of ten subscribed to their paper, while almost all Mennonite Brethren (MB) subscribed to theirs.

Sixty per cent of the respondents who received their denominational paper reported that they read all or most of them. Almost none said they did not read any of the papers they received. As a general observation, these findings regarding both receiving these materials and reading them seem to indicate a considerable commitment to these Mennonite means of communication.

As expected, Mennonite access and usage of television increased over time. By 1989, 95 per cent owned a television set, one-half owned VCRs, more than a third had cable TV, and one in five owned computers. Watching television also increased between 1972 and 1989, with only 7 per cent watching no TV in 1989. Use of radio, newspapers, and recorded music remained the same.

Integration of Local and Global Worlds

Since many Mennonites are well into the process of leaving the local sacred village and entering the global marketplace, we need to explore to what extent they see these as two separate worlds. Are they still identifying with Mennonite faith and are they in communication with and relating to its institutions? Are they socially involved with Mennonite friends and dates, or have they become a part of the diverse global village?

Separation of the Two Worlds

The traditional sacred canopy or local village represents a counter-culture, or a separation of life into sacred and profane values and spheres. Kauffman and Driedger (1991) asked their North American Mennonite respondents to what extent Mennonites in North America still think of themselves as being in two worlds in the 1990s, and found that at least nine out of ten respondents saw a clear difference between the 'kingdom of God' and the 'kingdom of this world,' and this finding did not vary much among the five denominations represented. Eight out of ten also thought that there was considerable tension between the church and the world. So it is clear that, even though most Mennonites in the 1990s have changed in such ways that they are no longer culturally identifiable, they still see themselves living in two worlds that are not the same. How, then, do they see themselves as being different?

Well over half said that they experienced at least some conflict between their Mennonite beliefs and practices, and the larger society.

Over half thought that Christians should avoid involvements in the 'kingdom of this world' as much as possible, and this again did not vary much by denomination. When we probed more specifically as to whether there was a contradiction between following Christ and entering leadership positions in government, only three out of ten felt the need to separate in this way. Obviously, there were varied interpretations of what 'separation' meant, and where this term applied, which we need to explore more.

Communal Identification with the Church

Mennonite origins were clearly religious. Do 1990s Mennonites still identify with these religious roots, and how much has this changed over a generation? Eight out of ten Mennonites said they fit in well with their congregation and prefer to remain in their own Mennonite church, and this has not changed in a generation between 1972 and 1989. About three-quarters prefer the name 'Mennonite,' were never a member of another congregation, and believe their denomination teaches the Word of God most accurately. So there is evidence of strong Mennonite identification, although it has slipped a bit since 1972. There is also more Mennonite denominational variation here, with Evangelical Mennonites (EMC) scoring lower than members of the Mennonite Church (MC).

Two out of three respondents came from backgrounds where their parents belonged to the same church although this, too, had slipped some over a generation. Over half were satisfied with being known as Mennonites, almost as many knew over half the members of their congregation, and almost half said that most of their best friends belonged to the same denomination. This illustrates that, for a basic core, there is solid social support for their church identification. In fact, one-quarter thought they would always remain a member of their Mennonite denomination. These general beliefs and practices suggest strong Mennonite identification, but what does it mean more specifically with respect to communications, organizational loyalties, and social relations?

Support of In-group Activities

Mennonite denominational differences were minor in their perspectives on two kingdoms, these differences began to show up in exami-

TABLE 5.3
Support Mennonite Communications, Organizations, and Social Relations

In-group identification	Per cent agreeing					
	MC	GC	BIC	MB	EMC	Total
Communications						
Should subscribe to a Mennonite newspaper	63	64	54	63	36	62
Should perpetuate Mennonite life through schools	48	49	39	42	23	46
Education in Mennonite school is very important	43	38	28	33	14	38
Should learn ethnic language if they have one	28	35	32	24	15	29
Organizations						
Mennonite organizations help me be active in my group	62	62	60	53	48	59
Mennonite organizations are relevant – not too in-bred	47	43	44	43	38	45
Social Relations						
Parents should discourage dating with non-Mennonites	39	30	29	28	25	34
Should have mostly Mennonite friends	19	30	13	9	8	15
Should not marry a non-Mennonite	18	11	11	9	4	14
Parents are less in favour of non-Mennonite friends	9	6	7	8	4	8

nation of communal identification, and they become fairly major in support of cultural and institutional organizations. Members of the Mennonite Church (MC) support Mennonite culture and institutions, but Evangelical Mennonites (EMC) support their own newspapers, schools, language, organizations, friends, and endogamy much less.

Six out of ten Mennonites subscribe to Mennonite newspapers and organizations, and almost half support Mennonite schools and think in-group organizations are relevant. Other in-group cultural activity is supported much less however. Only one-third think education in a Mennonite school is important, and that parents should discourage dating non-Mennonites. Only three in ten support learning the in-

TABLE 5.4
Membership in Community Organizations, 1972 and 1989

Type of organization	Per cent in 1989					Totals	
	MC	GC	MB	BIC	EMC	1972	1989
School service clubs	18	16	15	19	18	24	17
Youth groups	17	14	18	21	23	23	17
Farm organizations	10	11	6	8	15	12	9
Sports clubs	16	14	15	18	20	12	15
Professional or academic societies	17	18	20	15	16	11	18
Major political groups	8	10	10	19	10	7	10
Hobby or garden clubs	7	7	6	7	6	6	7
Literary, art, etc., groups	6	6	5	4	4	6	5
Business corporations (officers)	9	6	7	7	8	5	6
Labour unions	5	5	10	7	5	5	6
Service clubs (Rotary, etc.)	5	8	4	4	4	3	5
Fraternal groups (lodges)	2	3	0	3	1	2	2
College fraternities or sororities	2	2	1	3	3	1	2
Veterans' groups	1	2	1	2	2	1	1
Physical fitness clubs	14	11	13	11	13	*	13

*Not included in the 1972 survey

group language, and social relations have opened up to many others than Mennonites. Indeed, by 1989 there is relatively little taboo against marrying non-Mennonites, with only 14 per cent objecting to exogamy. Social relations especially, as well as communications, suggest that large numbers of Mennonites are increasingly opening up to relations with the larger society, to which we turn next.

Mennonite Membership in the Marketplace

Johann Driedger's shift of activities from the village to the marketplace was accompanied by a change in his cultural values. To what extent has that shift taken place in the five Mennonite denominations generally over time? In table 5.4 we see that roughly one-quarter of the respondents were involved in school service clubs and youth groups, and in farm organizations in 1972; membership had declined by 1989. This, we suggest, illustrates the general shift of most Mennonites from farming in the 1940s to less as they became urban professionals (Muppies).

As urbanization and professionalization increased by 1989, involvement in professional and academic societies also increased dramatically, as did involvement in sports and physical fitness clubs, political parties, and business corporations. It is clear that Mennonites are increasingly getting into hobby and garden clubs, labour unions, literary and art groups, service clubs, and a variety of other organizations. These many less focused activities diversify Mennonite interests, enhance other creative activities, and spawn a variety of new values.

Influence of the Media and Modernization

Having noted the scope and extent of Mennonite media usage, and the scope and extent of Mennonite media usage, and the changes in their values, let us examine the relationship between media access and television usage, and its effect on 'local village' values, and also examine the role of the media in the shift to 'global village' participation.

Effects on the Mennonite 'Local Village'

Media exposure has helped to break down the traditional insularity of Mennonites, and their separation from the world. Can we demonstrate such changes? We sorted salience of Anabaptist beliefs by designing interview statements such as 'True Christian believers can expect frequent persecution from the larger society.' We evaluated the extent of opposition to participation in war or war-promoting activities, and how this affected attitudes towards Church discipline. These factors combined were used as a measure that showed the highest negative correlation with media (in column one of table 5.5; Pearson's $r - .32$). Those who scored high on local village variables did not own TVs, radios, VCRs, videos, and computers, unlike those who scored low.

Almost as high in column one ($r -.31$) was the negative correlation between owning electronic media equipment and the respondents' moral attitudes, a scale made up of items referring to behavioural restrictions, such as smoking tobacco; attending movies rated for adults only; engaging in premarital sex, homosexual acts; masturbation; gambling; and dancing. A substantial negative correlation is also found for devotionalism ($r -.25$), which measures personal prayer and devotional activities. A negative correlation ($r -.21$) was also found between ownership of media devices and moral behaviour, including questions regarding patterns of consumption of alcohol and tobacco, and participation in dancing. The separatism scale is based on agreement to a series of statements asserting a fundamental contradiction between Mennonite Christian beliefs and the 'kingdom of this world,' correlated nega-

TABLE 5.5
Access and Use of the Media, by Local and Global
Village Variables, 1989

Variables	Media access	TV usage
'Local Village' Measures	(Pearson's *r*s)	
Anabaptism	−.32	.09
Moral attitudes	−.31	.07
Devotionalism	−.25	−.13
Moral behaviour	−.21	.00
Separatism	−.19	−.01
Separation Church/State	−.16	.02
Fundamentalism	−.15	−.05
Communalism	−.15	−.05
Associationalism	−.14	.15
Ethnicity	−.13	−.01
Orthodoxy	−.12	.01
Bible knowledge	−.12	−.04
Pacifism	−.12	.08
'Global Village' Measures		
Political action	.16	−.03
Shared ministry	.17	−.04
Greater roles for women	.18	−.00
Memberships	.22	−.05
Political participation	.22	−.06
Women leadership	.23	−.01

tively with media ownership (*r* −.18). Other negative correlations include separation of the Church and the State (*r* −.16); communalism (*r* −.15), which is concerned with importance and stability of church and denominational membership; and ethnic identity (*r* −.14), concerned with endogamy, choice of in-group friends, maintenance of the ethnic language, and participation in Mennonite organizations.

These scales represent a cluster of theological beliefs, morality, religiosity, and participation in the ethno-religious community, which together support solidarity and resist assimilation. The negative correlations between these measures and media access shows the antipathy between media ownership and these various dimensions of the traditional 'local village' life. It would seem that in homes where local-village measures are strong, Mennonite families are restricting access to the various forms of the media, and restricting their potential use owning fewer media devices.

In column two of table 5.5 we present measures of the actual usage of television, in terms of numbers of hours spent watching television per week. What is surprising and interesting is that these TV-usage measures do not correlate well with the media-access findings in column one. Whereas measures of access correlated negatively with all local village indicators, half of the TV-usage measures are not negative but positive. In fact, the major finding regarding TV usage and attachments to local village values is that they are unrelated (Pearson's r scores under .10). Only devotionalism (r −.15) is negatively related, similar to media access (r −.25). Surprisingly, associationalism (r −.15) is positively correlated with TV usage, but negatively related (r −.14) to media access.

Whereas media access correlates negatively with local village values as expected, use of television shows no clear pattern of relationship to Mennonite local-village values. These findings lend support to Innis's general hypothesis regarding the impact of new communication technologies, but do not appear to support McLuhan's hypothesis with regard to the influence of the experience of television viewing. By implication, these findings also support reports from psychologists that, on an experiential level, television does not involve audience members as much as do other media.

Evidence of 'Global Village' Attitudes

Similar relationships may be observed in the analysis of a second set of values that seek to identify a more active orientation, and a view of Mennonites located within the framework of a larger world. We see, in contrast to the negative correlations with the various measures of separatism and apartness, that these measures of active global involvement display substantial positive correlations with media access (ownership). Political participation, which includes willingness to vote in public elections, to hold political office, and to contact the State by writing, testifying, etc., is correlated positively with media usage. Two scales measuring the extent of participation of women (measures of openness to women in leadership and egalitarian family roles) were both positively associated with media access (r. 22). Political action (r .16), including questions about encouraging congregations to examine political candidates, encouraging ministers to discuss political issues from the pulpit, and engaging in political action more generally, were also positively associated with media access, as expected.

However, the results in column two indicate that there are no significant associations between television usage and global-village measures (all *r*s under .10). These results are all negative, compared with the positive associations between media access and global measures. On the other hand, McLuhan's idea that TV is a cool medium that leaves viewers uninvolved is not confirmed. The media-access measures collectively support a more active orientation to the world, characteristic of McLuhan's global village. Media access (owning more TV sets, radios, VCRs, and computers, and subscribing to more newspapers) is positively associated with global-village measures as expected, but greater television usage is not. Again, we find that there is more evidence of Innis's view of media access than of McLuhan's predictions of the importance of TV use.

Media Access and Modernization

We noted at the outset that Mennonites have relatively recently become more modern, moving to cities, pursuing higher education, and increased occupational and socio-economic status generally. We expect that media access and use will be an important factor in, if not a major indicator of, the shift towards modernization as well.

Using indicators of modernization (SES and urbanization), we found that the highest correlations were between media access and income. This shows that higher-status Mennonites own more media technology because they have the means to pay for such technology. Education, which is a part of the composite socio-economic-status measure, is a second factor, because the more educated seek the latest and best information. Occupation (*r* .12) also correlates positively with media access, because Mennonites in the professions and business give such access more priority than do farmers. As expected, modernization in the form of socio-economic status correlates positively with access to media technology.

Urbanization also correlates positively with media access; as Mennonites move to the city and become more exposed to others, they also purchase more television sets, radios, VCRs, and the like. Individualism, wanting privacy, reluctance about mutual admonition, seeing faith as a private matter and a personal choice, and following individual feelings also correlated positively with media access. Materialism, such as wanting to earn more money, dressing in the latest fashions, earning for security, working hard, saving money, and setting a nice home, also correlates positively with greater media access. The same is true for secularism, that is, being more open to secular messages, science, logic, reason, doubts, pleasure, and sensory stimulation, which also correlates positively with media access.

Age, however, is negatively associated with media access. Since nine out of ten Mennonites before the Second World War were still on the farm, and less well-to-do, it is not surprising that older Mennonites have been more reluctant to buy television, VCRs, and reading materials. We conclude that socio-economic status, urbanism, and age are three important modernization variables that influence access to the media.

Use of Television and Modernization

Earlier we learned that access to the media and actual use of media technology were two different matters. We suspect that other variables are operating, so let us examine the influence of modernization on actual TV use. While media access and modernization variables correlated mostly positively, in table 5.9 we see that television use and modernization correlated less strongly, and negatively. Of the socio-economic variables, education (r –.14), income (r –.19) and occupation (r –.09) are slightly negative in relation to television use. Higher-status Mennonites own more media technology, but use television less.

Urbanization (r .00) is not a factor at all, and individualism, materialism, and secularism are negatively correlated with TV use. This finding was a surprise, because it is the reverse of the findings related to media access, and we did not expect this. Mennonites who are more individualist (r –.17), materialist (r –.18), and secular (r –.14) do not use more television, presumably because they engage in other sources of stimulation and are less dependent on watching television. Age (r –.11) does not seem to be as important a factor in the amount of TV use as compared with media access either. McLuhan's contention that television use predicts modern influences is not confirmed.

Multivariate Analysis

It is clear that key modernization variables, such as socio-economic status(ses), urbanization and its concomitants, and age, are important influences on Mennonite media access and use, and these variables also influence 'local village' and 'global village' values, attitudes, and behaviour. SES, urbanism, and media access are positively correlated. Age is negatively correlated with SES and media access, and unrelated to urbanism and individualism.

Socio-economic status and individualism are negatively correlated with television use, and urbanism is unrelated to TV use. Age is not a significant factor in any of the variables (individualism, urbanism, TV use), but it is negatively correlated with SES.

Earlier we found that Mennonites identified with a dozen 'local village' variables, which were negatively correlated with media access, and hardly related to television usage. We found that local village variables correlated positively with moral behaviour (.31), ethnicity (30), devotionalism (.29), and moral attitudes (.28). Older Mennonites who grew up in rural farm enclaves were socialized strongly into 'local village' identity. On the other hand, younger Mennonites favoured women in leadership (–.23), shared ministry (–.19), greater community (–.19), and political participation (–.18) more, which favoured greater participation in the global arena. Elderly Mennonites identify more with the local village and they have less access to the media, and younger Mennonites have greater access to the media, and are significantly and positively associated with global-village affairs.

On the other hand, modernization variables such as education and socio-economic status correlated negatively with most local-village indicators, including fundamentalist theology (–.35), separation of Church and State (–.22), moral attitudes (–.21), and moral behaviour (–.18). The more educated were associated positively with global-village variables such as women in leadership (.40), shared ministry (.37), egalitarian family roles for women (.34), and political participation (.30). Socio-economic status tended to follow the same patterns as education, usually with somewhat lower correlations.

However, residence was not as influential. Urban Mennonites, like better-educated and higher-status Mennonites, tended to correlate negatively with local-village variables, and positively with global-village variables. Rural Mennonites were stronger on moral attitudes (–.20), fundamentalist theology (–.18), moral behaviour (–.16), and separation of Church and State (–.15). Urban Mennonites, though, were more involved in global-village activity, such as political participation (.23), egalitarian family roles for women (.21), shared ministry (.20), and supporting women in leadership (.20).

Conclusions

Harold Innis and Marshal McLuhan can both be considered pioneers in recognizing the impact of the media on communication in society and culture. Both shared the general expectation that media have contributed to the movement of humans from a more enclavic 'local village' to a more complex and open 'global village,' leading to a greater awareness of the larger social scene on a more global scale, with attendant changes in culture, values, attitudes, and behaviour.

We found that, between 1972 and 1989, Mennonites had become increasingly more exposed to the media, having acquired more media technology, and their use of television especially had increased. We found that increased access to media technology correlated negatively with strong Mennonite theological beliefs, moral attitudes and behaviour, associationism, communalism, and ethnicity. The 'local village' of Mennonite identity acted as a buffer, supporting distinctive religious and ethnic attitudes and behaviour.

On the other hand, increased media access was positively associated with 'global village' indicators such as openness to memberships, political participation, shared ministry, and greater roles for women in the family and in leadership. However, actual use of television correlated hardly at all with either local-village or global-village values, showing that media access and media use are two different issues, which raises questions about McLuhan's emphasis on sensory experience.

Modernization indicators such as income, socio-economic status, education and occupational status correlated positively with media access, as did urbanization, individualism, materialism, and secularization. However, age was negatively associated with access to media technology, with the young more involved than the elderly. Surprisingly, socio-economic-status indicators correlated weakly and negatively with TV use; urbanization was not influential at all; and individualism, materialism, and urbanization correlated negatively with TV use.

We conclude that the best predictor of local-village values is age. Older Mennonites who came from more enclavic rural local settings still held most to local-village Mennonite values. Education was negatively associated with these local-village Mennonite values, and residence was considerably less important. On the other hand, as education increased, openness to global-village values also increased, supported by greater socio-economic status, urbanism, and younger Mennonites.

We conclude that Mennonite access to and use of the media have increased over time as Mennonites have become more urban and educated. Local-village characteristics declined as media exposure increased. Increased access to the media has also led to more openness to participating in global village life. Increased education, modernization, and urbanization have resulted in greater access to the media, and encourage greater exposure to the global village. Young Mennonites are more exposed to the media, which has increased their involvement in the global village, but resulted in a decline in local-village identity.

We found that access to the media was much more influential than television use, which supports the predications of Innis more than those of McLuhan. Our findings do not support McLuhan's contention that television is a high-involvement medium. However, we found that access and availability of communication technology, as Innis proposed, transforms the nature of social relations.

6

The Politics of Homemaking and Career

The United Nations Population Conference, held in Cairo 5–13 September 1994, was dominated by the abortion debate.[1] The strong opposition to abortion and lashing out at the feminists by the Vatican could not be ignored, even though many Catholic countries did not share this view. Support for the Vatican's position from the Muslim countries also made it a significant issue in the debate. The feminists' argument was equally strong, not only on the pro-choice issue, but also on the need to recognize women as actors and decision makers (Keyfitz 1995). In the past, U.N. population conferences made an impact on only a few participants. But the 1994 conference had a much wider impact – not only because of the important role of the media, but also because of the changing social environment in which women are awakening to issues of social justice and individual human rights.

The abortion controversy, in particular, the reproductive health problems of women, created a special urgency. As Keyfitz (1995, 90) put it, 'There is a question for basic sociology here.' The question is: How does the debate on abortion correlate with many other elements of morality, individualism, and modern change? It is, of course, no accident that the Muslim and Catholic countries banded together to fight abortion. The changes discussed in previous chapters are also taking place in more preindustrial societies, which wish to maintain their patriarchal systems that often put women in traditional secondary roles. As well, they wish to maintain their rural sacred villages, where their cultures are threatened by the media that introduce global Western ideas. Urbanism is also on the rise, and an increase in the number of professional jobs has had an effect on the traditional agricultural way of life. Individualism is encouraged, which they see as deconstructing their patriarchal village patterns. Now, even family structures are changing, and abortion will enhance the woman's individualism and freedom, which challenges traditional male dominance.

How do these factors fit together in shaping modern thinking? The full test of an abortion debate requires a worldwide study of different societies in different stages of development. But that is much too large a study for us to attempt here. Mennonites are an ideal group to test the influences of a number of variables, including religious commitment, historic pacifism, socio-economic status, and degrees of emphasis on individualism (Driedger and Halli 1997). Since the Mennonites also represent a rural-agricultural, conservative religious group in North America, they represent a range of attitudes, as well as pacifism, which is crucial to our study. Mennonites' refusal to participate in war, we expect, means that Mennonites are more pro-life.

The Homemaking–Career Struggle

Kristin Luker (1984) claims that the abortion issue revolves less around the welfare of the foetus than around the social status of the woman and/or mother. Abortion represents 'two opposing visions of motherhood at war. Championed by "feminists" and "housewives," these two different views of motherhood represent in turn two very different kinds of social worlds' (Luker 1984, 193). Homemaking and career-making thus become competing statuses, which Luker says are the real social issues in the debate.

The challenge is to construct these homemaking and career-making empirical worlds, and to examine the extent to which pro-life and pro-choice do indeed correlate with other variables which together represent homemaking and career types. Which influences – homemaking or career-making – seems to be stronger? Can we provide a conceptual frame for these complex issues and sort the extent to which Luker and others have isolated major influences on pro-life and pro-choice attitudes?

Politics of Motherhood versus Career

Kristin Luker (1984, 194) claims that 'while on the surface it is the embryo's fate that seems to be at stake, the abortion debate is actually about the meanings of women's lives.' Women, like everyone else, rely on their strengths, so those with less education and training turn to homemaking and motherhood, where they concentrate their assets:

> ... for pro-life women the traditional division of life into separate male roles and female roles still works, but for pro-choice women it does not. Having made a commitment to the traditional female roles of wife, mother and homemaker, pro-life women are limited in those kinds of resources – education, class status, recent occupational experiences – they would need to compete in what has traditionally been a male sphere, namely the paid labor force. The average pro-choice woman, in contrast, is comparatively well endowed in exactly those resources. (Luker 1984, 200)

Socio-economic status is closely tied to the debate. According to Luker's studies, most pro-choice women are in the labour force, where they compete well with men, because they themselves have attained higher levels of education, have been able to compete for higher-status jobs, and earn substantial incomes that support a comfortable independent lifestyle. 'An astounding 94 percent of all pro-choice women work, and over half of them have incomes in the top 10 percent of all working women in this country (USA).' (Luker 1984, 198). 'Pro-life women, by contrast, are far less likely to work; 63 percent of them do not work in the paid labour force, and almost all of those who do are unmarried. Among pro-life married women, for example, only 14 percent report any personal income at all ... Half of pro-life women who do work earn less than $5,000 a year, and half earn between $5,000 and $10,000' (Luker 1984, 195).

These findings suggest that there are pro-life and pro-choice social types that emerge out of very different social environments. Urban, upper-middle-class pro-choice women in the labour force have become career-oriented; for them, motherhood is optional and only one of many choices. Women with lower socio-economic status in both the city and country, who are less educated and who stay at home to raise children, have fewer choices, and therefore concentrate on homemaking:

> ... Women who oppose abortion and seek to make it officially unavailable are declaring, both practically and symbolically, that women's reproduction roles should be given social primacy. Once an embryo is defined as a child and an abortion as the death of a person, almost everything else in a woman's life must 'go on hold' during the course of her pregnancy; any attempt to gain 'male' resources such as a job, an education, or other skills

must be subordinated to her uniquely female responsibility ... (Luker 1984, 200)

Religion and Pro-Life

Religious ideology is a major variable, independent of the politics of motherhood, which supports the family and homemaking, an important factor in formation of pro-life types. Luker's research showed that religious beliefs were perhaps the most significant factor in taking sides on abortion, similar to the findings of Glock, Ringer, and Babbie (1967). Almost three-quarters of the pro-choice respondents said formal religion was not important to them, and only 25 per cent said they went to church. Practically all pro-life respondents (91 per cent) said religion was important to them, with two-thirds attending church regularly (Luker 1984, 197). Luker also found that about 80 per cent of pro-lifers were Roman Catholic, a denomination that emphasizes sexual morality and family life.

In his *Abortion: The Clash of Absolutes* (1990), Laurence Tribe devotes considerable space to the role of ideology and religion in the debate, reviewing attitudes on abortion over time, comparing many countries. He suggests that the *Roe* v. *Wade* Supreme Court decision was an attempt to consider the welfare of both foetus and mother:

> Most Americans who look at the abortion issue see both a fetus and a pregnant woman. Too often, when activists on either side present their picture of the abortion issue, they leave room for only the fetus *or* the pregnant woman ... Those who oppose abortion often use a process of visualization to stir people's emotions. Yet what they ask us to visualize is an isolated picture of a fetus. Where is the person who develops, nurtures, and sustains the fetus we are looking at? Where is the woman? In this vision, she is insignificant, devalued. (Tribe 1990, 136).

Tribe suggests that motherhood and the foetus are closely intertwined with religion and a 'sacredness of life,' and must not be separated.

Pro-choice advocates focus more on the individual rights of a woman to develop her own life potential, while pro-life advocates focus on the foetus, linking the development of foetus potential with the required services of motherhood and the support of religious sanctity. Religion tends to restrict individual freedom in favour of traditional community sanctions. The Judaeo-Christian culture has been a significant source of limits on individual freedom, stressing as it does sacredness of human life, a focus that often conflicts with individual choice.

Pacifism and Opposition to Abortion

Cleghorn (1986) suggests that 'preservation of life' is a key factor, with homemaking and religion as supports for love, nurturing, and development of life. This seems to be in line with Luker's (1984, 194) contention that the abortion issue centres not on biological life (the embryo or foetus), but on social life (status, freedom). Too little work has been done to unscramble these biological and social quality-of-life distinctions.

It seems that if we select a group of people who are in principle against all killing, no matter what the biological or social circumstances, then Luker's claim that the abortion issue is about social, not biological, issues could be tested. Some historical religious peace groups, such as the Quakers, Church of the Brethren, Mennonites, Hutterites, and Amish, who are opposed in principle to all killing, including war, would make a good sample.

We would expect a group like the Mennonites, who are now about half rural and half urban, to be consistent with their historical peace position and favour pro-life (Driedger and Kraybill 1994). As Sider (1987) suggests, Mennonites should be consistent, and be pro-life, opposing abortion and nuclear war, and supporting the family and the poor (all potential for life). Or have modernization factors such as urbanism and increased social status resulted in reinterpretations of when life begins (before or after birth)? We contend that the pacifism factor can help sort Luker's contention that the issue on abortion is not the foetus, but the social status of women.

Social Class and Pro-Choice

Having discussed religion and pacifism as two factors that seem to correlate with homemaking and pro-life, what about factors (social class and individualism) that correlate with career-making and pro-choice? In line with Luker's findings, some suggest that the abortion controversy is shaped by class and cultural conflicts rooted in the person's place in the economy and the stratification system (Barnartt and Harris 1992; Clarke 1987). These scholars suggest that increased education and occupational status give the individual a sense of power of self-direction within a more liberal society that permits choice. They say that 'legalized abortion, in this perspective, is one means for achieving the conditions which will allow women to have dignity and reach fulfillment as persons' (Tamney, Johnson, and Burrton 1992: 35).

Peter Berger (1977) identifies as features of modernization abstraction, choice, individualism, and futurity. Rationality increases with education, choice forces innumerable daily decisions, while social nets distance individuals from their social groups. With increased education, people slip out of the conforming grip of traditional groups such as tribe, village, and family. This loosening from traditional moorings, we expect, will also change attitudes, shifting the focus from dependence upon the family as the major social net to the larger society and its many pluralist demands. Thus, we expect that attitudes on abortion will also change from pro-life to pro-choice as level of education increases.

Individualism and Pro-Choice

Robert Bellah and associates (1985) brought the discussion of individualism into a sociological context. They argue that individualism lies at the core of North American culture. While Americans do not celebrate individualism (as Adam Smith did), neither do they seem to agonize over it, as Max Weber did (Ainlay 1990). They discuss four forms of individualism, as noted in chapter 3. In the first two forms (biblical and civic), individualism is held in check by a shared religious and ethical community and commitment to civic participation. In the case of utilitarian and expressive individualism, the balance between commitment and individual interest is lost, and freedom to pursue material gain and self-gratification become dominant. We need to see the extent to which expressive and utilitarian individualism are factors in pro-choice abortion decisions because we expect that these forms of individualism will correlate highly with wanting a choice when faced with abortion.

Abortion: Changing Attitudes

Emancipatory strivings by women and other minorities have questioned traditional roles, thus subverting traditional sources of authority, and creating a legitimation crisis. The abortion debate vividly illustrates the tensions surrounding cultural transformation and legitimation. The U.S. Supreme Court *Roe* v. *Wade* decision transformed abortion from a relatively marginal and invisible technical matter into a public and moral issue (Luker 1984, 127). In the process, religious denominations have been forced to rethink their positions, which has resulted in a plethora of denominational statements on abortion. We expect that any sample of respondents will range along a black-and-white versus flexibility continuum. Can we sort which variables add to flexibility, and which to inflexible attitudes, on the issue?

Rural traditional societies emphasize the importance of the home, as well as homemaker roles for women. Mennonites have come from a long rural agricultural past, where gender roles were segregated. Now that half of them have become urban, they are an ideal group to test Luker's contention that homemaking and pro-life attitudes on abortion go together. Part of the sixteenth-century Protestant Reformation, Mennonites were a branch of the Anabaptists, who practised radical pacifism. This resulted in refusal to participate in war, which we expect will also make Mennonites more pro-life.

After the *Roe* v. *Wade* decision in 1973, highly publicized by the media, evangelical and conservative Protestants were involved in massive anti-abortion mobilization after 1973, and abortion became a serious issue of discussion among Mennonites. The Mennonite Brethren adopted a pro-life statement in 1972, as did the Evangelical Mennonite conference in 1973, the Mennonite Church in 1975, the General Conference Mennonite Church in 1980, Mennonite Central Committee Canada in 1982, and the Conference of Mennonites in Canada in 1988. Prior to passing these statements, extensive congregational and conference discussions were held, including distribution of abortion information. Mennonite discussion of and denominational statements regarding abortion between 1972 and 1989 will have resulted in Mennonite respondents becoming considerably more pro-life in all circumstances by 1989. Many of these Mennonite statements linked the Mennonite issue of pacifism with a pro-life stance on abortion as well.

Tamney, Johnson, and Burrton (1992, 25) develop a model using a series of the variables outlined above, and attempt to cluster them around pro-life and pro-choice polarities. We want to see whether we can expand their attempt, sorting some of the pro-life and pro-choice issues around 'homemaker' and 'career' polarities. We begin with the two homemaker and career-maker types, the first expected to be more pro-life, and the second more pro-choice. We expect that religion and pacifism will enhance pro-life positions under the homemaker type.

We also expect that high socio-economic status and strong individualism will influence career-makers to be more pro-choice. Let us summarize these expected relationships in the form of three hypotheses: (1) Post *Roe* v. *Wade* (1989) Mennonites (after denominational statements) will be more anti-abortion than 1972 respondents; (2) Homemakers (more religious and pacifist) will be more anti-abortion than career women; (3) Career women (higher status and individualism) will be more pro-choice than homemakers.

Sorting the Issues

First we present a comparison of national U.S. (1972 and 1985) and Mennonite data (1972 and 1989), to get some sense of the larger overall attitudes and trends on abortion (hypothesis 1). Second, we focus on the Mennonite data, which account for differences among Mennonites on anti-abortion and pro-choice attitudes for hypotheses 2 and 3.[2]

Trend Comparisons: U.S. and Mennonite Data

When asked 'Do you approve of abortion in the following circumstances?' almost nine out of ten of a national sample of Americans were pro-choice when the woman's health was in serious danger, but only four out of ten were pro-choice when a baby was not wanted. Circumstances were obviously an important factor, as seen in table 6.1. Responses did not vary significantly between 1972 and 1985 (Granbert and Granbert 1986). Indeed, the respondents seemed to make a distinction when faced with circumstances over which there was no control, and circumstances where the individual had a choice. Eight out of ten U.S. respondents wanted a choice when the mother's life was in danger, when rape had occurred, or when serious birth defects were likely. Less than half wanted a choice when social circumstances such as family income, legal marriage, and wanting the baby were the considerations. Legislation and other events in American life between 1972 and 1985 did not seem to affect general attitudinal changes.

The results of the Mennonite sample were very different. While three out of four Mennonites in 1972 favoured a choice when the woman's health was endangered, by 1989 this had dropped to 58 per cent. Mennonite educational discussion, and official pro-life denominational statements, seemed to have an effect over the seventeen years. Less than half the Mennonite respondents in 1972 favoured abortion in

TABLE 6.1
Percentage Pro-Choice on Legal Abortion

Pro-choice if:	National U.S. pro-choice*		Mennonite pro-choice	
	1972 (%)	1985 (%)	1972 (%)	1989 (%)
Woman's health is seriously endangered	87	89	73	58
Pregnant as a result of rape	79	81	46	31
Strong chance of serious defect in baby	79	79	48	23
Family cannot afford children	49	44	12	4
Woman not married and doesn't want to marry	43	41	9	4
Woman doesn't want the baby	40	40	8	5

*From Granbert and Granbert 1986

cases of rape or where chances of serious defects in the baby were strong, and these also dropped significantly by 1989. Hardly any Mennonites in both 1972 and 1989 were willing to consider choice options when low family incomes, absence of legal marriage, or unwanted babies were factors.

The abortion debate has dominated the media in the past twenty years, especially in North America. It has forced people to get involved in the controversy. The forces that lead to individualism and desire for choice seem not to have influenced Mennonites as much as they have the general U.S. population. Mennonite recent rural solidarity, and their long history of pacifism, seem to influence them in the direction of pro-life rather than pro-choice on abortion, especially when denominational discussion and official statements occurred between 1972 and 1989. Moral obligations to community seem to supersede individual choices. For many Mennonites who are pacifists, pro-choice is unacceptable because it reflects the interdependence of life and death.

Homemakers: Opposed to Abortion

Our earlier review of the literature suggested that homemaker-oriented and career-oriented respondents represent very different social worlds, which will result in quite different pro-life and pro-choice attitudes towards legal abortion. In table 6.2 we see, as Luker (1984, 6) predicted, that homemaker orientations correlated highly with pro-life attitudes. Three times as many who scored high as homemakers were against abortion; half were pro-life even when pregnancy resulted from a rape, or when the baby might have serious defects. More than nine out of ten were against abortion when families could not afford children, or when women wanted to remain unmarried or did not want the baby. As predicted, there were significant positive correlations between homemaking and anti-abortion in all six situations.

Anabaptist Beliefs and Pro-Life

Luker (1984, 6) and Tribe (1990, 16) both suggest that salience of religious beliefs will result in greater promotion of pro-life. In section B of table 6.2 we use a four-point scale of Anabaptist beliefs and find that, as adherence to Anabaptist beliefs rises, opposition to abortion also rises in each of the six circumstances posed. Four times as many respondents who score high on Anabaptist beliefs oppose abortion when the woman's health is seriously endangered. Twice as many who scored high on Anabaptism also opposed abortion in case of rape or defects in the baby. These differences were less pronounced for the last three social circumstances, but those who adhere to Anabaptist beliefs always scored higher on pro-life than those who scored low on Anabaptism. As expected in hypothesis 2, salience of religious beliefs clearly leads to greater opposition to abortion. Respondents who scored high on homemaking and high on Anabaptist theology had highly correlated pro-life profiles.

Pacifism and Opposition to Abortion

Since the Reformation in the sixteenth century, Mennonites have been one of the historic peace churches, so we expect that Mennonites who are theologically Anabaptist, and who are pacifistic, will more consistently wish to preserve life. Let us see to what extent pacifism and opposition to abortion correlate.

The data on pacifism in table 6.2 are surprising. Fewer Mennonites who scored high on pacifism (that is, favoured alternatives to joining the military, wanted no part in war, promoted peace, did not want to own stocks in companies producing war goods, and did not want to pay

TABLE 6.2
Percentage Who Oppose Abortion, by Measures of Homemaking, Theology, and Pacifism, 1989

Independent variables	Percent Who oppose abortion if:					
	Woman's health endangered	Raped	Baby defective	Can't afford baby	Not married	Baby unwanted
A. *Homemaker Orientation*						
High	22	49	52	92	92	92
Medium	15	46	53	90	91	92
Low	8	29	38	78	80	81
Z Value*	2.59**	5.06**	3.81**	7.23**	6.40**	5.96**
B. *Anabaptist Theology*						
High	24	59	63	93	94	94
Medium High	14	44	51	91	90	91
Medium Low	12	32	42	85	86	87
Low	6	23	28	74	75	75
Z Value	1.96**	6.19**	6.64**	7.86**	8.14**	8.16**
C. *Pacifism*						
High	9	37	41	81	79	83
Medium High	15	43	49	89	90	91
Medium Low	15	42	49	89	89	90
Low	16	42	51	88	88	87
Z Value	1.02	0.87	1.86**	2.36**	2.94**	1.38

*A test for difference of high–low proportions
**Statistically significant above the 0.05 level

war taxes) opposed abortion than those who scored in the medium and low ranges. J. Howard Kauffman (1989) found that, in most denominations, pacifism is a liberal position, opposed by fundamentalists and evangelicals generally. Kauffman, however, found that, in Mennonite circles, pacifism is supported by both liberals (as a social issue) and conservatives (as a traditional Anabaptist biblical position). Note in table 6.2 that none of the three low to medium-high positions for pacifism were significantly different. Also those respondents who scored high on pacifism had twice as many 'uncertain' responses as those who scored lower. This suggests that taking positions against paying war taxes (the fourth aspect of pacifism that put them in the 'high' category) is a radical step and makes many Mennonites uncomfortable.

These surprising results show that attitudes towards abortion can be interpreted in two ways. On the one hand, the foetus in the womb should not be destroyed, and/or, on the other hand, the foetus ought to be born into a safe social environment. For Mennonites who scored low to medium-high on pacifism, there was no significant difference in anti-abortion attitudes. Fewer highly pro-active Mennonites for peace actually opposed abortion. These findings show that, as pacifism increases, opposition to abortion does *not* increase. Our homemaker type is indeed strongly opposed to abortion, supported by strong Anabaptist beliefs, but not by pacifism. The negative opposition to abortion results on pacifism support Luker's contention that the abortion debate is not about saving life or the foetus, but about the social status of women/mothers. Indeed, a minority in all four positions on the pacifist scale (low to high) are opposed to abortion when the mother's health is endangered, and when pregnancy is caused by rape.

Career-Oriented Advocates of Pro-Choice

To measure our second type (career-maker), we could have assumed that the low end of the homemaker scale represented career-oriented women. However, to measure career orientation directly, we developed a career-orientation scale with four items, including female and male career equality, compatability of children and careers, importance of women's careers to the family, and being a full-time career woman. While the homemaker scale focused on the centrality of the family and the woman's central role in it, the career scale focused on women's work in the labour force, and their desire for more freedom.

We predicted that career women will be more pro-choice, which is clearly the case in table 6.3. Twice as many pro-career women (three-quarters) favoured pro-choice when the woman's health is endangered, and three times as many were pro-choice in the case of rape. The ratios between low and high career orientation increased with the other items, although the numbers in favour of abortion declined considerably. All of these significant differences show that indeed there is a strong correlation between having a pro-career orientation and being pro-choice on abortion, as predicted.

Our findings so far support the findings of Luker. We found homemaker and career types, the first committed to work inside the home and the second involved in the paid labour force. Homemakers were more pro-life and career-makers were more pro-choice. Does career-making correlate with independent factors such as socio-economic status and individualism?

Education and Pro-Choice

As Luker (1984) and Tamney, Johnson, and Burrton (1992, 25) suggest, we need to explore the extent to which socio-economic status correlates with pro-choice orientations. In table 6.3 we see that, as level of education rises, so do flexibility and openness to making choices on abortion. Respondents with graduate education wanted the right to choose abortion, more so than did those with only elementary education. Roughly twice as many of the most educated compared to the least educated wanted a choice and abortion to be available if the mother's health was endangered, if there was pregnancy due to rape, and if there was a chance of a serious defect in the baby.

The first choice (abortion if mother's health is endangered) involves two lives. A majority of the most educated chose to save the mother's life. Only one-third in 1989 wanted to choose in the case of rape, and only one in four in case of a serious defect in the baby. The educated again seemed to be more aware of the social consequences for the mother as well as the baby, and made greater allowance for choices. Almost none of the Mennonite respondents thought these choices should be extended to the impoverished, the unmarried, or those who did not want the baby.

Individualism and Pro-Choice

As Bellah et al. (1985, 28) had done, we designed utilitarian measures

TABLE 6.3
Percentage Who Are Pro-choice, by Measures of Career Orientation, Education, and Individualism, 1989

Independent variables	Percent Pro-Choice if:					
	Woman's health endangered	Raped	Baby defective	Can't afford baby	Not married	Baby unwanted
A. *Career Orientation*						
High	72	48	37	9	8	10
Medium	56	27	20	3	3	3
Low	38	15	9	0	1	1
Z Value*	9.06**	5.51**	3.84**	0.44	0.45	0.60
B. *Education*						
Graduate school	71	40	29	7	7	6
College	58	31	23	5	5	6
High school	53	29	22	3	3	3
Elementary	45	17	17	2	1	2
Z Value	5.66**	3.04**	1.70**	0.43	0.40	0.40
C. *Individualism*						
High	74	57	44	13	11	13
Medium high	59	32	25	3	4	4
Medium low	52	23	16	2	2	2
Low	52	20	14	3	3	3
Z Value	5.66**	6.39**	4.58**	1.07	0.91	0.11

*A test for difference of high–low proportions
**Statistically significant above the 0.05 level

of individualism that we expect will lead to more pro-choice in the abortion issue. In table 6.3 we see that those who score high on the individualism scale (including privacy of faith, facing ethical decisions alone, seeing religion as personal choice, not the business of the church, placing little importance on the congregation, and resisting admonition) are also significantly more pro-choice. Half of the respondents who scored low on individualism favoured choice if the woman's health was endangered, while three out of four who scored high on individualism did so. These ratios by low and high individualism increase as we move down through the other five items. Our findings reflect Bellah and colleagues' (1985) forms of utilitarian and expressive individualism, where the balance between individual choices and community commitment favours freedom of the self. As expected, when measures of individualism increase, positive attitudes towards choice in abortion also increase.

In table 6.4 we present the results of logit analysis of pro-choice attitudes, and the main effects of the covariantes. The results of the analyses are done separately for the six situations. The covariants are divided into two main categories: homemaker type and career-maker type. Among the homemaker type, the factors considered are homemaker, Anabaptism, and pacifism. The factors presented for the career-maker type are woman's career, individualism, and occupation. We also included the control variables such as education, income, age, and sex. Anabaptism and individualism showed the most significant and consistent relationships. The odds of pro-choice attitudes decreased to 8–17 per cent, depending on the variable, when the respondent scores were high on Anabaptist beliefs. On the other hand, when the respondent scores were high on individualism, pro-choice attitudes increase by as much as nearly six times, compared with the attitudes of those scoring low. These results provide unusually strong support for our homemaker and career-maker types. In fact, the results can throw light on the controversy that developed at the World Population Conference in 1994.

The variable individualism seems to represent the views of many feminists in Cairo who recognized women as individuals with their own views on matters related to reproductive health problems. These women wanted autonomy to protect their own bodies. There seems to be little compromise among those who score high on individualism. On the other hand, the Anabaptists seem to occupy the opposite end of the scale on this pro-choice issue. This was the position taken by the

TABLE 6.4
Results of Logit Analysis of Determinants of Pro-Choice Attitudes, by Six Circumstances, 1989

	Odds ratio of pro-choice attitudes by situation					
Covariates	Woman's health	Rape	Defective baby	Can't afford baby	Not married	Baby unwanted
Homemaker Type						
Homemaker – High	0.395†	0.637**	0.590**	0.299†	0.274†	0.683
– Medium	0.713*	1.163	0.963	0.513	0.401*	0.812
– Low	1.000	1.000	1.000	1.000	1.000	1.000
Anabaptism – High	0.105†	0.170†	0.080†	0.172†	0.106†	0.161†
– Med. high	0.259†	0.309†	0.167†	0.577	0.330**	0.492
– Med. low	0.328†	0.530†	0.328†	0.954	0.863	0.936
– Low	1.000	1.000	1.000	1.000	1.000	
Pacifism – High	1.000	1.000	1.000	1.000	1.000	1.000
– Med. high	2.175†	1.265	1.421	1.681	1.168	0.842
– Med. low	2.196†	1.709**	2.294†	2.247*	2.354**	1.401
– Low	3.492†	1.975**	3.675†	0.892	1.991	1.311
Career-Maker Type						
Woman's Career – High	1.000	1.000	1.000	1.000	1.000	1.000
– Med.	0.381†	0.534†	0.351†	0.108*	0.419	0.561
– Low	0.201†	0.217†	0.151†	0.061**	0.306*	0.278**
Individualism – High	1.811*	5.835†	5.025†	5.361†	3.567†	2.907**
– Med. high	1.403	4.158†	4.395†	5.210†	6.064†	5.525†
– Med. low	1.109	2.525†	1.954†	2.289†	1.735*	1.645*
– Low	1.000	1.000	1.000	1.000	1.000	1.000
Occupation – Professional	1.839*	1.653*	1.807**	0.341	1.195	1.501
– Business	1.951**	1.126	1.391	0.248	0.983	0.958
– Blue collar	1.702	1.140	1.392	0.640	1.039	1.810
– Farmer	1.000	1.000	1.000	1.000	1.000	1.000
Control Variables						
Education	0.774†	0.806†	0.856†	0.785**	0.744†	0.817**
Income	1.000	1.000	1.000	1.000	1.000	1.000
Age	0.966†	0.975†	0.950†	0.973†	0.990	0.994
Sex – male	0.654**	0.763*	0.712**	0.907	0.689	0.739
– female	1.000	1.000	1.000	1.000	1.000	1.000
CONSTANT	2.322†	2.572†	6.642†	9.318†	7.202†	5.230†
– 2 Log – Likelihood	915	1,302	1,127	433	451	529
Chi-Square	245†	368†	421†	153†	155†	134†
No. of observations	1,268	1,207	1,178	1,468	1,459	1,486

*P < 0.1; **P < 0.05; †P < 0.01

Vatican, and representatives of some Muslim countries at the Cairo conference. For those who scored high on Anabaptism, abortion is wrong. The Anabaptists seem to view abortion as a life-and-death matter, where they must choose life.

Ambivalence about abortion is common, but rarely voiced. For those Mennonites committed to individual rights, any discussion that compromises their right to choose as individuals is seen as unjust. So these results clearly define two poles among Mennonites – namely, the Anabaptist community versus individual rights.

Commitment to homemaking seems to create a social context compatible with Mennonite Anabaptist beliefs, which also correlates negatively with pro-choice of abortion. This is significant among those who score high on homemaking. The odds of being against choice of abortion also declined with increased adherence to pacifism, which was not clear in table 6.2 before controls were in place. We conclude that Anabaptist beliefs are the engine that drives Mennonite opposition to abortion, cradled in a homemaking context, where pacifism seems to flourish.

On the other hand, individualism seems to drive Mennonites to a need for greater choices with respect to many things, including abortion, with its many diverse situations. The right for a woman to make a career outside the home is a choice which many Mennonite women have made, and they are strongly inclined to keep their options on abortion open, as was expected. The odds of supporting a pro-choice position also increase to 65–84 per cent, from farmers to professionals. Professionals, especially, wish to have a choice on abortion, where unplanned-for or unwanted children would severely restrict their individual and career opportunities.

As far as control variables are concerned, they all show the expected relationships with pro-choice attitudes, with the exception of income. Surprisingly, income is not a significant predictor of pro-choice or pro-life attitudes. It may be because the effect of income is subsumed by the variables of occupation and education. In fact, education has an overriding influence on pro-choice attitudes. It is significant in all the different circumstances. Perhaps education is a proxy for many homemaker and career-maker variables, so that it also has its own independent effect. This could be because education encourages rational thought that includes perspective on alternative choices.

The variables of age and sex show insignificant relationships with pro-choice attitudes on abortion. However, as expected, younger Mennonites do support pro-choice when a woman's health is in danger, when rape occurs, and when there is danger of a defective baby. Though the support is statistically significant, the real differences are minimal. However, the support for choice in abortion tends to be 25 to 35 per cent less among Mennonite men than women. To some extent, this finding may reflect the historical patriarchal trend of men trying to control the lives of women by not granting them choices.

Conclusions

In the United States, a strong majority of 80 per cent or more favour a choice in whether to use abortion when the woman's health is in danger, when the pregnancy is the result of rape, or when there could be a serious defect in the baby, and this did not change in a generation. While a majority of Mennonite respondents also favoured a choice when the mother's health was in danger, they were much less open to choice in other circumstances, and openness to abortion dropped significantly by 1989 in all categories, quite unlike the U.S. findings. Reasons for this difference are of much interest.

We empirically constructed homemaking and career-orientation typologies to explore Luker's contention that abortion is not about the welfare of the foetus, but about the status and roles of women. We found that, in a North American sample of 3,000 Mennonites, these two typologies clearly existed. Respondents who fit the homemaker type were more religious, were significantly less educated and less individualistic, and were also opposed to abortion, as expected. Career-oriented respondents were more highly educated, placed more emphasis on individualism, and were also significantly more pro-choice, as expected.

Clearly, religion plays a central role when it comes to a choice in support of the homemaking, anti-abortion position, as Tribe (1990) predicted. Mennonite respondents who scored high on Anabaptist theological beliefs also opposed abortion most on all of the six dependent variables (the strongest and most consistent predictor of anti-abortion). As respondents scored down the Anabaptist scale to medium and low levels, opposition also declined, and the differences between high and low levels of belief were significant on all six forms of opposition to abortion. Theological salience is clearly an important factor in holding to Mennonite commitments, which clearly worked to make Mennonites different with respect to this issue.

We also predicted that pacifism would support homemaking, and that it would also result in opposition to abortion. The influence of this factor was not as independent, until we controlled for other factors, when it also became significant. While a majority of Mennonites are clearly committed to pacifism, there is a significant minority who are less sure about peace, especially those who have opted heavily for fundamentalism, which is often anti-peace. Many Mennonites do not see peace as part of a profile package, as Sider (1987) does.

On the other hand, individualism turned out to be the most important factor in promotion of choice in abortion. Mennonites in the professions were important supporters of a choice in abortion matters. As discussed in chapters 2 and 3, in order to have some control over their body and lives, women wished to keep their options on abortion open, especially when, because of rape, pregnancy was not of their own choosing. Serious defects in the baby would also require much extra work on the part of the family, and many were not willing to give up work outside the home to give the extra care required. Control of work and home situations seemed to be an important factor in having a choice.

Higher education was the most significant and most consistent predictor of a pro-choice position, presumably because the better-educated were more socially aware. Thus, they wanted the freedom to make decisions based on a variety of circumstances, weighing the many alternatives, which is really a postmodern notion. Situations are diverse, options are many, solutions are usually not black and white, and moral situations are often ambiguous, with few clear answers.

More than any other dependent variable, the desire for choice in case of rape was significant for all but one independent variable (income), which suggests that social circumstances must always be considered. However, there was less leeway for choice in less difficult social situations, such as not being married, and having an unwanted baby (the best example of unconditional abortion).

As Luker and we predicted, homemakers who were more religious, less educated, and less inclined to value individualism were significantly more likely to oppose abortion. Career-oriented persons who were more individualistic, less religious, and more educated were more likely to be pro-choice. The salience and quality of Anabaptism, and the reinforcement of these beliefs between 1972 and 1989, resulted in Mennonites being considerably more opposed to abortion than the national population, even though many have become more educated and more urban. Strong Anabaptist beliefs show that ideology can be a strong challenge to individualism, which is a counter-force to Luker's career-making status. Tribe's findings that religion is a strong force in pro-life attitudes is also confirmed.

PART III

RECONSTRUCTION FOR POSTMODERN DIVERSITY

7

Teens Growing Roots and Wings

A plaque hanging in a school principal's office reads: 'We give our children roots – and wings' (Bibby and Posterski 1985, 200). 'In this maze of the modern world' both are needed but, it is not always easy to find the right balance (Driedger and Bergen 1997). We examine, first, the roots, norms, and values of Mennonite teenagers, and then reflect on whether their roots prepare them adequately for life in the postmodern world. Growing well-grounded beliefs and values is the challenge, as the emerging generation of Mennonite teens leave their nests and fly.

Emerging Teen Trends

Bibby and Posterski (1985, 3; 1992) conclude that today's teenagers place much importance on people and relationships. Since teenagers must find their own peer networks, this requires letting them go sufficiently so that they can try their wings. In their concern to instil values and roots, adults often fail to let young people grow up; they suppress emergence.

The Nature of Emergence

In the rural past, young people on farms learned farming, housekeeping, and how to raise children. Growing up and having their own farm, household, and family represented a continuous transition from what they had learned early in life. Modernization has changed many things, and the rise of technology has made training and schooling essential. As schooling has expanded, from high school to college and further, the time between biological maturity and recognition of adult status has been lengthening. The term 'adolescence,' a period during which young people are neither children nor adults, describes this new stage of life (Bibby and Posterski 1985, 10).

The challenge for parents is that they want their children to adopt many of their values and roots, but schools have increasingly taken on the role of inculcating values, thereby subsuming the parental role. More limited time at home means fewer natural opportunities for parents and children to work together and share. Influence confined to off-hours at home does not leave as many natural opportunities for working and sharing together. Working parents and teens in school tend to become socialized in their respective environments, and the twain rarely meet. To make up for lost time, parents feel the need to press their values and traditions, and thus often can become rule-enforcing tyrants. Thus, adults and their institutions can become suppressors of emergence, rather than cooperate in facilitating changes.

Youth, on the other hand, are coming of age in 'a period of history of unequalled scientific and technological progress, a period Orwell and Huxley envisioned would be characterized by revolutionary changes in values, relationships, and family structure' (Bibby and Posterski 1985, 175). In these postmodern times, when NASA's rover is probing Mars, they sense that they face times that no previous generation has had to face. Bibby and Posterski (1985, 176) suggest, however, that such change is not a revolution, but a dramatic continuity between past and present. 'Traditional values regarding friendship, love, freedom, alongside honesty, hard work, and consideration, continue to be of paramount importance in their high-tech age.'

So, the problem is, to what extent are traditional roots valued by Mennonite youth? What norms and values do they adhere to? At the same time, where is their sense of freedom to explore and fly taking them? Since social relationships are of prime importance to today's youth, what is the nature of these relationships? Finally, to what extent are youth prepared to fit into institutions and the workplace, and become contributing members of society?

Learning to Fly in Relationships

Bibby and Posterski (1985) gathered the first comprehensive national survey of young people in Canada – 3,600 high school students between the ages of fifteen and nineteen. They followed up with a similar survey of 4,000 students across the country in 1992, to compare

TABLE 7.1
The Importance of Friends

'What I enjoy the most is ...'	%	'When something big goes wrong, I want to tell ———'	%	'When something great happens, I want to tell ———'	%
Friends	26	Friends	61	Friends	47
Sports	19	Family	22	Everyone	35
Sex	7	Mom	10	Family	15
Music	6	Dad	2	Mom	5
Partying	3	Other fam.	10	Dad	1
Reading	2	God	2	Other fam.	9
Family	1	Teachers/Couns.	1	Others	3
Other	36	Others	15		
Totals	100		100		100

Source: Bibby and Posterski 1992, p. 11

changes. They found that Canadian young people value relationships more than anything else. 'They want good interpersonal ties and they want to be loved' (Bibby and Posterski 1992, 9). They want individuals in their lives who care, and placed an increased emphasis on the individual, over the group, which is very postmodern.

The importance of friends is documented in table 7.1, which shows that respondents enjoy friends most, followed by sports – only 1 per cent listed family as very important. When something big goes wrong, they want to tell their friends (61 per cent) – family (22 per cent) is a poor second, divided mostly between Mom and other family members, with Dad hardly mentioned. When something great happens, they again want to tell their friends (47 per cent), or everyone (35 per cent), with the family (15 per cent) in third place (Bibby and Posterski 1992, 11). Bibby and Posterski (1992, 11) found that 'sadly, because some adults do not have particularly good relationships with teens, they help to fuel the widespread stereotype that young people are callous and detached ... Nothing could be farther from the truth. Such propaganda may be a salve for parents who are not connecting well with their teenagers. But it is out of touch with relational reality' (Bibby and Posterski 1992, 11).

What Teens and Adults Want

When it comes to what teens want out of life, about 85 per cent want

TABLE 7.2
Valued Goals of Teenagers and Adults

| | Percent saying 'very important' | | | |
| | Youth (Canadian) | | Adults (Canadian) | |
Valued goals	1984	1992	1985	1990
Freedom	84	86	89	85
Friendship	91	84	83	77
Being loved	87	80	83	81
Having choices	–	79	–	–
Success in what you do	78	76	66	64
Being respected	–	75	–	–
A comfortable life	75	70	66	63
Concern for others	–	62	–	63
Family life	65	60	84	83
Being a Canadian	50	45	68	61
Recognition	42	28	34	29
Cultural-group heritage	–	24	23	24
Being popular	21	22	9	–
Religious-group involvement	–	11	–	20

Source: Bibby and Posterski 1992, p. 15

freedom and friendship, a finding that has not changed much since 1984. Adults want the same. The need to 'be loved' is not far behind (see table 7.2). Youth and adults want the same. Success in what you do, being respected, and having a comfortable life followed, which youth accorded somewhat more importance than did adults.

Concern for others was also very important to two out of three youth and adults, whereas four in ten did not consider it important. But adults valued family life (84 and 86 per cent) as much as freedom, friendship, and being loved, which fewer youth valued. Religious-group involvement was important for only one in five adults, and for only 10 per cent of the youth. Clearly, importance of family life is declining among youth, and religious involvement is valued by very few. In 1992 just 18 per cent of Canada's fifteen- to nineteen-year-olds indicate that they are attending religious services on a weekly basis, down from 23 per cent in 1984 (Bibby and Posterski 1992, 50). Only 23 per cent regard themselves as committed Christians, and 3 per cent as committed to other religions, down from 39 per cent in 1984. Nevertheless, despite declining religious involvement, 79 per cent of the youth and 90 per cent of the adults still identified with a religious group, and most still wish to get married and buried in the church.

'Who' seems to be more important than 'where,' people are more important than programs, organizational structures must be warm, and the touch of a person is more powerful than an idea (Bibby and Posterski 1992, 254–7). Youth leaders are often frustrated, because relationships and building trust takes time, so that altering the course of history cannot be done in a weekend. Relationships are ends in themselves, and influence is limited to a few.

The Postmodern Sexual Revolution

With the development of the birth-control pill in the 1960s, fear of pregnancy declined, and general revolution in thinking about sex relations, including premarital sex, occurred. 'By 1975, 90 per cent of Canadians between the ages of 18 and 34 said they approved of premarital sex, in sharp contrast to only 65 per cent of people 35 to 54 and just 43 per cent of those 55 and older' (Bibby and Posterski 1992, 40). Estimates are that, by the year 2000, most Canadians will approve of premarital sex, with a minor core of 10 per cent continuing to be opposed.

In 1984, 80 per cent of youth and 77 per cent of adults in Canada approved of premarital sex if they were in love, which increased to 87 per cent of the youth and 80 per cent of adults in 1990. When they only 'liked each other,' 64 per cent of all Canadians approved in 1990, and 55 per cent of teenagers reported that they were sexually active. Approval of premarital sex was highest in Quebec. Seventy-seven per cent of the males, and 51 per cent of females approved when they liked each other, and males (62 per cent) were more active sexually than females (49 per cent). While males and females approved of premarital sex equally (88 and 86 per cent) when in love, females were more reluctant when the commitment of love was not present. While, in 1981, 350,000 Canadian couples had common-law relationships, by 1991 that figure had soared, to 1 million. Whereas cohabitation was frowned upon earlier, by the 1990s 88 per cent of youth in Canada thought it all right for a couple not married to live together (Bibby and Posterski 1992, 35). It will be interesting to see to what extent the sexual revolution has also influenced Mennonite youth.

Emerging Mennonite Youth

The norms of Mennonite persons born more than fifty years ago are much stronger in terms of in-group identity, moral behaviour, devotionalism, separation of Church and State, and religious beliefs than those of baby-boomers and their offspring born since 1945, as seen in table 7.3 (Kauffman and Driedger 1991).[1] On the other hand, boomers and 'Muppies' score higher on social relationships related to political action and concern for racial justice. They want a more significant role for women in Church leadership, and a more equal partnership in marriage. They are much more involved in memberships and use the media more. Values have changed, from an emphasis on in-group, normative relationships to greater concern with interactive social relationships, including justice, politics, and communication in a larger circle beyond the in-group. Whereas pre-boomers were concerned with tightening the flaps in their 'sacred canopy,' boomers and their teens call for more fresh air (Berger 1967). It is clearly a change from sectarianism to responsibility; from non-resistance to concerns for justice; from community solidarity to social networks. Note that the pendulum has already swung towards these teen values, because their parents, in the 30–49 age bracket, are much more like their teenagers than their grandparents, over 50 years of age (see table 7.3).

Focusing specifically on teenagers, table 7.3 indicates, in the top set of 'Older persons' values,' that except for moral behaviour, where one-third scored high, only one in five or less scored high on the dozen scales listed. Ethnic identity (language use, endogamy, in-group friends, use of Mennonite schools, organizations) and moral attitudes and behaviour scales (drinking, smoking, dancing, use of drugs) measure traditional normative values where about half the older adults scored high (Driedger 1995). On the other hand, at the bottom of the table we see that, under 'Younger persons' values,' almost half of Mennonite teenagers score high on political action (congregational discussion of issues, supporting candidates from the pulpit, encouraging action), and two to four out of ten score high on use of mass media, favour greater opportunities for women in leadership, and are more open to other races and non-Mennonite memberships. More adults over fifty support normative values, while those under fifty support more openness to the global village.

Not many studies have dealt with students in Mennonite high schools, but there are a few (Hess 1977; Kraybill 1977a, 1977b, 1978;

TABLE 7.3
Faith and Life Variables, Ranked by Correlation with Age, 1989

Variables/Scales	Age of the respondents					Pearson's *r*
	13–19	20–9	30–49	50–69	70+	
	(Percent scoring 'high')					
Older persons' values						
In-group identity	16	11	16	33	43	.31
Moral behaviour	35	15	17	41	53	.31
Church participation	11	22	36	29	17	.31
Devotionalism	7	12	16	27	31	.29
Moral attitudes	20	17	21	38	54	.28
Evangelism	8	9	16	24	27	.26
Separation of Church and State	17	19	21	32	51	.23
Serving others	6	19	29	37	37	.22
Stewardship	14	38	38	29	20	.18
Communalism	17	15	18	27	32	.16
Anabaptism	16	19	20	28	28	.16
Fundamentalism	11	16	20	30	36	.12
Common values						
General orthodoxy	57	72	71	80	82	.09
Separatism	11	16	17	18	18	.07
MCC support	13	19	22	19	25	.06
Bible knowledge	17	32	38	41	32	.03
Secularism	38	22	15	18	31	.03
Individualism	28	17	15	14	25	.02
Political participation	4	24	27	21	13	.01
Peacemaking	16	24	20	19	14	.01
Materialism	36	22	14	15	24	.01
Welfare attitudes	24	21	18	17	14	−.03
Ecumenism	29	31	26	28	29	−.04
Younger persons' values						
Greater roles for women	26	33	36	29	17	−.08
Political action	48	48	46	33	31	−.18
Use of mass media	22	14	19	9	2	−.18
Memberships	23	16	22	12	8	−.19
Women in leadership	34	44	42	29	11	−.23
Race relations	42	47	37	20	19	−.36
TOTALS Number	140	403	1,195	947	328	
Percentage	5	13	40	31	11	

Source: Kauffman and Driedger 1991, p. 268

Schludermann and Schludermann 1990). Shirin and Eduard Schludermann (1994) did a study of Mennonite high school students (Westgate and Mennonite Brethren Collegiate in Winnipeg) to compare values with Bibby and Posterski's (1985) Canadian national research. Using the half-dozen of the Bibby and Posterski's questions listed in table 7.2, the Schludermanns found that Mennonite students also scored highest on friendship (81 per cent) values, similar to Canadian youth in 1992 and adults in 1983. Mennonites (78 per cent) also valued being loved, as highly as Canadian youth (80 per cent). But that is where similarities ended. Only 58 per cent of Mennonite students in 1988 thought freedom was very important, which Canadian youth (86 per cent) ranked first. Surprisingly, family life was valued by fewer Mennonites (49 per cent) versus 60 per cent of Canadian youth and 83 per cent of adults. Only one in four Mennonites (24 per cent) thought a comfortable life was very important, nor was success (22 per cent) valued as much as Canadians did (70 and 63 per cent).

The Schludermanns (1994) also compared Mennonite students in Mennonite high schools with Catholic students in Catholic schools, and found that Catholic students in Winnipeg rated the six items discussed, roughly the same as Mennonites did in 1988. This suggests that students in denominational parochial schools seem to have quite different values from Canadian youth and adults in general. So it is important that we examine youth committed to the Church, to see their values might be quite different with respect to the values of Canadian youth and adults in general.

Roots and Values

If the values of Muppie youth have changed significantly, can we identify these and get some sense of where they are headed?

Biblical and Moral Roots

Using a sample of 3,795 churched youth aged thirteen to sixteen, drawn from thirteen evangelical denominations (including General Conference [GC] and Mennonite Church [MC] in North America), we see in table 7.4 that churched youth do have standards.[2] Eight out of ten respect the law, and two-thirds or more see the Bible as relevant and practical for daily guidance. The differences between MC and GC youth are minimal. Nor do Mennonite youth vary significantly from

TABLE 7.4
North American Norms and Values of Teens, 1994

	Percentage agreeing		
Teen norms and values	Total sample (N = 3,795)	GC (N = 307)	MC (N = 326)
Biblical and moral norms			
It is wrong to break the law when it hurts someone	80	78	83
Only the Bible provides a clear description of moral truth	72	58	73
The Bible is relevant for today's problems	68	68	73
The Bible provides practical standards for living	67	64	71
Moral standards today are not as high as they used to be	59	66	69
God sets limits; conflict with his laws has negative consequences	57	53	59
Freedom and relativism			
Every religion offers a different explanation of the meaning of life	59	61	59
Freedom means doing anything you want as long as it is legal	54	48	40
Truth means different things to different people; can't be sure	48	57	51
Nothing can be certain except experience in life	39	35	34
Lying is sometimes necessary	38	40	37
Intelligent way is to make the best choice based on feelings at the time	33	27	25
There is no 'absolute truth'; truth can be contradictory	29	35	27
Everything in life is negotiable	23	25	20
Whatever feels right is ok if it harms no one	22	24	17
Something is morally or ethically right if it works	16	14	11

Source: Churched youth survey by John McDowell Ministry, directed by Barna Research Group, Glendale, CA, 1993

other assemblies, Church of God, Nazarene, Foursquare, Free Methodist, Friends, Pentecostal, Salvation Army, Southern Baptist, and Wesleyan youth.

A majority agree that moral standards are not as high as they used to
be, and that God sets limits. While biblical standards are important to
them, and they view moral standards as being in decline, how do they
see freedom and relative forms of action? This is where it is difficult to
get a majority to agree. Over half agree that different religions offer a
variety of explanations for life, and that freedom is more than what is
legal. A minority admit that, on occasion, lying may be necessary, that
truth is often contradictory, and that negotiations in life are necessary,
depending on the circumstances.

More Mennonite adults scored high on normative biblical and moral
values (see table 7.4), while churched youth placed more emphasis on
social relationships. In our Canadian youth sample, we find that primary social relations seem to rank higher than most secondary relationships.

Primary social relationships are important to a large majority of
teens. Having one marriage partner is at the top of the list, and having
close personal relationships follows. A close relationship with God
seems to be part of this desirable package as well. Certainly adults
would have no problem with these high-minded desires, which also
include having a family, personal integrity, and a fulfilled sex life in
marriage.

Primary relations were more important than secondary relations.
Two out of three wanted to influence other people's lives, to be active
in the Church, and to make a difference in the world. Mennonite teenagers tend to follow others, except that they are less interested in being
active in the Church, making a difference in the world, having a high-
paying job and achieving fame, consistent with the Schludermanns'
(1994) findings.

Available Mentors and Brokers

Since youth seem to place less value on normative living and value
human relationships more, a key question is: What is the potential for
offering values in the form of mentors and friendship models? Three
out of four teens know adults who are valued as mentors. Mennonite
youth are even more fortunate.

Two out of three have a sufficiently high concept of themselves that they believe their contribution matters. They also think one person can make a difference, which suggests they have seen such mentors, and that their own worth has been sufficiently reinforced through social relationships. Indeed, they have such heroes and do model their lives after such persons. These experiences have been significantly reward-ing, and as a result they agree everyone needs such a hero. Role models are an important yardstick for forming social relationships, which teens value highly.

While over half think there is more to life than enjoyment, and that life is worth living, they admit that life is complex. Only one in three can agree that the future will be better than today. Youth in the post-modern 1990s are more sober about their options.

Self-Concept and Personal Identity

Strongly held values and supportive social relationships should lead to a positive self-concept and a positive identity. We ranked teen self-assessment of their strengths and weaknesses, and found the first dozen were positive and the last dozen negative. Most ranked high hopes, reliability, respect from others, and being an achiever among the top four strengths that teens aspired to. This finding did not vary by religious group. Almost as many thought of themselves as being reli-gious, which put their spiritual commitment in the top-five ranking.

The bottom dozen included mostly negative features, which they agreed applied to them. Half thought they were too busy, stressed out, and always tired. Four in ten admitted to being lazy. A third were lonely, disappointed, and sceptical, and mistrusted people. And one in five reported being angry with life, resentful, unmotivated, and lack-ing in purpose. In these regards, Mennonite youth were not signifi-cantly different from other evangelical youth. Considerable evidence supports a high level of realism across the range of positive and nega-tive evaluations.

The Wings of Social Relationships

In the first part of this chapter, we learned that, while adults favour normative behaviour more than do youth, youth value social relation-ships more than do adults. In the second part, we explored the extent and types of normative values youth do adhere to. We found that churched youth do have biblical and moral standards, they highly value primary relationships, they admire and follow adult mentors, and they have many positive strengths that suggest self-esteem and personal identity. This web of normative emphasis does suggest that today's youth have values to guide them. In the third part of this chapter, we explore more deeply the quality of the social relationships that youth emphasize and value more highly than do adults.

Family Relationships

The family always has been the cradle of human development, but sexual experimentation, divorce, and family abuse have put the family under great stress. Do modern youth want to raise their own families, do they value family support and relationships?

It is clear that most youth today think that God intended marriage to last a lifetime, and they do not expect their marriages to end in divorce (see table 7.5). Despite the openness to sexual experimentation found in Canada generally, three out of four want to be virgins when they marry, and those who no longer are virgins would like to be. As many feel that, overall, their family experience has been positive. About half want a marriage like their parents'. They are not unaware of family problems, and almost half seem to want to work to resolve any difficulties that arise. These data suggest that today's youth are not yet willing to give up on the family, and are planning to have families of their own. More Mennonite youth than the others felt their family experience was positive, and wanted their marriage to be like their parents'. They are obviously more conservative than Canadians in general.

Roughly two-thirds of evangelical churched youth, report that their parents seldom or never fight. Youth feel secure and loved, and say their parents usually trust them. This is also true for Mennonite teenagers.

Roughly half of today's youth report that their parents are seldom too strict, frequently set good examples for them, and usually do not expect more of them than is fair. This suggests that, for over half, standards and expectations of both parents and youth have been internalized and agreed upon. The source of these agreements seems to be love; half the youth feel their parents are really interested in them, and also trust them, because they allow their teenagers to do the things they want to do. The desires and values of both seem to mesh, driven by love and trust.

Almost half also agree that their parents seldom yell at them, and frequently spend time with them. One in four parents admit that they

TABLE 7.5
Attitudes towards a Strong Stable Marriage and Family, 1994

Family values	Percentage		
	Total sample (N = 3,795)	GC (N = 307)	MC (N = 326)
God intended for marriage to last a lifetime	90	89	93
Disagree we should expect that marriage will end in divorce	86	89	91
If I wasn't a virgin and could change the past I'd wait to have sex until after marriage	76	72	83
I would like to be a virgin at marriage	73	74	82
Overall I feel my family experience has been positive	72	81	84
I want a marriage like my parents	48	58	61
If the traditional family falls apart, society will collapse	47	39	49
Disagree parents out of love who have children shouldn't divorce	46	47	36
Disagree it is very hard to have a successful marriage today	44	50	49
Marriage problems have been exaggerated; most are healthy marriages	34	31	29

are frequently wrong or mistaken, which adds to give-and-take in communication. Alas, the other half of the parents and youth are not doing as well. This again suggests that, while many relationships are positive, many are not. In all of these parent–youth issues, there were no differences between Mennonites and other Church youth.

Demonstrations of Affection

We assume that love and affection begin in the family between parents and their children. As shown in table 7.6, we expect that this begins with fairness, respect, and interest in each other. Let us look deeper to see whether such positive relations also translate into love and affec-

TABLE 7.6
Teen–Parent Demonstrations of Love and Affection, 1994

	My father				My mother			
	Total (N = 3,795)	GC (N = 307)	MC (N = 326)		Total (N = 3,795)	GC (N = 307)	MC (N = 326)
We are very/fairly close	74	79	79		88	86	91
Never wonder whether he/she loves me	57	57	57		59	60	67
Feel proud of him/her	56	57	53		58	44	48
Shows his/her love for me	51	50	53		68	62	66
Show my love for him/her	41	31	32		52	37	36
Spends 30+ minutes with me weekly on things that matter	34	36	37		53	52	51
Seek advice from him/her	26	20	26		40	30	29
Do something special together	19	13	16		30	22	17
Talk about personal concerns	12	10	9		39	31	33

tion for each other, and how much this is demonstrated. Does this vary by type of parent, mother or father?

Three out of four are close to their fathers, as is shown in table 7.6. Nine out of ten feel close to mother. Over half never wonder about whether they are loved, and feel proud of their parents. About half say their father shows his love, while two out of three say Mother does so. Half also claim they show their love for their mother and spend at least a special half-hour or more with her each week; fewer do so with their father.

We see that closeness, being loved, pride, showing love, spending time, seeking advice, acting and talking together are more commonly expressed about mothers than about fathers. The expectation that mother has closer relations with her children than father is clearly borne out in the total sample.

Mennonite youth do not show love for mother and father as much as do other non-Mennonite youth. Fewer Mennonite teenagers also feel proud of their mother, and they do not seek her advice as much, nor do they do something special with her as much as do other youth. This clearly shows that Mennonite teenagers do not give their mothers the same status they accord their fathers, which is not the case for other youth. Two out of three MC teenagers never doubt the love of both parents, a finding that is significantly higher than for GCs and others. These Mennonite data are distinctly different from those for other church youth, as well as for general Canadian findings.

Gender and Sex Relations

Ours is a much more permissive society than those in the past, revolutionized by the media and the car. The electronic revolution has opened up communication via computer, fax, e-mail, and the Internet, offering the potential for previously unimagined networks of interpersonal relations. The car has expanded physical mobility, and the potential for multivariate spatial relationships.

Societal and Mennonite differences are especially evident in the sexual revolution. Three out of four youth (see table 7.7) want to be virgins when they get married, but modern society provides more opportunities for members of the opposite sex to be alone together. Do their morals and actions match? Most youth find holding hands acceptable, and two out of three approve of kissing and embracing when in love. Their reported actions match their ideals fairly closely.

TABLE 7.7
Attitudes and Behaviour of Teenagers with the Opposite Sex, 1994

Which of the following are acceptable or have you done with the opposite sex?	Acceptable in love			Have done		
	Total sample (N = 3,795)	GC (N = 307)	MC (N = 326)	Total sample (N = 3,795)	GC (N = 307)	MC (N = 326)
	Percentages					
Held hands	85	90	88	89	82	89
Embrace and some kissing	68	73	69	73	64	67
Heavy 'French' kissing	33	36	31	53	42	45
Fondling of breasts	10	10	9	34	31	31
Fondling of genitals	9	9	8	26	23	21
Sexual intercourse	7	6	5	16	8	8

Heavy 'French' kissing is where a discrepancy between ideals and reported actions begin to show (see table 7.7). One-third do not approve of such behaviour when in love, but half have engaged in it. Only one in ten approve of fondling of breasts, but a third have engaged in it. One-quarter of evangelical churched youth have engaged in fondling of genitals, while few approve of the practice, even for those who are in love. Almost no teenagers approve of sexual intercourse when in love. Half as many Mennonite as non-Mennonite youth have engaged in intercourse, that is, under 10 per cent. These data clearly show that while premarital sex is still largely taboo, non-Mennonite youth are finding it more difficult to abide by these ideals.

In many ways these findings sound incredible, compared with the findings for Canadian youth in the study by Bibby and Posterski (1992). Questions about the appropriateness of holding hands, when 80 to 90 per cent of Canadians approve of premarital sex, seems to hark back to Puritan days. Are these churched youth so much a part of premodern culture that they have not yet joined the postmodern age? Or are religious subcultures this effective in raising youth in a counter-culture of different values? Although 55 per cent of Canadian teenagers reported that they were sexually active before marriage, only 8 to 16 per cent of churched youth reported such an experience or experiences. Religious commitments are certainly paramount for these youth, and prevent them from engaging in sexual activity as freely as Canadian youth.

Institutions Connecting Roots and Wings

In the 1960s there was a general resurgence of individualism and a wholesale rejection by many of social institutions that have since been greatly modified. Teachers in schools had to revamp their methods of teaching; with the young Kennedys in power, the media began to put image-making centre-stage in politics, a legacy the Clintons have inherited. The 1950's surge in church memberships began to decline. Since then, we have begun to question more our religious, political, economic, and educational institutions.

Church Institutions

If relationships are most important to today's youth, can they find social opportunities in the churches? Almost all evangelical youth made a personal commitment to Jesus Christ that is still important to

TABLE 7.8
Religious Beliefs and Activity of Teens, 1994

	Percentage		
Religious beliefs and behaviour	Total sample (N = 3,795)	GC (N = 307)	MC (N = 326)
Made a personal commitment to Jesus Christ that is still important	86	78	82
God is the all-powerful, all-knowing creator who rules world today	85	84	85
Attend a church youth group weekly	84	83	82
Attend church services every week	82	78	86
Attend a Sunday school class weekly	78	83	87
I will go to heaven because I have accepted Christ as Saviour	75	74	80
Pray to God daily	65	67	67
My Christian faith is very important in my life today	64	53	56
Read the Bible every week or more	48	45	55
Attend a Bible study group weekly	43	37	37
Lead a small group	17	8	8

them; they believe God the creator is still in control (see table 7.8). Eight or nine out of ten are members of a youth group in the church. They also attend church services, as well as Sunday school, weekly. The church is offering these teenagers networks of weekly activity, and they are supported by their church-going parents.

The salience of their beliefs is somewhat diminished, which suggests that some of their weekly church activity is a family routine into which they are locked. Three-quarters believe they will go to heaven because they accept Christ. Two-thirds claim their faith is important for daily life, and as many pray to God daily. Less than half read their Bible and attend a Bible study group every week. Seventeen per cent lead a small group – half as many Mennonites do. Generally, Mennonite youth follow the larger evangelical pattern, except that somewhat fewer consider their faith important, more attend Sunday school, and fewer attend Bible study and lead groups. The social relationships centred around the church are surprisingly strong, although we need to remind ourselves that these are youth committed to the church, a subculture that differs greatly from Canadian youth in general.

The Political Arena

In the strident 1960s we were riding the demographic baby-boom bulge, when there were always more mouths to feed, more students to teach, more jobs to be filled to sustain the escalating economic spiral. How things have changed! The economy is less buoyant; birth rates and population are in decline; businesses, schools, and professions are facing cutbacks; and jobs are hard to find. In the interim, young people have become compliant and conservative, as compared with their 1960s counterparts. Youth are more serious and are uncertain of their chances to compete in our every-changing world. Postmodern youth are more aware of problems that are not likely to soon disappear.

These conservative attitudes are also apparent in the political arena. We usually think of youth as being more liberal while adults become more conservative. Our 1989 North American data show that three out of four adult Mennonites voted for conservative Republicans in the United States, and over half of the teenagers who could vote did so as well (Kauffman and Driedger).[3] True, twice as many teens voted for liberal Republicans and Democrats, which does follow expectations, but the numbers are surprisingly small – one or two in ten. What's noteworthy is that teens do not differ significantly from their parents in this area.

Twice as many in the 1970s voted for the most conservative Social Credit Party in Canada, but more youth than the elderly voted Progressive Conservative. The one-third in the 1970s who voted Liberal are a phenomenon related to immigration history, as Liberal governments often helped Mennonites emigrate to Canada. Twice as many (one-quarter) of teens voted for the New Democratic Party, which is the most socialist, left of centre. Youth did vote more for liberal parties in both countries, but well over half to three-quarters voted conservative. This seems to correlate with an image of today's youth as focused on equality between the sexes and among the races. In sum, today's youth are much more conservative than were their 1960s counterparts, and are more conservative than their boomer parents on some issues.

Peace and the Military

To what extent have distinctive peace tenets been passed on, and how does this vary by age? Driedger and Kraybill (1994) found that a major shift has occurred, from non-resistance to active peacemaking over the fifty years since the Second World War. Before the war, nine out of ten Mennonites were on the farm, but since then half have moved to cities, are more educated and more mobile, all indicators of increased modernization. Have these modern forces eroded the distinctive search for peace?

In table 7.14 we see that the traditional alternative-service position to war is still the first choice of two-thirds of those over thirty, but fewer than half of the teenagers would choose that alternative. There is a significant dip among youth in their teens on alternatives to the military. Less than 10 per cent would choose to refuse to register or to be inducted, which shows that more radical alternatives of the past may no longer work. Uncertainty is up, however, with one-quarter of teens not sure what their choice might be. This is a very substantial group, which suggests either that peace education is not happening, or what is being done is not working. Choices for direct military service are inching up as age decreases. Almost half of Mennonite teenagers would choose some form of military alternative, or are not sure of their position, compared with one-quarter to one-third who are over thirty. Again there is evidence that teenagers, especially, are not hearing the peace message. The most distinctive Mennonite peace message appears to be in decline, a phenomenon we examine more closely in chapter 10.

Conclusions

We began by saying that both roots, which provide security, and wings, which allow for the exploration of the larger world, are necessary for youth to thrive. Bibby and Posterski (1985) found that national Canadian youth enjoy their friends most, and relegate a much smaller place to the family, which is becoming much busier and more fragile. Most youth and adults highly valued freedom, friendship, and being loved. Family life and concern for others were in decline, and involvement in religion was minimal. The 1960s brought about the sexual revolution, so that by the 1990s almost all Canadian youth and adults approved of premarital sex, part of the quest for freedom, friendship, and love.

Comparing Mennonite adults and youth, we found that, while older Mennonites scored higher than youth on doctrinal and moral norms, youth valued political involvement, communication, and social relations more. They wanted more openness, communication, and relationships.

In the rural past, traditionally the emphasis was on roots; however, in the postmodern world, youth must change with the times, which requires strong wings to negotiate new challenges. We found that older adults had developed their roots (norms, standards) well, while youth were clearly more concerned with social relationships.

We also found that youth who are connected to the church are by no means without roots. Almost all have made religious commitments, and attend activities regularly. Many also foster a meaningful devotional life. They clearly have biblical and moral values, and meaningful social relationships, including with adult mentors, and have developed positive self-concepts and identities. Family life continues to provide a sense of rootedness for youth as well. A majority feel secure and loved at home, where their parents trust them. Many want marriages like their parents'. However, while they aspire to having families of their own and want these relationships to succeed, they are realistic about some of the difficulties that lie ahead.

Most seem to have the roots of biblical norms and family values, which ground youth for life in the modern world. Their ideals remain high. They desire a clear purpose for life, want to make a difference in the world, expect to have a traditional family, hope for a comfortable lifestyle. Achieving fame, having a high-paying job, and being active in the church are significantly less important. In their relationships with the opposite sex, their standards are high and their behaviour does match their ideals.

A goodly number are quite realistic about the future and admit they are often too confused, too busy, stressed out, and tired. About half disagree that the main purpose in life is enjoyment and fulfilment, wonder whether life is worth living, feel life is too complex, and feel alone in times of trouble or crisis. Only a third feel the future will be better than the present. They are less optimistic about the present. They have a sense that life will not be easy in the postmodern world.

Our research has isolated a number of issues that clearly require research. Biblical and devotional norms are in decline among youth, part of a firm system of roots. While adults stress norms more, youth focus more on relationships. How can the relational roots of youth be strengthened? Family relationships are robust, but family structures are changing. Can the family remain a touchstone for the sense of being loved and feeling secure? Mennonite youth seem to have more difficulty relating deeply to their parents than do others. Why do Mennonite youth show less affection? The biological and social pressures of the sex drive will become increasingly more difficult to manage. What can be done to help youth live up to their ideals? Youth seem to be well locked-into the Church and its activities. How can that level of interest and involvement be maintained or increased for those who are unconnected? Youth are increasingly ambivalent about peace and Anabaptist beliefs. How can this theology be more effectively communicated? How come youth are so conservative politically, when in the 1960s they were so radical and wanted change everywhere?

8

Blending Educational Monastery and Marketplace

John Yoder (1995, 146) suggests that Mennonite schools often began as Bible schools, designed on the buffered monastery model and fostering an alternative lifestyle and set of values to the larger society. In the educational monastery, Mennonite faith and life can be developed and expressed within a segregated enclavic social, intellectual, and religious community. However, no institutions exist in total isolation; to be viable they must develop relationships with the larger marketplace. Yoder (1955, 147) concludes that, with time, schools tend to evolve towards a 'progressive opening of doors in the monastic walls that facilitate ease of movement in and out.' Thus, the interface between monastery and marketplace expands.

Paul Toews (1995) has collected essays that trace the birth, origins, community, and changes that have occurred at Fresno College as it has moved from monastery to marketplace. In this chapter we wish to present the Fresno model and select several key elements of the school community that change. Types of students who enroll, and their degree of commitment to the 'collegium' or community of peers, are examined, in order to do a comparison of sixteen Mennonite colleges and seminaries in North America. To manage a study of many schools comparatively, it is not possible to consider all the variables the Fresno scholars discussed. But we shall make a selection of key variables to see whether there are important differences.

Yoder's Monastery–Marketplace Model

Paul Toews (1995) has edited a volume containing eight articles written by faculty of Fresno Pacific College to celebrate fifty years of Mennonite higher education in California. These essays trace the vision, origins, community development, prophetic mission, and revisions as they have expanded from monastery-like parochial Bible school education, to graduate education in the marketplace, as John Yoder (1995, 133) aptly terms it.

Yoder (1995, 133) traces three major strands, clearly identifiable in the weaving of the Fresno experiment. The first began as the Pacific Bible Institute, where a small group of Mennonite Brethren faculty and students focused on Bible training as the means to a more effective service to the Church for ministers, youth workers, Christian educators, and missionaries. The second 'focus shifted to a more or less classical undergraduate curriculum within the context of a Christian community committed to an Anabaptist view of the church and the world as a paradigm through which to interpret the liberal arts' (Toews 1995, 134). And the third began in the 1960s, as the focus shifted to serve society, by development of education on a graduate level, involving pre-service, in-service, and professional-development programs in elementary and high schools of Fresno county. This 'pragmatic vision was also driven by the need of the college to reach a higher level of financial stability. The revenue from the professional programs provided genuine relief for the hard-pressed college budget, while at the same time trying to meet the needs of an increasingly dysfunctional society' (Yoder 1995, 135).

Yoder continues:

> Christian monasteries were established in medieval Europe as an expression of a particular set of ideas about religious order and service. They were places of learning as well as reflection, contemplation and retreat ... The monastery models an alternative lifestyle and set of values to the larger society and culture ...; faith is both developed and expressed in the context of community ... a kind of social, intellectual and religious center. (Yoder 1995, 146)

The Bible schools that Mennonites and others often created as pioneers with limited resources began as a type of monastery, but most have either closed their doors, as needs changed, or evolved into liberal-arts colleges.

To remain viable, and in touch with the needs of their changing and supporting Mennonite community, Mennonite schools shifted and/or expanded to increasingly include training in the ideas, relationships, and interchange with the larger community outside. 'Like the monastery, the Christian liberal arts college represents a particular expression of religious order and community ... The word "college" itself derives from the Latin "collegium" – a community of peers committed to a common enterprise and to each other' (Yoder 1995, 147). Thus, the college is a place to broker in-group identity and community, as well as to minister to the ideas and needs of the larger community, where the college makes concrete the ideas the monastery values.

The three stages suggested by Yoder in the Fresno case are likewise echoed in Thomas Askew's (1987, 137–52) discussion of evangelical colleges in North America. He identifies three phases of development: the insular, Church-focused institution; the corporate definition of consolidation and credentialing; and the professionalization of networks. James Juhnke (1992) likewise traces three generations of leadership that tend to parallel the Yoder and Askew stages: the founding generation preoccupied with relationships to a conservative, rural constituency; a middle generation that accomplished accreditation to keep the progressive wings interested and coming; and a more recent postwar generation who are increasingly entering the arenas of professionalization and bureaucratization. Robert Enns (1995, 67) calls this 'the secularization process' and it is increasingly entering Mennonite communities.

Yoder (1995, 147) sees 'the monastic metaphor as a way of characterizing the Fresno College story and suggests a series of outwardly expanding circles developed as the college moved from its more insular Bible institute beginnings, to the liberal arts focus and then still further to the present day graduate level professional programs.' The metaphor suggests a progressive opening of doors that ease movement beyond the monastic walls. Indeed, Yoder (1995, 148) sees the dialectic between ideology and program, between the in-group and out-group, as 'salting and lighting' in both the marketplace and the monastery. In this chapter we explore, using only a few indicators, to what extent this monastery–marketplace model is operating in the other fifteen Mennonite colleges and seminaries in North America.

Examining Components of Community

Throughout Paul Toews's (1995) edited volume, the contributors hark back to basic aims of Fresno Pacific College, and being a Christian Anabaptist–Mennonite community is always among them. Sociologist Robert Enns (1995, 66–88) focuses on the identity dilemmas faced at Fresno in maintaining 'community,' as the school has changed over fifty years. His first point is that numerical growth has escalated, which has brought about a diversification of faculty, students, and programs, and this has resulted in increasingly diverse needs. From a student population of 257 and faculty of 17 in 1966, before the college's programs increased in its second, liberal-arts stage, Fresno has grown to an enrolment of 642 undergraduates, 129 teacher-education students, 674 graduate students, and 11,883 part-time professional-development students, and 91 faculty. This large increase in students has greatly affected the nature of community life and institutional identity (Enns 1996, 75–7). 'The Mennonite Brethren presence in the student population decreased from approximately four out of five students to fewer than one in five.' Barely half of the faculty in 1993 were of Mennonite background, and only one-third of the faculty had attended a Mennonite college in their undergraduate studies.

Enns (1995, 83–6) reports that the 1992 accreditation 'team viewed Fresno Pacific College's most pressing problems as all stemming from a single unresolved issue: the need to articulate a mission for the college which can unify its presently disparate components and serve as a meaningful guide for the coming decade.' The team thought the college could not afford the luxury of drifting through the next years without refining its mission. We shall explore two of the demographic indicators Enns explored for Fresno Pacific: (1) growth of student populations, and (2) proportion of Mennonite students, comparing the sixteen Mennonite colleges and seminaries in North America. We shall see whether the demographics suggest that other schools are facing problems of 'community' identity, as Fresno is.

Demographic Openings to the Marketplace

We suggest that demographic changes in the size of Mennonite families are an important factor in Mennonite schools opening up to the marketplace. Let us examine these demographic trends to gain some comparative sense of how the seven Mennonite colleges in the United States, the three Mennonite seminaries, and the six Canadian colleges have responded. Geographical locations of these sixteen schools are shown in figure 8.1 (Driedger 1997).

U.S. College Enrolments

The seven U.S. Mennonite colleges (Eastern Mennonite, Bluffton,

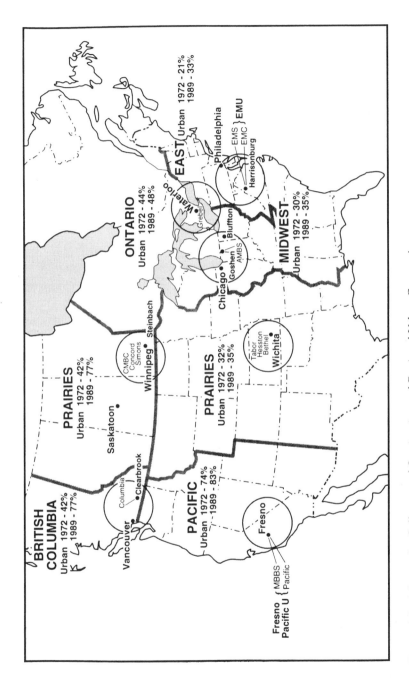

Figure 8.1　Mennonite Colleges and Seminaries and Regional Urban Comparisons

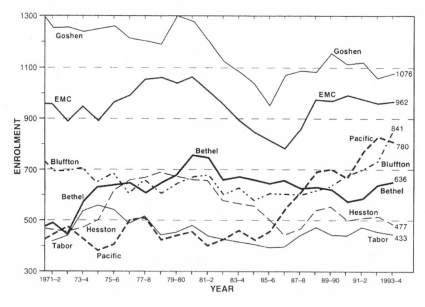

Figure 8.2   Mennonite U.S. College Enrolment Statistics, 1971–1994

Goshen, Bethel, Hesston, Tabor, and Fresno Pacific), all but Fresno Pacific located in small towns, have largely been regional schools, drawing support and students from their local constituencies. They were fairly independent operations, linked more or less to denominational networks of the three largest Mennonite denominations (Mennonite Church [MC], General Conference Mennonite [GC], and Mennonite Brethren [MB]. Since these seven colleges centre Mennonite constituencies in four general areas (East, Midwest, Prairies, Pacific) of the United States, similarities and differences in their opening up to the marketplace will be instructive. In figure 8.2, using total student (TS) figures, we see that the ranking order has remained the same since 1970, except that Pacific College has moved from sixth to fourth in size.[1] In 1970 Goshen College enrolled the largest number, with about three times as many students as Tabor, the smallest, and that ratio has remained much the same.

The enrolments of the two largest colleges, Goshen and Eastern Mennonite, each with 1,000 students or more, have fluctuated considerably. Enrolments in both schools began to rise in the mid-1960s, and this rise continued until 1980, when there was a sharp decline that lasted for a half-dozen years. After the mid-1980s this decline was arrested, and enrolments rose again, stabilizing at 1,000–1,100 students. The 1993/4 enrolments are very similar to the enrolments twenty years earlier. The enrolment patterns of these two largest Mennonite Church schools in the Midwest and East remarkably rise and fall together, which suggests that demographic factors were operating, and not regional or social factors.

Examination of the three Kansas colleges (Bethel, Hesston, and Tabor) shows that Hesston, the other U.S. Mennonite Church college, follows its sister Goshen and Eastern Mennonite (EMC) patterns quite closely. Hesston enrolments rise until 1979, a drop in the mid-1980s, and a slight rise and stabilization again at 1970 levels in the 1990s. Enrolments in the largest U.S. prairie college, Bethel, follow the rise and fall of the three MC colleges into the early 1980s, but the drop was not as severe in the mid-1980s. Unlike the three Mennonite Church (MC) colleges, the General Conference (GC) Bethel stabilized at an enrolment above 600 in 1993/4, considerably higher than in 1970. This slightly different pattern suggests that other factors such as leadership may have stemmed Bethel's decline sooner, which resulted in a gain of 150 students over twenty years (30 per cent).

The enrolment in the Mennonite Brethren (MB) Tabor College began to rise in the 1970s, attaining a record 558 students in 1974, but this rise was not sustained into the 1980s. Enrolment soon levelled off, to around 400 students, and stayed at that number, with few rises and falls, for the next twenty years. The 433-student enrolment in 1993 was very similar to the 412 students in 1971. Together, the three GC, MC, and MB colleges in Kansas began with an enrolment of 1,357 students in 1970–1 and ended in 1993 with a joint total of 1,546, a rise of roughly 200.

While these five 1971 college enrolments in the United States did not change much in twenty-five years, Pacific and Bluffton colleges have increased in size. Bluffton College, also located in the Midwest, began with 700 students in 1970, and climbed to 841 students in 1993, an increase of 140 students. The enrolment profile is different from that of any of the other colleges. In 1970 Bluffton was the third-largest in the United States, but when Goshen and EMC enrolments climbed, Bluffton dropped, and did not recover to 1970 levels for twenty years, until 1991. In the last two years, 1992–3, enrolments escalated by 140 students. The increase is largely due to opening up to non-Mennonite students, so that only about 10 per cent were Mennonites, a phenomenon

TABLE 8.1
Mennonite College and Seminary Enrolments
(Full-time Equivalent), 1970–1993

Schools	1970	1975	1980	1985	1990	1993
USA						
Pacific	381	408	623	708	891	1,068
Hesston	451	586	617	450	464	447
Bethel	486	627	736	592	553	617
Tabor	362	437	453	356	393	389
Goshen	1,215	1,167	1,203	893	1,031	966
Bluffton	711	676	626	554	612	800
EMC	927	936	1,036	789	921	920
Canada						
Columbia	189	266	199	159	181	240
Steinbach	56	73	79	74	76	70
CMBC	106	145	167	181	177	194
Concord	85	161	144	161	133	139
Simɔns					18	53
Grebel	138	151	342	420	399	358
Seminaries						
EMS	30	52	64	54	65	81
AMBS	59	110	134	140	117	85
MBBS	37	83	124	103	91	91

we will explore in more detail later. The Mennonite Brethren Pacific College in Fresno, California, represents the most dramatic rise, starting with 420 students in 1970, and almost doubling, to 780 students, in 1993. This rise began less than ten years ago, an enrolment profile very different from the others. The demographic rise in the early 1980s and the slump in the mid-1980s, seem not to have affected Pacific. Increased numbers of non-Mennonite students are also a major factor here; both Bluffton and Fresno have smaller Mennonite hinterlands to draw from.

Total student (TS) enrolments used in figure 8.2 are one way of comparing the annual demographic rise and fall of student enrolments. To deal with full-time (FT) and part-time (PT) enrolment figures, we present comparative full-time equivalent (FTE) statistics in table 8.1, which reflect a more complete count of actual courses taken by students.[2] The general enrolment profiles of the seven U.S. colleges, shown in figures 6.2 and table 6.1, are similar, so we will not go over the full-time equivalent (FTE) again. These full-time equivalent figures are reported in five-year intervals, so we can compare all sixteen Mennonite schools in one table.

Graduate Education in Seminaries

Fifty years ago, when Mennonite Biblical Seminary and Goshen Biblical Seminary began, these two seminaries, representing the two largest Mennonite conferences, had the continent largely to themselves. They were the only institutions of Mennonite graduate education. In those days they wrestled with problems of finding competent faculty with PhDs to teach, and persuading their constituencies to send students to institutions offering what was considered 'too much liberal book-learning,' which farmers didn't need.

A glance at a map of North America shows us that Associated Mennonite Biblical Seminary (AMBS) is in the centre of the continent, where its constituent Mennonite Church (MC) and General Conference (GC) congregations are located (figure 8.1). While Mennonite colleges are confined to recruiting from their local regions, is it still possible to think of Mennonite theological graduate training on a continental scale? After 1957, when AMBS left Chicago for Elkhart, Mennonite Biblical Seminary (MBS) and Goshen Biblical Seminary (GBS) joined to become the Associated Mennonite Biblical Seminary (AMBS), seemingly a formidable graduate institution that could compete for graduate students. In 1971, three seminaries – AMBS in Elkhart; Indiana, Eastern Mennonite Seminary (EMS), located in Harrisonburg, Virginia; and Mennonite Brethren Biblical Seminary (MBBS), located in Fresno, California – were already established, each having fifty students or more, By 1993, the average seminary enrolments for these three was 112–85 (TS) and 81–91 (FTE) students each. The profiles, however, vary profoundly.

Between 1970 and 1983, the GC–MC Associated Mennonite Biblical Seminary (AMBS) total student (TS) enrolment tripled, from 80 to a record 244 students, the largest increase of any Mennonite school in North America. Centrally located, the new campus, joining the MBS and GBS faculties and students, in Elkhart, recruited young faculty who were coming into their own as scholars and churchmen, which created an exhilarating momentum. They were riding the demographic baby-boom roller-coaster, as did Goshen, EMC, Bethel, and

Hesston, and also experienced the same decline after the early 1980s. Like Goshen and EMC, who were able to stop the enrolment drop by the mid-1980s, AMBS seemed to be stemming the drop for a few years in the later 1980s, but recently the downward plunge has continued, unlike in any other Mennonite school. This decline cannot be explained only by demographic factors. The well-known faculty have retired, replaced by new faculty; rural Indiana seems isolated when Mennonites are increasingly moving to cities; and EMS and MBBS are challenging on the east and west flanks. In the meantime, Eastern Mennonite Seminary (EMS) in the east, and Mennonite Brethren Biblical Seminary in the west, have also tripled their total student (TS) enrolments, from some 50 students in 1971 to 112 and 185, respectively, now in the AMBS range. The enrolments of these two seminaries did not escalate in the 1980s as that of AMBS did, but increased steadily, with modest increments and few major rises or dips. It appears that the MC EMS is drawing students to the east, and the MB MBBS drawing students to the west, away from AMBS, increasingly squeezing AMBS into a Middle America regional role. These trends are changing the roles of the three seminaries profoundly, and the downward adjustments are most difficult for AMBS.

It was Harold Bender and the Anabaptist Vision that drew MBS away from Chicago to Elkhart (near Goshen). AMBS had three Mennonite World Conference presidents and churchmen on its faculty (Harold Bender, Erland Waltner, and Ross Bender), and numerous well-published high-profile scholars, such as Harold Bender, John C. Wenger, Howard Charles, John Howard Yoder, William Klassen, C.J. Dyck, who helped draw students in the 1970s. In the 1980s, many of these retired or left, so that a complete change of faculty has occurred. For example, in 1983, 70 students from Goshen College (ten miles away) attended AMBS, while ten years later, in 1993, this figure had dropped to 25; students attending EMC dropped from 21 to 14 during the same period. Since then, the EMS and MBBS have located on their respective Eastern Mennonite University (EMU) and Fresno Pacific University (FPU) campuses, as they have boosted their Eastern Mennonite Seminary and Mennonite Brethren Biblical Seminary enrolments. AMBS has, however, retained a higher (74 per cent) Mennonite student enrolment than EMS (53 per cent) and MBBS (45 per cent). While AMBS was the continental Mennonite seminary in the 1960s, in the 1990s this has changed to a threeway race, where the seminaries are increasingly becoming regionalized, like the colleges.

Canadian Colleges

Canadian Mennonite colleges are much younger than the American ones. The first Mennonite Brethren Bible College (MBBC) was established in Winnipeg in 1944. Canadian Mennonite Bible College (CMBC) was established by the Conference of Mennonites in Canada (GC) three years later, in 1947, in the same city. The other four colleges – Conrad Grebel College (CGC), in Waterloo, Ontario, Columbia Bible College (CBC), in Clearbrook, British Columbia; and two more (Steinbach Bible College [SCB] and Menno Simons College [MSC]), also in Manitoba, were started later.

The earliest and largest two Canadian colleges in Winnipeg, representing the two largest Canadian GC and MB denominations, are still smaller than the American ones, and have similarities to the early beginnings of the U.S. schools. The total student (TS) enrolment profile of CMBC is very similar to that of Goshen and EMC, beginning with 120 students in 1971/2, reaching a maximum of 230 in the early 1980s after which enrolment dropped by about 20 per cent, with a recovery to well over 200 students by 1993. The difference is that, while the Goshen and EMC levels of enrolment in 1970 and 1993 are roughly the same, CMBC ended up with almost twice as many students twenty years later, a dramatic early rise, but a less dramatic drop later.

The profile of the MBBC, also in Winnipeg, is remarkably similar; in the 1970s, it drew students from across Canada, as did CMBC, as the Mennonite Brethren national school. However, in the early 1990s, MBBC experienced trends similar to those evident in MB colleges in the American West, where a population shift of Mennonite Brethren from the prairies to the Pacific Coast occurred; more MBs now live in British Columbia than on the prairies. Since then they have established Columbia Bible College in Clearbrook, B.C., and very recently declared their allegiances to their provincial school, rather than to the former national MBBC. The MBBC has since changed its name to Concord College, becoming a more regionalized Church prairie college. This has, however, resulted in fewer full-time students and a decline in Mennonite students.[3] Like the American colleges, Concord is increasingly becoming more regional.

Two Mennonite Bible schools run formerly by the Mennonite Brethren and General Conference Mennonites in British Columbia have now been amalgamated and been upgraded to a college – Columbia Bible

College (CBC) – where the two denominations run this Mennonite college jointly. Similar to Pacific College in Fresno, Columbia Bible College (CBC) has recently experienced rising enrolments as the college is increasingly more open to cooperation with other Mennonites, and has opened its doors to non-Mennonites. Similar to the American Pacific Coast Mennonites, three out of four B.C. Mennonites are urban, with the result that the competition in the marketplace is greater.

Mennonite Brethren and General Conference Mennonites in Ontario actually began this inter-Mennonite market cooperation in education by establishing Conrad Grebel College in Waterloo, a metropolitan centre such as Winnipeg. Conrad Grebel College was the first to locate on a university campus, a major opening to the marketplace. Its location is one of several indications of its openness; as well, Grebel faculty are teaching courses as part of the university curriculum; Grebel College is in charge of the music department of the campus; and it is one of several residential colleges open to non-Mennonite students. We have used students living in Conrad Grebel dormitories as the enrolment count for the college.

Menno Simons College (MSC) in Winnipeg is the latest new college, opening up to the marketplace, as did Conrad Grebel, on a university campus (the University of Winnipeg), where founding a Mennonite chair earlier had already laid some groundwork for Mennonite courses and classes. MSC is the third Mennonite College in Winnipeg, concentrating on conflict studies, not theology as the other two Winnipeg colleges do, and enrolments are still quite small.

Steinbach Bible College (SBC) is more monastery-like and traditional, located in a small town, as are the American colleges. SBC was established recently, and is the only college run by four more conservative groups (Evangelical Mennonite Church, Evangelical Mennonite Mission Church, Evangelical Mennonite Brethren, and the Sommerfelder Church). It is the only college not run by the three largest (MC, GC, MB) conferences. SBC enrolments began with 56 students in 1970, grew to 149 in 1983, and dropped to 83 in 1993. Enrolments have grown by 50 per cent since 1970. Roughly nine out of ten students are Mennonite, and about 70 per cent are full-time. CMBC, Concord, SBC, and Menno Simons colleges, all in Manitoba, are at present discussing the potential for greater cooperation, as a federation of colleges.

Factors that Support the Monastic Community

As Mennonites increasingly become more urban, as family sizes decline, as increased socio-economic status and mobility provide more open educational options, can Mennonite colleges continue to draw Mennonite students? Before 1980, larger Mennonite families helped feed the demographic baby boom, and rising enrolments. Since 1980, enrolments have dipped, and Mennonite schools have been scrambling to keep their expanded campuses filled with students. Many of these schools have turned increasingly to part-time and non-Mennonite students, a new opening to the marketplace. Let us illustrate by examining full-time and Mennonite student enrolment trends.

Full-time Student Enrolments

With Yoder, we expect that schools which are able to keep full-time students housed in campus dormitories on the periphery of small towns will be able to generate activities and social opportunities that enhance community solidarity. This ability reinforces the function of the educational monastery. The six U.S. Mennonite colleges located in small towns were able to maintain full-time student enrolments in the 90–5 per cent range in 1970, and this figure had only slightly declined by 1993. Pacific College in the larger metropolis of Fresno began with a similar full-time count in 1970, but declined to under 50 per cent full-time by 1985. If full-time student enrolment is a good indicator of potential community solidarity, small towns seem to be an effective location for Mennonite educational monasteries.

Steinbach Bible College, located in the small town of Steinbach, follows the American pattern. Columbia Bible College, also located originally in the small town of Clearbrook, B.C., began the same way in 1970, but slipped to two-thirds full-time in 1993, when Clearbrook's population also exploded. Canadian Mennonite Bible College (CMBC), located in the metropolis of Winnipeg, was able to keep up full-time enrolments also, by drawing students from across Canada, and housing them in dormitories that were fairly segregated, in the suburb of Tuxedo – a new urban pattern that needs to be examined further. Concord College, which began in Winnipeg as Mennonite Brethren Bible College, soon declined to 50 per cent full-time enrolment, and has dropped drastically, to 33 per cent full-time, since it became Concord College. Menno Simons College in Winnipeg, and Conrad Grebel College, in Waterloo, like CMBC and Concord, are both located in cities. Conrad Grebel has dormitories on campus and is able to create community on campus, but Menno Simons does not. Menno Simons also has no full-time students to boost a sense of community.

Eastern Mennonite Seminary (EMS), located in the small city of Harrisonburg, Virginia, located on the same campus as EMC as part of Eastern Mennonite University, began in 1970 with a strong full-time student count of 85 per cent, an enrolment figure similar to that of the small-town colleges, but dropped to 54 per cent full-time by 1993. Associated Mennonite Biblical Seminary (AMBS), located in a similar small city, Elkhart, Indiana, had only 60 per cent full-time students in 1970, and dropped to 45 per cent full-time by 1993. Mennonite Brethren Biblical Seminary (MBBS), located in the metropolis of Fresno, California, began with three out of four students being full-time in 1970; this figure dropped to 53 per cent in 1993. All of the three seminaries have increasingly enrolled part-time students, which Yoder (1995) suggests does not enhance community solidarity on extended monasterial campuses. Many Mennonite schools are opening up to more part-time students. Are they also opening up to more non-Mennonite students?

Mennonite Student Enrolments

American small-town Mennonite colleges have been very effective for a century in retaining full-time students in campus dormitories, which creates a small-town monastery-like community. However, with urbanization, demographics have changed, with a decrease in size for rural as well as urban families, so that, since 1980, there has not been a sufficient number of Mennonite students to keep Mennonite colleges growing. Colleges have used different strategies to boost enrolments. Mennonite colleges are now opening their monastery walls to attract more students.

The Board of Education of the Mennonite Church has been monitoring levels of Mennonite student enrolments, and has set limits, below which its three American colleges (Goshen, EMC, Hesston) must not drop. Earlier Mennonite levels were set at 65 per cent, but by 1994 that figure had dropped to 55 per cent. This policy is intended to retain a monastery-like community without being forced to open the doors to the larger student marketplace. Other colleges have not been held to such standards.

In table 8.2 we see that the three Mennonite Church colleges, Hesston, Eastern Mennonite, and Goshen, all held their Mennonite enrolments to the 75–85 per cent range in 1970. Bethel College was also within that range in 1970. However, by 1993 the proportion of Menno-

TABLE 8.2
Mennonite College Enrolments (Percentage Mennonite),
1970–1993

Schools	1970	1975	1980	1985	1990	1993
U.S.A.						
Pacific	31	29	19	17	13	11
Hesston	88	79	86	69	59	55
Bethel	82	79	74	68	55	45
Tabor	69	64	58	49	42	44
Goshen	74	67	75	73	69	64
Bluffton	30	25	20	15	12	10
EMC	83	69	63	71	72	69
Canada						
Columbia	91	88	89	87	83	69
Steinbach	70	81	89	90	94	87
CMBC	90	89	88	91	85	86
Concord	60	68	70	67	48	40
Simons					40	40
Grebel	41	31	51	48	65	54
Seminaries						
EMS	57	44	41	61	68	53
AMBS	79	77	77	88	79	71
MBBS	50	45	46	68	62	45

nite students had dropped considerably. The MC board policy held Eastern Mennonite and Goshen enrolments to roughly two-thirds Mennonite, but Hesston College, competing with two other Mennonite colleges in Kansas, dropped its proportion to 55 per cent. All other American colleges dropped their Mennonite enrolment proportions below 50 per cent. Without a policy, Bethel College could not keep up with the Mennonite Church college standards, although it held on until 1985, after which it dropped to 45 per cent. Bluffton and Pacific colleges, with relatively smaller Mennonite rural hinterlands, began in 1970 at one-third Mennonite and fell to 10 per cent by 1993. These are clear examples that opening up to the marketplace for larger student enrolments lowers the proportion of Mennonite students in the college community.

While American college Mennonite ratios are dropping, Canada's Steinbach Bible College, supported by more conservative rural Menno-nites, has actually increased Mennonite proportions, from 70 per cent in 1970 to 87 per cent in 1993. Columbia, the other small-town college in Clearbrook, dropped from 91 to 69 per cent over twenty-five years, as the city population grew. Of the metropolitan colleges, CMBC in Winnipeg has retained its Mennonite ratio in the 1980s, but Concord, its sister college, dropped well below 50 per cent since 1985. Colleges on university campuses, such as Conrad Grebel, have actually brought Mennonite student proportions above 50 per cent since 1985 with added dormitory facilities, but Menno Simons College, without dormitory facilities, has a level below 50 per cent.

It is clear that demographic forces are pressing all Mennonite schools to open up to more non-Mennonite students in the marketplace. The Mennonite Church American colleges, Steinbach (SBC), and CMBC in Winnipeg seem to be holding a sizeable Mennonite student majority, while the others are increasingly opening up to the marketplace. Pacific and Bluffton colleges, especially, are recruiting non-Mennonite students in large numbers. It is the trend that Yoder (1995) found led to changes in the monastery-like community vision, and which the California study commission said needed more focus and planning.

The three Mennonite seminary enrolments have been relatively steady over twenty-five years, but at quite different levels. In 1970, four out of five students at Associated Mennonite Biblical Seminary were Mennonite, and this proportion held until 1993. Eastern Mennonite Seminary began in 1970 with a little more than half Mennonite, dropped below half for a decade, and brought its Mennonite proportion up to two-thirds in the 1980s, with a drop to 53 per cent in 1993. Half of the Mennonite Brethren Biblical Seminary students were Mennonite in 1970; this figure dropped to under half for a decade, rose to two-thirds Mennonite in the 1980s, and declined sharply to 45 per cent in 1993. While enrolments of full-time students at AMBS are dropping, the proportion of Mennonite students is being maintained. While enrolments of full-time students at EMS and MBBS are dropping, those seminaries are also struggling to keep a majority of Mennonite students on campus, as total student enrolments rise.

Opening Up to the Marketplace

While Mennonite schools with large Mennonite hinterlands are still able to draw large numbers of full-time Mennonite students, many are opening up to new ways of extending their services to others in the marketplace. Let us briefly examine a few of these new trends.

Graduate Teacher Training

In 1967, Fresno Pacific College established a policy that 60 per cent of the enrolment should be Mennonite Brethren students, because increasing numbers of non-Mennonite students were enroling, and the proportion of Mennonite students was dropping (Wiebe 1994, 101). This policy, however, resulted in a decline in total student enrolments. To counteract this decline, the college enlarged its fifth-year teacher training course in 1967, and inaugurated a teacher education program with graduate credits in selected courses. By 1974 this program had developed into an MA in 'teaching' (Wiebe 1994, 135). By 1993, Fresno Pacific had enrolled 780 undergraduate, 129 post-baccalaureate, and 592 graduate students, for a total enrolment of 1,501 students. Thus, the college and graduate school continued to grow, but the proportion of Mennonite students dropped to 11 per cent. Fresno Pacific College promoted these changes 'because the teaching profession provides a constant opportunity for personal interaction making possible the demonstration of Christian principles ...' (Wiebe 1994, 101).

Recently, two other colleges have followed Fresno Pacific's lead, offering graduate education. In 1994, Eastern Mennonite University began a graduate teacher-education program, with 33 students enrolled, and in 1995 Bluffton College began a similar program, with 25 graduate students enrolled (Preheim 1995). Fresno and Bluffton have the smallest Mennonite hinterlands from which to draw students, and their Mennonite student proportions have also dropped, to 10 per cent. They are entering the marketplace with educational services well beyond what is customarily offered by the traditional Mennonite monastery.

University Teaching by Colleges

While Fresno Pacific, Bluffton, and Eastern Mennonite have expanded their curricula to include graduate work, they have done so from their own private campuses, where they have control over their space, dormitories, classrooms, and activities. By the 1960s, Canadian Mennonite Bible College (CMBC) and Mennonite Brethren Bible College (MBBC), both located on their own campuses in the metropolis of Winnipeg, expanded their offerings by becoming teaching centres of the University of Manitoba and the University of Winnipeg, respectively. University courses were now taught on the Mennonite college campuses, for which students received credit towards university degrees. These courses were usually taught by Mennonite teachers. These colleges, too, had control of their space, dormitories, curriculum, and activities on their own private campuses. These two Mennonite colleges are also full members of the Winnipeg Theological Consortium with the University of Winnipeg, St Andrews College (Orthodox), and Catherine Booth College (Salvation Army), which offer a graduate degree in theology.

These variations became extended when two colleges, Conrad Grebel and Menno Simons, were founded at the University of Waterloo in the 1970s, and the University of Winnipeg in the 1980s, respectively. About 3,000 University of Waterloo students take one or more courses annually at Conrad Grebel College, 113 live in the campus Grebel dorm residence, and some 60 students are associates of the college (Tiessen 1995, 6–7). Menno Simons College, located on the campus of the University of Winnipeg since the 1980s, has no campus of its own, but is located on one floor of a university building. Several faculty teach Mennonite-related courses in which general students enroll. It is the newest and most open version of a Mennonite presence on a city university campus being of service in the marketplace.

The Influence of Universities

Since Dutch/Russian Mennonites (a heritage shared by 90 per cent of Mennonites in Canada) have always tended to be less sectarian and more urban than the Swiss, they have been more inclined to consider going to university, especially since Mennonite colleges were not an option until the 1940s. Thus, a smaller percentage of Canadian Mennonites attend Mennonite schools, and more attend universities in nearby metropolitan centres (Canada's universities are located in Winnipeg, Vancouver, Waterloo, Saskatoon, Calgary, Toronto, Edmonton, Regina, and London). To illustrate, with two of Manitoba's three universities and well over half its population located in Winnipeg, the 22,000 Mennonites in that city have easy and cheap access to university education. The 1992–3 University of Manitoba directory lists 179 faculty and staff, and 1,595 students with Mennonite names, more than any Mennonite college in North America (representing 5 per cent of the university population).[4] Mennonite enrolments can be found in universities in Vancouver, Waterloo, and Saskatoon, near Mennonite population concentrations. Mennonite schools have to compete with these universities in the marketplace, which is increasingly a factor in the United

States as well. Universities are able to offer a wider range of options, which is likely to appeal to more mobile, education-conscious Mennonites. This phenomenon affects the three Mennonite seminaries in Elkhart, Harrisonburg, and Fresno as well.

Consolidation and Cooperation

While Fresno Pacific College and Bluffton College have extended their services well into the marketplace, two counter-trends exist that suggest consolidation and more Mennonite educational cooperation. Eastern Mennonite University (EMU) has reorganized its college and seminary along with their other graduate programs under the umbrella of Eastern Mennonite University, which is an example of more diversity of undergraduates and graduate programs. Since then, Fresno Pacific has become Fresno Pacific University, with the encouragement of the California study commission, following EMU's lead, to also become a university and expand its offerings even more.

The joining of Mennonite Biblical Seminary and Goshen College Biblical Seminary on a new campus in Elkhart, Indiana, in 1957 was the first instance of graduate-educational cooperation among Mennonites. Conrad Grebel College in Waterloo, Ontario, was the first cooperative Mennonite college-educational project undertaken by the Mennonite Church and General Conference Mennonites, which pooled their resources and students to form a viable Anabaptist school.

In British Columbia, Columbia Bible College was formed when the Mennonite Brethren and General Conference Mennonite Bible schools were joined. In this way they have enlarged the Mennonite demographic pool from which to draw full-time Mennonite students. Steinbach Bible College is supported by four smaller Mennonite groups, which enhances their strength to support a Bible college of their own. Three Mennonite colleges in Manitoba (CMBC, Concord, and Menno Simons) have decided to join together to form a federation of Mennonite colleges. Will the three Kansas Mennonite colleges follow with similar discussions? These seem to be counter-moves intended to help consolidate resources in order to bolster Mennonite community solidarity and help to balance the monastery–marketplace dialectic.

Nurturing the Monastery–Marketplace Dialectic

Is an educational community with a core purpose still needed? What evidence is there that Mennonite schools have been able to enhance beliefs and activity?

Changing Generational Values

Mennonite values are changing, the modern marketplace encroaches and Mennonites are becoming more educated, more urban, and more mobile. While 9 out of 10 Mennonites before the Second World War were rural, now one half live in cities. To what extent can we discern sets of values that are changing as new generations emerge and older ones decline?

In chapter 7 we discussed the finding that persons born more than fifty years ago were much stronger on in-group identity, moral behaviour, devotionalism, separation of Church and State, and religious beliefs than persons born since 1945. On the other hand, post–Second World War Mennonites score higher on political action and concern for racial justice. They wanted a more significant role for women in Church leadership, for example, and a more equal partnership in marriage. They were much more involved in the larger community. Values are changing, from more closed in-group, normative orientations, to greater concern for justice, politics, and communication in a larger, more open circle, beyond the in-group. Whereas pre-war Mennonites were concerned with securing their 'sacred canopy' or monastery, postwar Mennonites call for more openness (Driedger 1993). Thus, the general pressures to open up the educational monastery is strong, and it should not be surprising that Mennonite schools are trying to enter the marketplace to serve both their own constituency's needs and the needs of others around them.

Effective Anabaptist–Mennonite Schooling

How effective have Mennonite schools been, and have they been able to attract Mennonite students with strong Anabaptist–Mennonite values? Kauffman and Driedger (1991) sorted their sample of 3,083 North American Mennonites into two groups: those who had attended Mennonite schools and those who had not. As seen in table 8.3, those who attended Mennonite high schools, colleges, and seminaries scored higher on Christian values compared with those who attended non-Mennonite schools. The differences are significant. These data suggest that the ability of these schools to draw already committed students and further educate them in Christian values is significant.

TABLE 8.3
Mennonite Attitudes, by Types of Mennonite Schools Attended, 1989

Scored high on:	Non-Mennonite college (N = 603) (%)	Mennonite high school (N = 531) (%)	Mennonite college (N = 581) (%)	Mennonite seminary (N = 160) (%)
Beliefs				
Bible knowledge	35	51	62	86
General orthodoxy	75	72	60	56
Anabaptism	14	27	31	52
Religious Practice				
Church participation	29	30	43	69
Devotionalism	18	21	28	43
Stewardship	23	31	33	41
Moral and Ethical Issues				
Women in church leadership	39	28	63	70
Pacifism	15	23	36	58
In-group Identity				
Support of church colleges	40	56	73	80
Ethnicity	9	30	37	37
Communalism	15	16	18	50
Openness to the Larger Society				
Ecumenism				61
Political action	50	40	49	41
Political participation	36	31	24	19
Concomitants of Modernization				
Personal independence	26	21	21	13
Secularism	17	16	16	6
Materialism	16	15	14	0
Individualism	18	14	14	0

Those who attended a Mennonite seminary scored much higher on Bible knowledge and Anabaptist beliefs, and attending a Mennonite high school or college helped raise scores for these beliefs as well.

Generally, participation in religious practice also rises steadily with increased Mennonite education. Those with Mennonite seminary training especially include many with high scores on church and Sunday school participation. We would expect this, since seminarians are trained to focus on such participation, but the increments of participation among Mennonite high school and college students are significant as well.

A majority of those who attended a Mennonite seminary also scored high on moral and ethical issues, such as supporting women in Church leadership, more significant roles for women in the home, positive relations between the races, and pacifism. Mennonite education boosted moral emphases, except for women in leadership, which fewer Mennonite high school students supported.

A very large majority of seminarians support church colleges, and a majority of the Mennonite high school and college students did so as well. There was less support for ethnicity, and church schools seem to get more support than does the MCC. This strong support from Mennonite school alumni underlines the importance of Mennonite education.

Political action and participation decline with increased Mennonite schooling. Similar declines occur in the four indicators of modernization. We see that openness to the marketplace and modernization scores are generally low, and they do not vary greatly among those who attended Mennonite or non-Mennonite high schools and colleges. Almost none who attended seminary scored high on modernization. These data suggest that Mennonite schools have successfully attracted, and helped promote, Anabaptist–Mennonite beliefs and practice. The many Mennonite schools at various levels form a cooperative net of leadership training that promotes Anabaptist–Mennonite values.

Conclusions

John Yoder suggests that Fresno Pacific College developed from a small in-group Bible school run by Mennonites for Mennonites in a monastery-like way, to a large multipurpose undergraduate and graduate school increasingly involved in the marketplace and the needs of others. In fifty years Fresno Pacific changed from monastery to marketplace, evolving through three distinct stages: (1) the Bible institute, (2) the Christian liberal-arts college, and (3) the institution offering graduate education for all. In the process, the 'collegium of peers has seen many changes from a small gemeinschaft community focused on Bible study, to increased inclusion of others where in the 1990s only a minority of the faculty and students are Mennonite' (Yoder 1995, 146). We used this model to see whether the fifteen other Mennonite colleges and seminaries in North America went through a similar process.

Tracing enrolments of the sixteen Mennonite schools over twenty-five years, we found that, when Mennonites were rural and raised larger families, enrolments climbed in these schools until the early 1980s, when there was a sharp decline after the baby boom. Most Mennonite schools since then have scrambled for students in order to keep their expanded faculty and facilities occupied. This resulted in pressures to find non-Mennonite students, and develop new programs to attract students and funds. In the process, Mennonite schools changed in a variety of ways so that, by the 1990s, distinct types of schools were emerging.

Older Mennonite schools located in large rural agricultural Mennonite hinterlands, such as Goshen, Eastern Mennonite, Hesston, Bethel, and Tabor, weathered the demographic pressures by maintaining largely full-time enrolments of students, a majority of them Mennonite. These schools have remained largely Christian liberal-arts colleges in the intermediate stage of development, halfway between the monastery and the marketplace, maintaining a strong Anabaptist–Mennonite community of education. These schools are challenged to offer sufficient variety of education for the changing times to continue to attract Mennonite students.

Mennonite schools such as Bluffton and Fresno Pacific, located in relatively small Mennonite hinterlands, soon found that their pool of Mennonite students from which to draw was limited, and they began to increase recruitment of non-Mennonite students. By the 1990s both had enlarged their student enrolments greatly, but only 10 per cent of these students were Mennonite. Thus, the original purpose of the educational monastery to prepare leaders for the Mennonite in-group, evolved to the broader service role of offering a liberal-arts education to others in the marketplace. However, these schools are challenged by the need to retain some form of Anabaptist identity and community.

To strengthen potential for Anabaptist graduate education, the Chicago and Goshen Mennonite seminaries amalgamated the two schools in Elkhart in 1957 to form the Associated Mennonite Biblical Seminary. As in Elkhart, the two largest Mennonite groups also joined to form Conrad Grebel College in Waterloo. The Mennonite Brethren and General Conference Mennonites likewise joined to form Columbia Bible College in Clearbrook, to enlarge the demographic pool in order to maintain a Mennonite educational community. Four smaller Mennonite groups also cooperated to increase their strength in supporting Steinbach Bible College in Manitoba. And the latest cooperation is now developing between the General Conference Mennonites and the Mennonite Brethren to share a campus in Tuxedo, where strengths can be pooled to enhance Mennonite education.

It is clear that from this comparison of sixteen Mennonite schools that they are all changing and diversifying. Postmodern features of diversity, pluralism, deconstruction, reconstruction, and difference are much in evidence, as they seek to survive, to remain relevant in an electronic age. The extent to which the metanarrative of religion, science, and the enlightenment is changing can be assessed only with more qualitative research of curriculum and educational philosophy. As numbers of part-time students increase, pressures for variety in educational options will also increase. As Mennonite enrolments drop to 10 per cent or less, it will be hard to retain the beliefs and values of the Anabaptist–Mennonite monastery, as a part of the monastery–marketplace dialectic.

9

The Emergence of Women as New Leaders

In the early days of the Anabaptist movement, women often took on leadership roles, some performing the functions of ordained ministers (Driedger and Friesen 1995). However, as Mennonites became more rural, they returned to patriarchal values, which did not include ordained ministry for women. Recently, Kauffman and Driedger (1991) have found that urban, professional, and upwardly mobile Mennonites have again become much more open to women serving in all positions of Church leadership. Based on the recent experience of Mennonite women in the pastoral ministry, let us explore the extent to which modern Mennonites in North America accept the idea of women serving in Church leadership and examine whether these attitudes in fact do vary according to upward social mobility. But, first, we need to sketch the changing historical contexts.

Changing Social Contexts

The early Anabaptists were also radical reformers, in Europe in the sixteenth century, when they included changing roles for women. However, this soon changed where patriarchal patterns again prevailed. Since the 1960s, the women's movement has again revolutionized women's roles.

Status of Anabaptist Women

As Harold S. Bender (1959, 972) has pointed out, women played an important role in the early Anabaptist movement because the emphasis upon voluntary membership, adult baptism, and personal commitment 'inevitably opened up new perspectives for [them].' Later, however, 'after the creative period of Anabaptism was past, the settled communities and congregations reverted more to the typical patriarchal attitude of European culture' (Bender 1959, 972). 'The court records in the Swiss–South German areas as well as in Holland show that they could and did give vigorous and intelligent independent testimonies of their own to their faith, and shared martyrdom unflinchingly with the men ...' (Bender 1959, 972).

Like Bender, N. van der Zijpp (1959, 973) found that women played an important role in early Dutch Anabaptism. Zijpp reported that some women – for example, Aeffgen Lystyncx and Elizabeth Dirks, who was called a 'Leeraresse,' or preacher – taught in Anabaptist meetings. Zijpp (1959) also noted that many women died as martyrs. In Amsterdam, 33 out of the 106 martyrs executed were women. 'Soetken Gerrits of Rotterdam, and Vrou Gerrets of Medemblik published hymnals. Soon after persecution was ended, c1570, women are named as deaconesses, and from the early 17th century also as trustees of orphanages and old people's homes' (Zijpp 1959, 973). However, by the seventeenth century women had no voting power and were not eligible on church boards in the Netherlands where practices had again reverted back to common social practices of the day.

Dutch Anabaptists were somewhat more open so that by 1865, some of the Dutch congregations gave women the right to vote in choosing a pastor, and soon after that women were granted suffrage.

> In 1900 in 113 congregations the women had full suffrage, in 30 only in the case of calling a pastor, and in 12 no suffrage at all. At present (1959) in nearly all the congregations women have complete right of voting and in nearly all they are eligible to be members of the church boards. Such women trustees were first found in 1905 at Middleburg, and about the same time at Dordrecht and Leiden. At present all but a few congregations have women trustees. (Zijpp 1959, 973)

However, as Mennonites left Holland and settled in isolated areas farther east, in Prussia and Russia, they seemed to fall back into traditional patterns (Krahn 1959, 973). Wives became busy raising large families and keeping up with the obligations of the farm. The congregational meeting was typically referred to as 'Brudershaft' ('meeting of brothers'), and only males attended. With women taking over the teaching of Sunday school classes, the 'Brudershaft' was gradually 'invaded' by the women. The traditional seating arrangements of women on one side and men on the other was part of the Protestant pattern preserved in rural settings, until more education, urbanization, and professionalization changed such patterns of segregation.

More recent work by Marilyn G. Peters, Anneke Welcker, and M.M. Mattijssen-Bertman Doorwert (1990) also shows the considerable involvement of early Anabaptist women in Church leadership. According to Peters and colleagues, in the midst of the sixteenth-century patriarchal society Anabaptist women held worship services, taught the Scriptures, distributed the sacraments, were elders and prophets, went on evangelistic tours, debated with theologians – and died for their faith. Peters et al. point out that about one-third of the 930 martyrs listed in the *Martyrs' Mirror* are women.

In general, however, Anabaptist women who lived during the seventeenth, eighteenth, and nineteenth centuries had no voting power and were not eligible to serve on Church boards (van der Zypp 1959, 973). In Swiss–South German areas, 'the patriarchal type family life prevailed, with women in a respected, responsible position in the home, but "silent" in church life, in ecclesiastical government, and church work' (Bender 1959, 73). Dutch women leaders proved to be the only exceptions within Anabaptist patriarchal practice during this period.

Today the Dutch Mennonites continue to support women in leadership roles in the Church. As Peters and colleagues (1990, 933) point out, depending on their qualifications and experience, women have responsibility at all levels in the congregations, and in the denomination at large. For example, in 1987, out of a total of 93 ordained pastors, 33 were women. One woman has chaired the Alegemene Doopsgezinde Societeit (General Mennonite Conference), and a larger number have held executive positions. In fact, the Dutch Mennonites were the first denomination in the Netherlands to ordain women ministers.

However, various Mennonite groups in North America 'have vastly different understandings and practices regarding women' (Peters et al. 1990, 934). Both the Mennonite Church and the General Conference Mennonite Church have ordained women as pastors since 1978 and 1980, respectively, but the Mennonite Brethren do not ordain women as pastors, although a growing number have completed seminary training and are serving in various capacities, including pastoral staff positions (Peters et al. 1990, 934). Like Peters and colleagues, Kauffman and Harder (1975) and Kauffman and Driedger (1991) found enormous differences in the attitudes of their respondents to surveys of five Mennonite denominations representing 80 per cent of all Mennonites in North America. Some denominations ordained women, others did not; but these studies indicate that urban, educated, and professional Mennonites were more open to women in Church ministry.

The Agricultural Patriarchal Iron Cage

Mennonites have migrated throughout history, first in the sixteenth century, when they were persecuted and had to run for their lives, and later when they needed more agricultural land because of their large families. Women suffered during these many moves, where they were expected to leave the safety of familiar homes, and friends and relatives, and migrate into often unknown new settlements, far away from civilization, doctors, and medical help. This happened again and again over a 500-year span, as they moved eastward from Holland to Prussia, and then to Russia; westward again, to Canada and the United States; northward, to Alberta and British Columbia; and southward, into Mexico, Belize, Bolivia, and Paraguay.

One of the cruel aspects of the patriarchal 'iron cage,' was the religious belief of many conservative Mennonites that family planning was a sin. Thus, six to eight children was considered a small family, while ten, twelve, and as many as fifteen to eighteen children was not uncommon. Many women in that traditional agricultural environment were pregnant most of their early adult lives. Pioneer farm life was very difficult, with husbands sometimes away from home, trying to earn extra money, while wives struggled to tend the children, cows, livestock, and crops as best they could.

Katherine Martens and Heidi Harms interviewed twenty-six such Mennonite women and published the results in *In Her Own Voice: Childbirth Stories from Mennonite Women* (1997). It is a heartfelt set of accounts of the fears, joys, pains, and sometimes tragedies of women who suffered in these pioneer traditional settings, when midwives often took the place of doctors, and families who could not afford to have another addition kept having children. 'I wonder to what extent our attitude to childbirth in the Western world is still affected by the Old Testament curse that women should give birth in pain. If childbearing is our lot in life – our punishment, even, for a sin that is vaguely equated with being female – talking about it brings up the shadow of that sin' (Martens and Harms 1997, viii).

Many in this collection are 'exceptional stories, the ones told in low voices in the kitchen, [where] there is the assumption that birth stories will be "horror stories"' (Martens and Harms 1997, viii). The vulnerability of women who were pregnant most of their lives, who were isolated in patriarchal 'iron cages,' is evident everywhere in these women's stories, as attested by the volume editors: 'I learned to accept my father's statements because he had authority over me, my mother's because she had jurisdiction over the girls, my brothers' because they were older and they were men, my sisters' because they were older, my doctor's because he knew better than I what was good for me, and my husband's because he was in a scientific profession' (Martens and Harms 1997, xx). In addition, in traditional settings, there were the Church fathers who knew what was right, who had 'shunning' and 'excommunication' powers over all who were living in a well-defined, but segregated village setting, where conformity was the unwritten law.

Katie Funk Wiebe (1992) interviewed fifteen Mennonite Brethren women and her *Women among the Brethren* traces the stories of births, sickness, deaths, hard work, travel, waiting, praying – a litany of obligations demanding patient endurance. It includes many stories about extended periods of separation from their men (part of their patient suffering) while they were often pregnant, trying to manage the farm, in a long-grass wilderness. These are also stories of women who were looking for places to live their religious beliefs in peace and freedom. These are reminders of how it used to be. In striking contrast, we must sketch a summary of the development of the postmodern women's movement, and the options available to women since the Second World War.

The Feminist Movement

It is some thirty years since Betty Friedan published *The Feminine Mystique*, which created a great stir in 1965, when the birth-control pill was also introduced, and when we were in the midst of a cultural and sexual revolution. Since the 1970s an extensive literature has developed outlining the various feminist perspectives on the changing family (Nett 1988, 15). Jaggar and Struhl (1978) wrote a book on five feminist frameworks (conservatism, liberalism, traditional Marxism, radical feminism, socialist feminism) that provide alternative theoretical accounts of the relations between women and men.

Conservatism denies that women are oppressed, and claims that human nature is essentially the same in all times and places, that human interests, desires, abilities, and needs are determined by innate factors (Jaggar and Struhl 1978, 69). Human biology is considered a major factor in causing differences between the sexes, and these therefore cannot be changed. Feminists dispute this contention.

Liberal feminism had its origin in the 'social contract' theories of the sixteenth and seventeenth centuries and the publication in 1792 of Mary Wollstonecraft's *A Vindication of the Rights of Women* (Jaggar and Struhl 1978, 70). Wollstonecraft declared that women's capacity to reason would be equal to that of men if they were given equal education, and therefore they would have equal opportunity to exercise their talents unhindered by restraints of law or custom. When discrimination has been eliminated, women will also be liberated. Many are still waiting.

Marxist feminism rejects the importance of biology in gender differences, and points instead to the difference in functions imposed by the societies in which humans live. 'Rejecting the biologism of conservatives, Marxists reject the liberal's belief that it is possible for people to have genuine equality of opportunity for the development of their potential while they remain within a class society where the many produce the wealth but the wealth and power end up in the hands of a few' (Jaggar and Struhl 1978, 71). Marxists locate the origins of women's oppression in the economic system, where the means of production are in the hands of the few (mostly men). The importance of political and economic power on the macro level can be seen as also important on the micro level.

Radical feminism insists that the oppression of women is fundamental to all societies and at all times in the past. It is the most difficult oppression to eradicate or change, it causes the most suffering to its victims, and it is a model for all other oppression (Jaggar and Struhl 1978, 71–2). There seems to be general agreement by radical feminists on women's oppression being widespread, fundamental, and difficult to change, but they differ on the extent of the suffering caused and whether it is a model for other forms of oppression.

Jaggar and Struhl (1978, 72–3) describe *socialist feminism* as beginning

with basic acceptance of the historical materialist approach that was begun by Marx and Engels. It argues, however, that the traditional Marxist analysis needs to be enriched if it is to be thoroughly adequate for understanding the multifaceted nature of women's oppression. By placing an emphasis on understanding the cultural institutions (the family, heterosexual intercourse, etc.) that play a major role in oppressing women, this theory incorporates the central radical feminist insights; by insisting on analyzing these institutions within the context of class society, socialist feminism continues to employ a fundamentally Marxist method.

Socialist feminists recommend that problems such as abortion, poverty, and degradation need to be studied among the various social classes and among different racial groups to understand the variations in social class and male oppression. They agree that sexism is at least as fundamental as economic oppression (Cuneo 1990, 198–9). Socialist feminists see the family as an integral part of other economic, political, and social systems; they consider that domestic 'unproductive' labour must be recognized, and that household duties must be shared. There is an interconnectedness of home and work, private and public, personal and political, family and economic systems (Clement 1988, 74–5).

Meg Luxton's book *More Than a Labour of Love* (1980) showed the interrelationships between women's roles in Flin Flon, Manitoba, a small city of 10,000 people. It was a case study of three generations of housewives, and showed how domestic labour in a mining town changed when industrial capitalism entered the area. Flin Flon was a company town, and both men and women were dependent on the company for work. The only alternatives for women, as they could not work in the mine, were low-paying, insecure, and monotonous jobs, or marriage.

Fifty years ago there were few labour-saving devices, and housework was carried out in less modern conditions. As time spent on housework decreased with the use of vacuum cleaners and other devices, time spent on bringing up children increased even though families were smaller (Luxton 1980, 82–4). Over three generations the number of women working outside the home changed: very few did so in the first generation, more were working in the second generation, and about half the women were in the labour force in the third generation. Despite these changes, household schedules were largely arranged around the rotating work shifts of the men, and wives, even when working outside the home, continued to be primarily responsible for the emotional well-being of their husbands, as well as coping with the housework and taking care of the children. Men helped relatively little in the household, even when women were in the labour force, although this situation had improved somewhat by the third generation (Luxton 1980, 184–7).

Trade unions and pro-labour political parties provide greater organizational support for men than for women. Women feel more alone in their struggle to obtain respect for the work they do in the home and to get full-time jobs (Cuneo 1990, 8–11). As Luxton points out, 'challenging the way domestic labor is organized means challenging the most basic structures of male-dominated industrial society' (1980, 222). Luxton (1980, 231) concluded from her study that 'working-class women are starting to realize that the present form of the family holds them back ... The demands that these women are making to improve their daily lives require fundamental changes in the way society is organized.' These power struggles are part of the process of changing roles for all members of the family.

Profound changes have also taken place in Mennonite families, where there has been a shift of the workplace from the farm to the business or professional's office (Wilson 1991). Education and training have increasingly been transferred to schools, where children learn in more formal settings, rather than as informal apprentices near home. Mate selection is no longer under family control, but is now a matter of individual freedom. Roles are no longer as rigidly segmented into male and female, so that single women are now more economically independent, and mothers are working outside the home. With over half the women in the work force, men must increasingly share duties in the household, as well as helping to raise the children (Wilson 1991). To gain an understanding of the extent to which Mennonites in various walks of life are aware of these changes, let us examine the extent to which members accept increased roles for women in Church leadership, and also what it is like for female pastors to take leadership roles in churches where patriarchy was dominant only a generation or two ago.

Acceptance of Women in Pastoral Leadership

To explore the changing attitudes of Mennonites towards women, we shall examine Sauder's 1993 sample of Mennonite women who were then in the ordained pastoral ministry. We compare Sauder's (1993) findings with the experiences of American male and female ministers in nine denominations listed in a study done by Jack Carroll, Barbara Hargrove, and Adair Lummis (1983). We expected that: (1) as urbanization and education rise, openness to women in pastoral ministry will increase; and (2) the majority of Mennonite women ministers will compare favourably with other ordained non-Mennonite male and female clergy.

Attitudes towards Female Leadership

Since Mennonites have recently become more educated, urban, and professional, we expect that their openness to female ordination will increase. Using the North American samples collected by Kauffman and associates in 1972 and 1989, we find that, as Mennonites became more urban (from one-third to one-half between 1972 and 1989), more favoured women in the ministry.[1]

Table 9.1 shows that roughly twice as many in 1989 were aware of women being discriminated against as in 1972. Half of the respondents in 1989 thought that larger numbers of qualified women should be elected or appointed to Church committees and boards (up from one-third in 1972). Almost half thought their denominations should allow the ordination of women to the ministry in 1989; this figure had increased threefold since 1972, when only 17 per cent agreed. These differences in one generation were highly significant.[2] So it is clear that Mennonites, who were mostly agriculturalists fifty years ago, were opening up to much more involvement of women in non-traditional areas.

Favourable attitudes to the expanding roles of women increased for all five denominations. General Conference Mennonites scored highest, and Evangelical Mennonites lowest. However, while more Mennonite Brethren were open to greater female involvement in committees and boards, in 1989 only one in four agreed to the ordination of women to the ministry. EMCs had changed very little between 1972 and 1989. It is clear that Mennonite attitudes'vary. Evangelical Mennonites are changing more slowly because they score more highly on fundamentalism, which takes more literally Paul's biblical admonition that wives are to be subject to their husbands. This more patriarchal interpretation is more accepted by fundamentalist theology, in contrast to Anabaptist interpretations. Church affairs are dominated by men, especially power positions such as ministerial functions.

Types of Leadership Positions

Women have always been active in the church, teaching Sunday

TABLE 9.1
Mennonite Attitudes to Expanding Roles of Women, 1972 and 1989

| | Denominations (percentage answering yes) | | | | | | | | | | Total yes answers | |
| | GC | | MC | | MB | | BIC | | EMC | | 1972 (N = 3,591) | 1989 (N = 3,083) |
	'72	'89	'72	'89	'72	'89	'72	'89	'72	'89		
Are women being discriminated against and denied basic rights?	20	36	15	31	14	32	12	21	10	16	16	32
Should larger numbers of qualified women be elected to church boards?	40	58	29	50	26	53	36	50	22	38	32	52
Should your denomination allow the ordination of women to the ministry?	30	59	12	45	12	27	17	38	12	15	17	44

Source: For 1972 data, Kauffman and Harder 1975. For 1989 data, Kauffman and Driedger 1991.

school, working with children, and serving food – all of which were considered women's roles fifty years ago in the rural communities. Earlier, gender roles were more segmented, into male and female work, but that tendency has changed enormously recently. Over half of Mennonite women are now in the workforce, families are smaller, and gender roles increasingly change as work at home is shared by both women and men. As table 9.2 suggests, this change is also altering attitudes towards the roles of women in the Church.

In Table 9.2, we present some attitudinal findings. We asked which of the fourteen types of leadership qualified women might take in the local congregation. Three-quarters agreed that serving as deaconness was appropriate, while only one-third approved of women conducting ordinations. Well over half of the respondents agreed that women could engage in non-ordained Church functions.

Less than half thought it was appropriate for women to chair the board of elders; preach; or conduct communion, funerals, weddings, baptisms, and ordinations. These leadership positions seem to involve greater power and suggest a clear dividing line between being chair of a church council or chair of a board or elders. Ordination seems to be the symbol of power that many do not wish to grant to women. In the past, ordination was granted only to men who entered the ministry of a local church. However, as the Church began overseas mission work, women who were married to ordained ministers took on increasingly more male roles, and they, too, were ordained as missionaries. Single women became heads of schools, hospitals, and the like, and the result was that male–female lines in the division of Church work became much less clear. Since then these segmented gender roles have also begun to change, especially in city churches, where more egalitarian pressures have led to acceptance of changing leadership patterns.

Differences of Acceptance as Related to Education

Table 9.2 shows that three-quarters of men and women favour women serving as deaconesses. However, below the power line referred to above, significantly fewer women think it appropriate for women to undertake more powerful tasks, such as preaching and conducting communion, funerals, ordinations, weddings, and baptisms. In regard to all fourteen positions, women are less willing than men to grant status to females. This is a very interesting finding because it shows that not only men wield patriarchal power, but more women support such

TABLE 9.2
Responsibilities Appropriate for Women in Leadership, by Gender and Education, 1989

Leadership positions	Gender		Education					1989 Total (N = 3,014)
	Male (N = 1,401)	Female (N = 1,613)	Elementary (N = 299)	High school (N = 1,193)	College (N = 873)	Graduate school (N = 649)		
			(Percentages)					
Deaconess/deacon	76	76	53	65	87	93		76
Worship leader	73	70	44	64	81	88		71
Minister of Christian education	72	67	35	60	82	88		69
Read Scripture in worship service	71	66	46	58	79	85		68
Youth minister	65	59	29	54	72	80		62
Chairperson, church council	63	62	36	56	70	77		62
Chairperson, board of elders	52	46	23	40	56	70		49
Preaching	50	41	17	32	56	69		45
Conduct communion service	48	38	15	30	54	67		43
Conduct funerals	46	37	13	28	51	66		41
Ordained minister	46	37	15	28	50	63		40
Conduct weddings	46	35	13	27	50	64		40
Conduct baptisms	45	36	14	28	50	65		40
Conduct ordinations	41	33	14	25	46	59		37

Source: For 1989 totals, Kauffman and Driedger 1991, 263

patriarchal roles for men. Note that acceptance of women in deaconess work is equally supported by men and women. However, as we move down the line of positions, women are increasingly more conservative, so that by the time we get to the most powerful position of conducting ordinations, women are significantly more reluctant than men to grant such powers to women. Women seem to have been socialized into accepting patriarchy even more than men have been, and these values are hard to change.

Education is a major factor in leadership status. A majority of Mennonites with elementary education did not agree to women serving as congregational leaders (except as deaconesses). On the other hand, two-thirds or more of the respondents with graduate education favoured women serving in all positions. Clearly, congregations with well-educated members are much more open to calling upon women pastors to perform all congregational tasks. Rural–urban results were similar, with urban Mennonites favouring more female involvement, and rural respondents not doing so. Hence more urban churches call women, because they have a larger proportion of educated members.

We expect that as Mennonites become increasingly more educated and urban, women will also find more leadership opportunities in the churches. Preaching seems to be a central symbol of status. A majority of those with at least a college education accept women preaching and performing all of the other functions normally conferred by ordination. Significantly fewer of those with less than college education accept such leadership by women.

The place of women in ordained ministry was hotly debated among Mennonite Brethren (MB) in 1993, when their denominational conference again restricted women's ministry to unordained functions, as is consistent with our findings in table 9.2.[3] The role of women in the Mennonite Brethren church is increasingly an issue in works by MB women writers such as Katie Funk Wiebe (1992), Gloria Neufeld Redekop (1990), and Marilyn Peters (1990).

Seminary Leadership Preparation

Before the Second World War, nine out of ten Mennonites were on the farm, but the war changed that, with men (and a few women) going into alternative service and into the military, where they were exposed to the outside world. Having seen the larger world, Mennonites increasingly decided to go to school, and it soon became apparent that

Mennonite seminary education for the ministry was necessary. General Conference Mennonites started the Mennonite Biblical Seminary in Chicago during the war, after the Witmarsum Seminary in Ohio had folded. The Mennonite Church likewise began Goshen College Seminary in the 1940s, and the Mennonite Brethren also began their seminary in Fresno, California, in the 1940s. Some Mennonite women attended these Mennonite seminaries, but few entered the ministry before 1980. When the author attended Mennonite Biblical Seminary in Chicago in 1954–7 about 20 per cent of the student body were women. When Dorothy Nickel Friesen attended AMBS in 1971–4, the ratio of men to women had increased very little (Driedger and Friesen 1995). Only two women graduates earned degrees during those three years (classes of 1972, 1973, and 1974). By 1993–4 half of the AMBS students were women (AMBS enrolment reports, 1994). Thirty-three women graduates earned degrees in the classes of 1992, 1993, and 1995. All respondents who attended seminary in the 1950–60s in Sauder's (1993) survey (N –134) reported that fewer than 20 per cent of the students were women; two-thirds attending in the 1970s reported fewer than 20 per cent women; only students of the 1980s reported that 20–40 per cent of the seminary student body were women. So it is quite obvious that Mennonite women are increasingly attending seminary, first as the wives of men who are training for the ministry, doing so for their own personal spiritual growth, or to prepare for educational leadership in congregations. However, such exposure also increasingly suggests that women, too, could enter pastoral leadership roles, and as successfully as men. Thus, theological education, which now includes as many women as men students, will inevitably lead to churches' needing trained pastors calling women to lead them, especially in cities where Mennonites are more educated, and more exposed to egalitarian life at work and play.

In a sample of non-Mennonite men and women clergy in 1983, three-quarters of the men trained to be pastors, while two-thirds of the women attended seminary for personal spiritual growth or to seek vocational discernment.[4] Renee Sauder's 1993 survey of 134 Mennonite women pastors showed that, like non-Mennonite clergywomen, Mennonite women entered seminary classes for personal spiritual reasons and only one in four attended seminary to prepare for the ministry.[5] Women were seeking spiritual growth, while men were preparing for pastoral work, but this finding will likely shift over time to preparation for the ministry.

Support for Entering the Ministry

In the early years of seminary education, relatively few women were encouraged to go to the seminary; by the 1980s and 1990s, this had changed considerably. In the 1983 American Protestant study, almost all pastors encouraged men who are now in the ministry to attend, and three out of four encouraged women who were in American Baptist, Lutheran, Christian, Episcopal, Presbyterian, United Church of Canada, and Methodist Protestant churches. Eight out of ten Mennonite pastors also encouraged Mennonite female pastors to go to seminary.

U.S. clergymen also reported that their families supported their decision to enter the seminary, but only two-thirds of U.S. clergywomen received such support from their families. Fewer Mennonite female pastors reported that they were encouraged by their families to enter the seminary. The lower levels of family support for women desiring to enter the seminary must be attributable to the families' reading of congregational reluctance to accept women in such leadership, and to the families' sense of the difficulties that this attitude would cause the women.

Best friends supported Mennonite women the most, and U.S. clergymen supported them the least. Generally, most pastors, families, and best friends supported both men and women in entering the seminary, although there were variations. Such support augurs well for the future pastoral ministry of both men and women.

The inner call was by far the most important reason why eight out of ten Mennonite female pastors entered the ministry. The U.S. study did not specify this alternative. Half of the American clergymen reported that their home ministers had encouraged them to enter the ministry. Friends had the greatest influence on American clergywomen. Conference ministers and seminary faculty were less influential than ministers, friends, and family. In the 1990s, as Mennonite women become more upwardly mobile, more and more entered the seminary to strengthen their own spiritual growth, and in some cases to prepare for the ordained ministry.

Women in Congregational Leadership

Few women have served as pastors in Christian churches, including Mennonite churches. However, Renee Sauder (1993) found 186 Mennonite women who had such pastoral experience in Mennonite churches; 134 of them completed questionnaires in a survey she conducted.

Bridging the Barriers

Entering the congregational ministry was not without problems, as we would expect, seeing that most churches have been exposed to a long history of male dominance in leadership. Only one-quarter of the 134 Mennonite female pastors reported that they had been hired full-time in their first placement; two-thirds were part-time, and 7 per cent worked without pay (Sauder 1993, 5). This finding did not change greatly in subsequent pastoral assignments. One in five reported that the Church experienced internal strife because they were called, although two-thirds said such strife subsided later. Only 8 per cent reported that they had been ordained within the first year. For over half, ordination took one to two years, and for the rest it took three or more years (for 10 per cent it took more than seven years). Clearly, the patriarchal 'iron cage' is not easily dismantled. More than a third reported opposition to their ordination within the congregation, but almost no opposition from the conference minister (Sauder 1993). While the conference leaders may be more open to women serving as ministers, some congregational members are not. Three out of four female pastors had held district or conference or denominational church-wide positions on committees or boards, and thus experienced increased openness in the church structures.

Eight out of ten of these 134 pastors served congregations in cities with a population of 2,500 or more; more than a third served in metropolitan centres of 100,000 or more. Two-thirds of Mennonite women were placed in mostly small urban congregations with under 200 members (40 per cent had fewer than 100 members). Almost all of these congregations comprised a majority of middle- and upper-middle-class members who were at least moderately liberal theologically. Three out of four thought that their congregation would consider calling another woman if they left, and half of those who had left said their congregation had actually hired another woman. However, almost two-thirds of the respondents thought it might be difficult for them to get another pastoral position. It requires a clear call to serve, and dedication to serving as a female pastor, when opposition seems so pervasive.

Experiences of Female Pastors

What were the personal experiences of these female pastors? How effective did these 134 feel they were? Were they able to work with

TABLE 9.3
Experiences of Pastors in Serving Congregations

	Percentage		
Experiences with congregation	U.S. clergymen 1983	U.S. clergywomen 1983	Mennonite women pastors 1993
Felt accepted, liked by congregation	91	90	90
Physically healthy and energetic	82	79	72
Sufficient money to live comfortably	61	72	70
Accomplishing things in ministry	53	64	45
Can separate work and private life	48	47	29
Felt lonely and isolated	9	14	11
Trouble with some lay leaders	8	13	8
Bored, frustrated by job limits	8	9	5
Thought about leaving this work	4	10	8

senior pastors? Where did they turn for support when conflicts arose? And how much support did they get from their spouses? Again we are fortunate that Sauder used many questions from Carroll, Hargrove, and Lummis (1985) in her survey. Thus we can compare U.S. male and female clergy and Mennonite women pastors. Nine out of ten in all three groups felt accepted in their congregations (see table 9.3). Very few in each group thought about leaving. All seemed committed to pastoral leadership.

Half or more of the American male and female clergy felt accepted, energetic, and comfortable, and were certain they had accomplished much in their ministry. Roughly one in ten American clergy felt lonely, frustrated, and troubled, or considered leaving. The experiences of Mennonite female pastors followed the general pattern, although fewer felt they had accomplished much, and more found it difficult to separate private life and work. Did their Mennonite congregations expect too much, or did they not recognize their work enough? We do not know. Pastoral work can be very demanding, so it is not surprising to see that only one in three (29 per cent) Mennonite women pastors were able to separate their work from their private life. Mennonite congregations, especially smaller ones, in which women serve can be bottomless pits of work, where it always feels like much more needs to be done. Add to that the boundless demands of children and family at home, and it is not surprising that most found it hard to juggle what

TABLE 9.4
How Effective Do You Feel You Are/Were with Your Latest Congregation?

	Percentage answering 'very/quite'		
	U.S. clergymen 1983	U.S. clergywomen 1983	Mennonite women pastors 1993
Preaching sermons	97	97	90
Leading worship	97	97	90
Crisis ministry	90	88	63
Visitation	89	89	71
Teaching adults	87	88	70
Pastoral counseling	86	86	55
Motivating others	70	73	51
Recruiting members	68	61	18
Managing church budget	67	44	14
Teaching children	64	75	51
Stimulating service	60	58	32

essentially were two jobs. However, very few complained about being lonely, having trouble with laypeople, or being bored, and almost none thought about leaving the ministry.

How Effective Did Clergy Feel They Were?

Almost all U.S. clergymen and women felt effective in preaching, leading worship, crisis ministry, visitation, teaching adults, and pastoral counselling (see table 9.4). Their high ratings of themselves is impressive. This did not differ for men and women. These clergy from nine Protestant denominations felt at ease with themselves and their work. Did their seminaries train them so well in these more professional institutional duties? Were their routines more ordered and their expectations more unified, so that congregational expectations and clergy aspirations correlated well?

American clergymen and -women rated themselves considerably lower on a second set of five items: motivating others, recruiting members, managing the church budget, teaching children, and stimulating service of their members. Were these same clergy less confident outside their more formal institutional structures, when they were expected to assert individual initiative in less structured settings?

Interestingly, U.S. clergywomen reinforced many stereotypes that women are less skilled in handling money and better skilled than males in handling children. Generally, however, U.S. male and female assessments of personal effectiveness show little difference.

Although Mennonite female pastors share the confidence of U.S. clergy in preaching and leading worship, they score lower than both American male and female clergy on every one of the eleven categories (Anderson 1990). Unfortunately we do not have data for male Mennonite pastors. Nine out of ten female Mennonite pastors score high on the two most structured forms of preaching and worship, but scores drop significantly on all other activities. Only seven out of ten feel they are effective in visitation and teaching adults, considerably fewer than among American clergy. Barely half feel they are effective in counselling, motivating others, and teaching children, a much lower proportion than among American clergy. Very few indicated confidence in managing church budgets, recruiting members, and stimulating members to serve. The differences in relation to American clergy are striking. Have Mennonite families and schools not encouraged and educated female pastors to be confident? Are Mennonite congregations so much harder to satisfy and serve? Or are Mennonite women pastors just more realistic in their assessments of their work; that is, are they simply more honest and less political? Or do they get more feedback serving smaller churches? Or have Mennonite women emerged so recently out of patriarchal settings that their self-concepts are not yet well developed? Would male Mennonite pastors be more similar to non-Mennonite pastors or to female Mennonite pastors? More research needs to be done.

Associations with Senior Staff

Of the 134 women who served as pastors in Sauder's (1993) sample, 30 were lead pastors in their church, 10 were co-pastors with a non-spouse, 43 were co-pastors with their husbands, 21 were associates, 8 were assistants, 3 were Christian education directors, 4 were lay ministers, 4 were interim pastors, and 11 were team pastors. Thus, the 134 women found themselves in a variety of roles, interacting with a variety of co-workers, and having quite different statuses. Whereas in the past we have tended to ignore such status differences, today we are much more aware of them. In addition, these 134 were stratified into 54 per cent who were ordained, 31 per cent licensed, 8 per cent commis-

TABLE 9.5
Experiences of Associate/Assistant Pastors with Senior Pastors

	Percentage		
	U.S. clergymen 1983	U.S. clergywomen 1983	Mennonite women pastors 1993
Been an associate/assistant minister	56	61	52
Often discussed ministry in church	53	62	66
Personality, style, values important	40	56	48
Difficulties in being associate important	21	34	25
Senior often threatened by me	16	25	7
Being a woman important factor in conflict		24	11
Senior often made good suggestions	6	20	11
Senior often over-protective	5	12	6
Senior often overly critical	6	7	3

sioned, and 7 per cent not officially recognized. Some could perform all the functions required of a minister, while other had more limited job descriptions.

What were the experiences of women who worked as associates or assistants with the senior minister? Table 9.5 shows that over half of both the women and men had been associate or assistant ministers at one time in their lives of service. More than half had discussed the ministry of the church with the senior minister. Women more so than men thought that personality, style, and values were important in working together. Interestingly, U.S. clergymen and Mennonite women pastors thought more alike on most items than did American clergymen and American clergywomen. More U.S. clergywomen reported difficulties in social relations resulting from being an associate and being a woman (Nuechterlein and Hahn 1990). They also thought senior ministers were threatened more often and were more overprotective. Especially senior clergymen seemed to be less comfortable working with women. One in four reported that they had experienced sexual harassment, both by congregational members and by staff and pastoral colleagues (Sauder 1993).

The ministry involves some conflict, especially when pastors are faced with tragedy, illness, moral transgressions, despair, and death. In a congregation where they have been hired to render emotional, spiritual, and social support, where do clergy turn when they need help? American clergymen and -women turned first to their spouses and family. (We do not have comparable information for Mennonite clergy.) About half also turned to parishioners or staff in the Church. Mennonite female pastors turned more to friends outside the Church, to ministers, or to a denominational executive. Since they served smaller churches, perhaps they were more reluctant to share with the congregational members because of the potential for gossip that characterizes tighter communities.

The Roles of Spouses

In times of conflict, American clergy most often turned to their spouses. To what extent did spouses support the pastors to whom they were married, and what form did this support take? Over half of the clergy reported that their spouses were active in the Church. Two-thirds of the women reported that their spouses were employed full-time (40 per cent of the clergymen). Indeed, the spouses of female ministers were significantly different from the wives of clergymen in that half of the former were also ordained, most supported the ministry of their wives, and most gave these careers equal priority. Over half reported that parishioners appreciated the work of spouses in the Church (Mennonites somewhat less). In the case of U.S. clergymen, only 4 per cent of their spouses were ordained; fewer of these spouses (40 per cent) were employed full-time, which meant that careers took precedence less often; fewer of these wives respected their husbands' employment; and fewer also supported their husbands in their ministry. We conclude that women in ministry receive support from their spouses more often than do American clergymen. This support should make female pastors more effective and happier in their work.

The most striking differences in comparing the three sets of clergy was that the spouses of very few U.S. clergymen (4 per cent) were also in the ministry, while 45 per cent of the Mennonite and 60 per cent of the U.S. clergywomen were also ministers. Since so many of the women and their husbands were both in pastoral work, three out of four also thought that both careers should take equal priority. Since they were in the same kinds of occupation, they seemed to better understand the importance of teamwork. So it is also understandable that a large majority of the women clergy also reported that their spouses supported their work. There seemed to be more teamwork. This partnership of spouses in the ministry explains the reports of U.S. clergymen that almost none of their spouses was in the ministry, and therefore there was less feeling of both careers being equal, and that fewer spouses supported the men who were in the ministry. In sum, feelings of partnership were less pronounced.

Conclusions

Voluntary membership, adult baptism, and personal commitment opened up new perspectives for early Anabaptist women and enabled them to become leaders in the Anabaptist movement. Both Bender and Peters found that the patriarchal society in the sixteenth century gave way to new ideological insights that transformed family and social structures, thereby opening up greater opportunities for all in the Church. Later, as Mennonites became more rural, they again reverted to more patriarchal role patterns, whereby women were restricted in their church-leadership opportunities.

In the twentieth century, van der Zijpp and Peters found that Doopsgesinde women in Holland were among the first to gain suffrage and to serve as ordained pastors. This, we contend, was due not only to their theology, but also to their increased urbanization. We have argued that as Mennonites become increasingly more urban, educated, and professional in North America, they, too, became more open to increased leadership of women in the Church. Indeed, that is the case. As education and urbanization have increased, Mennonites have favoured significantly greater involvement of women in leadership, including full ordination and the rights of such official status.

The 1960s revolutionized many things, and the feminist movement was among these major changes. Betty Friedan's *Feminine Mystique* led the crusade against a patriarchal system that confined women to the home, under the authority of men. Now that a majority of women are in the labour market, both men and women are increasingly exposed to more egalitarian gender relations. Women are increasingly finding their niche in higher-level occupations, which is changing both the status and the roles of both women and men. Opportunities for women in the pastoral ministry is one such place of change.

Using Sauder's sample of Mennonite women who had experience in the pastoral ministry, we found that, compared with experiences of other clergy in the United States, most Mennonite women entered the ministry following an inner call, which grew out of personal spiritual growth.

Once these Mennonite women became pastors, they – like most other American clergy – felt accepted and comfortable in their work. They felt effective in preaching, leading worship, and teaching, but less effective in administrative work. Mennonite experiences were also very similar to those of other American clergy working with senior co-pastors. Almost all Mennonite husbands supported their female spouses in the ministry, more so than did the spouses of both male and female American clergy.

In order to make comparisons, future research should include information on both male and female Mennonite pastors. Such research should also include more demographic indicators and measures of religiosity, so that more sophisticated trends research can be done. We were fortunate that we could compare our Mennonite data with those on the experiences of American male and female clergy. While openness to women serving in the ministry in our postmodern society has greatly increased over what it was in previous generations, we expect that, with expansion of education, urbanization, and professionalization, North American Mennonites, like Dutch Mennonites, will increasingly accept full ordination of women in the ministry of the church.

10

Peacemaking as Ultimate Extension

The discovery of sixteenth-century Anabaptist polygenesis and their plural visions by Stayer and others (1975) has brought new excitement to historical theological studies since 1975. J.R. Burkholder's (1991, 5–7) typology of Mennonite peace theologies promises a similar new path to exploring contemporary postmodern Mennonite diversity. These developments are also entirely in tune with multicultural trends in sociological studies of minorities today (Driedger 1987, 1989, 1996). We suggest that these trends are a reflection of the postmodern social context in which Mennonites now find themselves, as half of them have become urban. Theologians focus on theological nuances and trends; sociologists ask what social reasons there are for such contemporary plural interpretations.

In this chapter, we use Burkholder's (1991) plural peace typology as a model to guide our discussion, demonstrate that both urbanization and theology affect political and peace attitudes over time, and provide empirical evidence of these trends and types between 1972 and 1989.

Diversification of Peace Perspectives

In his sketch of ten theological peace types, J.R. Burkholder (1991) uses a more inductive method, selecting representative peace positions of major Mennonite figures, similar to Richard Niebuhr's (1951) *Christ and Culture* and John Howard Yoder's (1971) *Nevertheless*. He agrees that a more deductive approach can also be helpful, but fears that it 'squeezes the life out of subjects' and tends to force organization. Let us develop the analysis in the deductive direction, putting it

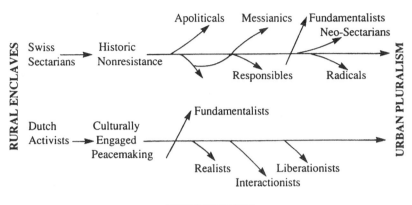

Figure 10.1   Major Swiss Sectarian and Dutch Activist Theologies of Mennonite Participation in Society

into a sociohistorical frame to provide greater opportunity to explain recent changes in peace trends (Driedger 1992). The inductive method that yielded ten types is helpful, but it is necessary to see the larger context in order to see why these types have emerged, how they are related at present, and provide clues to where all this might lead us in the future.

Using Burkholder's ten types, plus the elaborations of these types by Burkholder, Friesen, Schroeder, Harder, Gingerich, Barrett, Redekop, Suderman, and Schipani, we present a sociohistorical flow chart (figure 10.1; Burkholder and Gingerich 1991, 50–83). An examination of the information given uncovered a more dynamic model, with two major sociohistorical Swiss Sectarian and Dutch Activist streams beginning in rural enclaves and moving towards increased urban pluralism. These provide us with four cells – rural non-involved, rural involved, urban non-involved, and urban involved (Driedger 1992).

Swiss Anabaptists who emerged from continental Switzerland and southern Germany were less influenced by the commercial, industrial, and urban environment along the Baltic, north European coast, where Dutch Anabaptists emerged (Driedger and Kauffman 1982, 269–90). Although both have developed their solidarities in rural enclaves for the past hundreds of years, Dutch Mennonites moved to Ukraine, where they developed their own Mennonite commonwealth, with greater entrepreneurial and social independence. These Dutch Russian Mennonites later came to settle west of the Mississippi in the United States and in Canada. Swiss Mennonites developed their rural enclaves mostly east of the Mississippi.

Historic Swiss Sectarian Non-resistance

Historic non-resistance became the baseline peace position of the Mennonite Church developed by Guy F. Hershberger (1944), Harold S. Bender, and John C. Wenger, all located at Goshen, Indiana (Burkholder and Redekop 1976). Burkholder (1991, 6) describes this position as stressing the literal obedience of the teachings of Jesus, conscientious objection to military service, seeking alternatives to violence, and reluctance to reform the social order. Developed and tested in rural Goshen during the Second World War, when most Mennonites were in agriculture, and when not many MCC and alternative-service workers had yet returned from seeing the larger world, it represented an unchanging agricultural rural enclavic view of the segregated Mennonite community.[1] This basically conservative non-involved stance was consistent with the Schleitheim confession, which came out of Switzerland, and it was modified to be in tune with the rural Mennonite Church, where it was largely accepted.

As shown in figure 10.1, most of Burkholder's ten types were led by Swiss-origin Mennonites, and generally the early types that have gained adherents have tended to favour non-involvement. Apolitical non-resistance represents the most conservative two-kingdom version of historic non-resistance, often favouring Old Testament political categories, and it basically does not approve of political activity by the Church.

Pacifism of the Messianic community, for John Howard Yoder, seems to be a natural extension of the historic non-resistant type based on obedience to Christ as Lord, possible through the redemptive power of loving one's enemy. The titles of some of Yoder's books such as *The Christian Witness to the State* (1964), *The Politics of Jesus* (1972), and *The Priestly Kingdom* (1984), propose witness and involvement largely from a renewed Christian monastery community, with limited forays into the larger society. This modified version of a more messianic message, which only selectively involved the larger society, was expanded by the Concern group, and seemed to appeal to both younger Mennonite intellectuals and some of the conservative community in the 1960s. As a result, their writings received a strong hearing. In contrast, J. Lawrence Burkholder's appeal for social responsibility and greater engagement in society, made at about the same time that Yoder was writing, received little support in the Mennonite Church, as it was seemingly at odds with their rural historic non-resistance, because it wrestled with ethical compromise (Driedger and Kraybill 1994). Whereas Yoder's writings appealed to Swiss sectarians, Lawrence Burkholder's (1984) dissertation written in the 1950s (and not published until 1989) was not well received. Burkholder's plea for more responsibility to society was largely quashed. To what extent his ideas will receive a better hearing among Dutch activists, or will appeal more to urban Mennonites, remains to be seen.

In the meantime, the fundamentalist intrusion has increasingly had its influence on the Mennonite Swiss sectarians, and historically non-resistance has often suffered. Harold Bender's Anabaptist vision sought to hold together the outreach and non-resistance emphases of early evangelical Anabaptists, which kept many concerned with evangelism within the larger fold. However, the Fundamentalist movement is often very patriotic, especially during wars, and we need to see to what extent this influence has eroded the historical non-resistance position among Mennonites. Except for concerns with individual morality such as abortion and use of alcohol and the like, fundamentalists have shied away from greater social concerns because they see society as unregenerated (Marsden 1991). More recently, the modern evangelical movement has become less exclusive and more involved in social issues (Wuthnow 1981, 1987, 1988a).[2]

Almost two-thirds (63 per cent) of the Swiss Mennonites in 1989 were still rural, the most rural of the five groups surveyed (Kauffman and Driedger 1991). However, they, too, are moving towards more urbanization, and there seem to be a variety of peace probes trying to cope with their original two-kingdom background. It is too early to tell whether Ted Koontz's neo-sectarian pacifism, which seeks a modified two-kingdom ethic, will draw many adherents (Schipani 1991). Radical pacifism by proponents such as Dale Brown and Ron Sider who favour more non-violent public political-action movements seem to have limited appeal for some, but will urbanites buy it more? Where Swiss sectarians will focus as they become more urban later than most others is not yet clear.

Dutch–Russian Culturally Engaged Peacemaking

Lauren Friesen makes a good case for culturally engaged peace-making, represented by largely Dutch–Russian Mennonites in the Newton area; it is plotted as a second major stream of peace theology in figure 10.1 (Friesen 1991). It is not clear which of Burkholder's ten types this represents, but it seems to fit with non-violent statesmanship and realist pacifism. I find Lauren Friesen's description of the 'Russian Mennonite trajectory' involving C.H. Wedel, David Goertz, C.H.P. Krehbiel, P.H. Hiebert, Edmund G. Kaufman, and Gordon Kaufman quite convincing (Friesen 1991).[3] Friesen's imagery represents the more acculturated Dutch–Russian Mennonites who chose Kansas rather than Manitoba for major settlement in the 1870s, where they founded the first Mennonite college (Bethel).

Friesen (1991) and Juhnke (1989) claim that German idealism and historicism led these early Western American Mennonite pioneers to think more dialectically, since their faith and culture were in tension with the larger society around them. Thus, their Mennonite faith and culture were in dialogue, or in the process of exchange, with the society around them more engaged in networking. In Russia, too, they had had considerable autonomy in religious, economic, and political affairs, and they did not see these issues in black and white, two-kingdom terms. C.H. Wedel proposed that 'Gemeindechristentum' meant that church members actively engaged in the arts, literature, and culture, part of the larger society. Mennonites could participate in society more, and also offer their peace witness as a contribution, involved in vigorous engagement with, rather than withdrawal, from the world. Goerz was employed by Johann Cornies in economic development in Ukraine; Krehbiel, the founder of the *Mennonite Weekly Review*, ran for state senator; Edmund Kaufman gave peace a prominent place in his mission work in China, and later as president of Bethel College; and Gordon Kaufman sought to apply this theology in his work at Harvard, teaching at the Divinity School, and is now a leading theologian (Friesen 1991, 17).

Some of the leaders of this 'Russian Mennonite trajectory' were reluctant to use the term 'non-resistance' (the term is commonly used in Goshen), because they were more interested in responsible participation in the larger society from a 'Gemeindechristentum' base. In their Russian colonies, they were involved in developing ethics, and in responsible community-building, which entails many of the tasks the larger society also was engaged in. Culturally engaged peacemaking, rather than pacifism, seems to be an apt label for this major Dutch–Russian Mennonite stream. Duane Friesen, also located in Kansas, seems to advocate a modern version of that same stream which Burkholder labels 'political non-violence,' or realist pacifism, also plotted in figure 10.1, as representing more recent openness to involvement in society (Friesen 1991, 7).

The Dutch Activist stream does not have as many early varieties of peace advocates as do the Swiss sectarians, which is interesting. Is it because the Dutch Activists have assimilated more with a less salient position, or does the Swiss two-kingdom theology have more problems relating to a larger society prone to schism and fragmentation? We expect that our data will help clarify some of this.

The fundamentalist theological intrusion pressing for less involvement is also evident among the Dutch Activists, so we have plotted this interjection in the Dutch Activist stream also. It is clear that we will need to test the influence of fundamentalism on peace in both streams.

Burkholder plots the contributions of Frank Epp and John Redekop as Canadian pacifism, which I think is too general and regional (Burkholder 1991, 7). I have relabelled Canadian pacifism 'Interactionist peacemaking,' a natural extension of Dutch–Russian activism, since a large majority of Mennonites in Canada are of northern European heritage. I agree with Burkholder that they have much in common with the political and social responsibility types and that they see the democratic state as a positive arena for Christian participation. John Redekop makes the case that opportunities for participation are greater in Canada, that Canadian Mennonites have a more positive view of the state, seeing government more as a servant; as a consequence, Canadian Mennonites are less reluctant to use government funds, for example. There is continuity between Kansas and Manitoba Mennonites in that the engaged moved to Kansas and the conservatives moved to Manitoba, when they first came to North America in the 1870s. However, since then, large migrations in the 1920s and 1950s of more acculturated and urban European Mennonites has brought about greater openness to societal involvement in Manitoba. Redekop (1991) suggests that the more politically active Dutch–Russian Canadian Mennonites have been able to work within government because Canadian politics is less ideological, and has less potential for conflict with Mennonite faith.

Liberation pacifism proposed by Arnold Snyder, Mark Neufeld, and Perry Yoder, which sides with the poor and oppressed, may be increasingly more difficult for middle-class urban Mennonites to adopt (Suderman 1991). More and more groups are demanding justice in the larger society, a justice which will appeal more to third-world Mennonites, who are poor. MCC service continues to introduce Mennonites in fifty countries to the needs of the poor. Will 'rich' North American Mennonites have the will and commitment to side with the poor? Mixed reactions to Hugo Zorrilla's call to justice still leave this question unanswered (Zorrilla 1988).

In our attempt to plot the ten types presented by J.R. Burkholder in figure 10.1, we suggest that the Swiss sectarians have a strong tendency towards non-involvement. They have been more rural since the sixteenth century, and the Mennonite Church was still two-thirds rural in 1989. Will this change as they urbanize? Perhaps, but their theology is also more oriented towards two kingdoms. The effect of theology and urbanization needs to be tested. Dutch Activists have generally been more urban; in 1989 they were about two-thirds urban, and their theology, which is more in line with the Dortrecht confession, developed in northern Europe, has always allowed for more cultural engagement. We expect that Mennonite Church sectarians will be less willing to engage in politics than are Dutch Activists. Which stream has managed to keep Anabaptist peace concerns most alive?

From Non-resistance to Peacemaking

In 1944, during the Second World War, Harold Bender presented his landmark paper on Anabaptist discipleship to the American Church historical society. That same year, Guy Hershberger published his well-known *War, Peace and Non-resistance*. Both came out of Goshen, a rural Swiss Mennonite community, under the national American threat of conscription and war. Both works have become classics, products of profound anguish and struggle as to what to do in a time of crisis. They were Moses and Aaron who led Mennonites through the Red Sea, and many followed.

Driedger and Kraybill (1994, 77) did a word study of Hershberger's (1944) *War, Peace and Non-resistance*, based on Jesus' words 'Resist not evil,' found in Matthew's gospel (5: 39) and dominant in Hershberger's work. 'Non-resistance' was used 427 times, and is the dominant symbol and theme in Hershberger's classic works. Symbols of the passive, such as pacifism, suffering, obedience, non-violence, and submission, supported the non-resistant symbolism. Active peacemaking, politics,

TABLE 10.1
Text Coverage of Concepts in the *Mennonite Encyclopedia*, in Numbers of Text Columns, by Year

Concepts	Number of text columns	
	1955	1990
Non-resistance	18	2
Conscientious objector	15	7
Non-conformity	15	4
Church and State	14	7
Relief work	14	6
Simplicity	5	0
Love	3	4
Litigation	3	0
Pacifism	1	0
Civil disobedience	0	2
Justice	0	4
Development work	0	6
Politics (and related)*	0	12
Peace (and related)**	0	13

Note: 1955 data is for vol. 1–4; 1990 data pertain only to vol. 5.
*Politics, political attitudes, and political activism
**Peace, peace activism, peace education, peace studies, and lobbying

witness, and responsibility faded into insignificance, appearing fewer than 10 times in the entire volume.

However, only six years later, after Mennonite youth had come home from alternative service and the war, the Winona Lake conference statement reflected a major turn away from safe non-resistance to active engaged love, service, discipleship, society, and witness under a new-found Lordship of Christ. Their God changed from a parochial sectarian meek Jesus to the Lord of the universe who reigned over all. A profound change was taking place: non-resistance was turning into active responsibility. Mennonite youth in their service saw that there was a world out there that needed active love.

When Driedger and Kraybill (1994, 153) examined key peace topics in the four-volume *Mennonite Encyclopedia* published in 1955, and compared the four with the fifth volume (published in 1990), they found the enormous change documented in table 10.1. They found eighteen columns of text devoted to non-resistance in the 1955 encyclopedia, edited by Swiss Mennonite Harold Bender; the next most prominent subjects were: conscientious objections (15 columns), non-conformity (15 columns), Church and State (14 columns), and relief work (14 columns); peace, politics, development work, justice, and civil disobedience received no mention. In volume 5, edited by Dutch Mennonite C.J. Dyck, peace (13 columns) and politics (12 columns) lead the way, with the other subjects falling far behind. Non-resistance received only two columns of coverage. The change over the past fifty years has been enormous. A 1986 MCC brochure on peacemaking showed concepts of peace (36 mentions), peacemaking (27), justice (16), reconciliation (13), love (11) leading the way, with no mention of non-resistance. Factors which brought about this change need further examination.

Changing Theological and Political Attitudes

Our discussion thus far in this work has shown that theology is an important factor in differentiating Mennonite attitudes. We have also sensed that political attitudes are an important part of increased diversity and changes towards pluralism. Let us explore these two factors further to discover how they effect change. We expect that types of theological beliefs will affect political action.

Theology and Draft Choices

Since theology seems to be a major factor in choices for peace, we developed General Orthodoxy, Anabaptist, and Fundamentalist theology scales (Kauffman and Driedger 1991). We cannot present the details of each of the three scales, but want to use the Anabaptist and Fundamentalist versions to show the enormous theological influence on attitudes to peace. In table 10.2 we see that roughly eight out of ten Mennonites surveyed in both 1972 and 1989 chose the three top non-military options, while about two out of ten chose military service. Almost all who scored high on Anabaptism (93 per cent) chose non-military alternatives, while 6 out of 10 (60 per cent) who were low on Anabaptism chose military options. Commitment to the Anabaptist way supports alternative service very strongly.

When we examined who these low-scoring Anabaptist Mennonites were, we found that they held strongly to fundamentalist beliefs that were usually negatively correlated with peace concerns. In this chapter, we explore how fundamentalism is not only a drag on peace, but tends

TABLE 10.2
Draft Choices, by Anabaptist Theology

Which position would you take if faced with the military draft?	Anabaptist theology scale				Totals	
	Low	Lower Middle	Upper Middle	High	1972	1989
		(Percent in 1989)				
Refuse to register	2	2	4	5	1	4
Register, but refuse induction	1	3	5	6	2	4
Alternative service	37	66	78	82	80	70
Non-combantant military service	30	20	11	7	11	15
Military service	30	9	2	0	6	7
Number	353	647	928	35		2,570
Total percentage	14	25	36	5		100

to lead its adherents to be negatively inclined towards peace; in fact, many of them are opposed to the Anabaptist peace position. We also found that the larger Mennonite denominations were most strongly Anabaptist, and the smaller denominations most strongly fundamentalist. The Mennonite Brethren (MB) were usually in the middle. One of the reasons the Mennonite Church respondents (MCs) strongly chose peace alternatives to military service is because they were strongly Anabaptist theologically, while so many Evangelical Mennonites (EMCs) chose the military options because they were strongly fundamentalist. The intrusion of fundamentalism into the Swiss historical non-resistance and Dutch culturally engaged mainstreams (see figure 10.1) has had the strongest effect in the smaller denominations, especially on their peace theology, a phenomenon that needs more discussion.

We expect that, as Anabaptist theology scale scores increase, concerns for peacemaking also increase. Fundamentalism depresses and seriously opposes peacemaking. We also expect that MCs and GCs will be strongest on Anabaptist theology and most positive towards peacemaking, while EMCs will be weakest in both.

Anabaptist versus Fundamentalist Beliefs

Let us expand on and explore the theological implications. Less educated, rural Mennonites were fairly successful in preserving their sectarian peace position in segregated community enclaves. However, as they were separated from the larger society, their peacemaking beliefs could not be easily shared. Now that Mennonites are becoming more educated and urban, and are re-entering the pluralist society around them, they are in the process of reconstructing their theology to encompass the larger world and its needs. Fundamentalists are tempted to take Mennonites out of the world and its problems by attending more exclusively to their individual needs of the soul and the spirit. Anabaptists have always sought to build meaningful fellowships of believers in a changing society, to demonstrate the kingdom of peace and justice.

The early Anabaptists took the Sermon on the Mount and Jesus' prayer to be 'in the world but not of it' (John 17: 16) seriously. This 'in but not of' gospel required a dialectical give-and-take, outreach, and response which varied by context in diverse society. They understood outreach in the form of evangelism, and dealing with the troubles people found themselves in socially, as two major tasks in responding to both spiritual and social need. A comparison of the Anabaptist and fundamentalist theologies will serve to illustrate varied theological emphases.

As seen in figure 10.2, evangelism and peacemaking are not correlated at all ($r = .00$), meaning that they seem to be two separate tasks of winning others to the church as followers of Jesus, and serving society in a peaceful way outside of the congregation of believers.[4] Anabaptists and fundamentalist are positively associated with evangelism ($r = .26$ and .24). On the other hand, while Anabaptism is strongly associated with peacemaking, fundamentalism is ($r = -.30$) negatively associated with peacemaking. Anabaptists are committed to both tasks; fundamentalists only to the first. This, we suggest, represents two very different perspectives, which Robert Wuthnow (1981, 1987) calls 'Dualist' and 'Wholist' concepts of the world and which he has continued to pursue in his writings, in *Meaning and Moral Order* (1987), *The Restructuring of American Religion,* (1988a) and *The Struggle for America's Soul: Evangelicals, Liberals, and Secularism* (1988b). These two perspectives are also at war within the bosom of the Mennonite churches. The basic theological task, it seems, is to deal with these divergent views of what building the Kingdom of God is all about.

Anabaptist Mennonites saw their task in a more wholistic way, which included evangelism (.26), serving others (.29), work in MCC (.16), welfare for others (.14), racial justice (.07), and peacemaking (.48), greatly expanded upon by Kauffman and Driedger (1991). What was

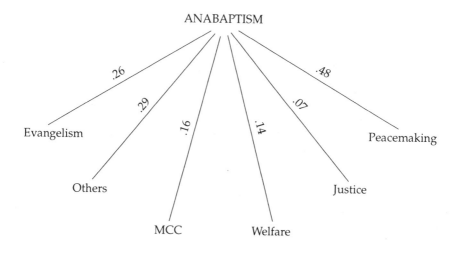

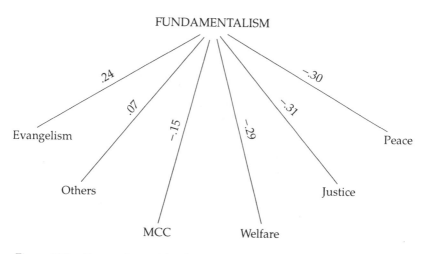

Figure 10.2   Comparison of Anabaptist and Fundamentalist Theologies and Their Associations with Six Issues

radical about early Anabaptist theology was that many explicitly included peacemaking as a prerequisite for discipleship, along with evangelism, so followers would be forced to take both the Church and the world seriously. It is this insistence on blending a process of 'in but not of' theology which strikes us as being postmodern.

When wars came, Mennonites, even in ethnic enclaves separated from the world, were forced to deal with the larger demands of society, such as alternative service, which according to Albert N. Keim (1990) and Klippenstein (1979) cost them millions of dollars during the Second World War. While many youth in the 1940s were ill prepared to give reasons for their faith, they were forced out of their communities to demonstrate their positions according to the original Anabaptist visions. Since then, helping others (.29) in their local communities has blossomed into a $35-million outreach involving 1,000 workers in fifty countries working in the 'Name of Christ' under the Mennonite Central Committee (.16). The disaster of world-war conscription was turned into Christian service, which has grown unabated since. MCC workers, having seen the injustices of war, famine, racial discrimination, and despair, have returned to Mennonite congregations for the last fifty years to reinterpret (deconstruct and reconstruct) the larger vision of early Anabaptists. Present-day postmodern Mennonite Anabaptists now also better understand the 'in but not of' Sermon on the Mount (Matthew 5–7) dialectic: 'It has been said, but I say unto you.' Jesus' sayings here are remarkably deconstructionist.

Figure 10.2 also shows that Mennonite fundamentalists, like the Anabaptists, are committed to evangelism (.24), but much less to serving others (.07). Contrary to the positive linkages of the Anabaptists to societal service and outreach, fundamentalists are negatively associated with MCC service (–.15), welfare for others (–.29), racial injustice (–.31), and peace-making (–.30). Service to society and the world outside of the church is missing. More seriously, they are strongly against such social services. The 'in but not of' dialectic is not possible because fundamentalists see the world as their enemy, while Anabaptists see others as fellow unfortunates in need of love, and part of God's creation, and thus able to benefit from networking efforts. More recent Evangelicals are working at more active involvement in the world to right this imbalance (Wuthnow 1989). The Anabaptist 'in but not of' dialectic remains intact, as they stand with one foot in the church and the other in the world, trying to engage in postmodern processes.

Mennonites have often cited their indebtedness to leaders of the recent past, such as the Benders, Millers, Hieberts, Thiessens, Janzs, and Dycks, who had 'courage to spare,' in their own ways encouraging the vital 'in but not of' dialectic. While in the past that dialectic was often seen in two-kingdom terms, with too much emphasis placed on polar opposites, Mennonites are coming out of enclavic settings, trying to fine-tune the relationships of evangelism, service, relief, welfare, justice, politics, and peacemaking (rather than the non-resistance and pacifism of the past). The ten peace types presented by J.R. Burkholder provide us with alternative perspectives on peace.

Swiss/Dutch Political Differentations

As predicted earlier, Dutch Mennonites were more willing to participate in the political process than Swiss Mennonites, with those of other backgrounds more like the Dutch than like the Swiss. While three out of four or more generally favoured voting in elections, studying issues, holding office, and witnessing to the state, this number dropped to half or less when asked more specifically about political action, endorsing candidates, and discussing politics from the pulpit.

Willingness to act politically does not, however, necessarily mean that such action will enhance Mennonite identity, or help others. While more Dutch Mennonites actually voted than did their Swiss counterparts. Other Mennonites voted more for liberal Democrats and the New Democrats. On composite political attitude and participation indexes, Other Mennonite attitudes and behaviour were more similar to that of Dutch Mennonites. Driedger and Kauffman's (1982) and Juhnke's (1989) predictions that Dutch Mennonites were open to more political involvement are confirmed.

Political Participation by Denomination

The number of Mennonites favouring greater political participation has increased over the past generation (table 10.3). Whereas three out of four favoured voting in public elections in 1972, by 1989 almost all thought Mennonites should vote. While less than one-half voted in most elections in 1972, by 1989 two-thirds did so. Willingness to participate in the political process has increased dramatically in one generation.

Denominationally, attitudes towards political participation are the reverse of trends towards non-resistance. Almost all EMCs (Evangelical Mennonite Church) consistently favour more participation on all items, a finding considerably higher than for MCs (Mennonite Church). For example, twice as many EMCs voted as MCs, and 50 per cent more EMCs than MCs favoured holding governmental offices at the local, state, provincial, and national levels. Rural sectarianism seemed to hold the MCs back, while greater recruitment of non-

TABLE 10.3
Political Participation of Mennonites, by Denomination, 1972 and 1989

	Percentages 1989					Totals	
	MC	GC	MB	BIC	EMC	1972	1989
Should vote in public elections	72	88	94	95	96	76	84
Should witness directly to the state	73	74	79	77	83	61	76
Church should try to influence the actions of government	64	68	75	74	68	56	70
Members may hold governmental office	63	83	90	92	95	62	68
Voted in most elections in recent years	45	64	84	85	87	46	65
Held an elective or appointive ofice in government	3	3	6	3	5	3	4

heritage members seemed to enhance EMC involvement. Postmodern diversity among Mennonites and 'différance' is certainly evident.

Lauren Friesen's (1991) predictions that culturally engaged Russian Mennonites will be more open and active in political issues were also confirmed. Comparing American Mennonites east and west of the Mississippi, we found that more Westerners favoured voting, study, holding office, witnessing to the state, political action, endorsing candidates, and discussing politics from the pulpit. Western Mennonites also voted more, a few more favoured liberal Democrats, and twice as many held political office.

John Redekop's (1991) predictions that Canadian Mennonites who are largely of Dutch heritage, dealing with a less threatening non-militarily focused government, will be more active politically is also confirmed. Both Eastern and Western Canadian Mennonites are more open to political involvement than Eastern American Mennonites. Western American Mennonite attitudes are more like Canadian attitudes, presumably because of their common Dutch–Russian culturally engaged tendencies. More Canadians also vote, but Western Canadians vote the most conservatively (62 per cent) and Eastern Canadians most liberally (18 per cent), i.e., for New Democrats. How do we explain this East–West Canadian split?

Effects of Education and Urbanization

Increased education and urbanization have also changed political attitudes. Openness to political participation and action increased on all indicators between 1972 and 1989. Two-thirds in 1989 reported that they voted in most elections, and most thought Mennonites should vote, should witness to governments, and should hold office if they wished. This varied greatly between elementary educated members, who were less open, and those who had a college and graduate education, almost all of whom favoured such participation.

When asked whether such political action was acceptable in their local congregation, this openness dropped below half, especially when they were asked about endorsing particular candidates and discussing political issues from the pulpit. Three times as many of the most educated favoured political action and discussion of political issues from the pulpit, compared with those who were least educated.

We do not have the space here to present the details on urbanization, where the effects were very similar to the effects of education (Kauffman and Driedger 1991). Almost all large-city Mennonites, who also were more educated, tended to favour political participation, while farm respondents (also less educated) were more reluctant. Again, this difference was especially significant on the political-action questions, with few rural Mennonites in favour of political action in their local church. Since MCs are the most rural and have the least education, this is also reflected in their more conservative attitudes towards politics.

Theology correlated negatively with education. Strong Anabaptists were less open to political participation and action, and strong fundamentalists reacted in roughly the same way. Mennonites committed strongly to Christian beliefs of any variety were less open to political involvement. These differences were not as great and as significant as were education and urbanization, but they were negative. On the other hand, as predicted, as Mennonites become more educated and urban, they become more politically involved. Also as expected, MCs who are most rural are least politically active; Mennonites who are more urban are more open to political involvement.

Emergence of Plural Peace Types

It is not possible here to trace each of the 10 types presented in figure

10.1, but we can present trends represented in the four rural–urban and involved–non-involved cells.

Ranking Items and Attitudes

In table 10.4, we have ranked a dozen items by the extent to which Mennonites in our samples supported peace. Interestingly, four general categories, from traditional to radical attitudes, emerge. Roughly eight out of 10 members of the Mennonite Church held to more traditional peace attitudes advocated by Hershberger, while only half to two-thirds of the EMCs did. As expected, the Goshen non-resistance tradition was strongest among MCs. These traditional attitudes decline slightly between 1972 and 1989.

Somewhat fewer Mennonites supported John Howard Yoder's position on peace witness, but two-thirds or more were in favour of Yoder's position, especially GCs and MCs. Support for Yoder's peace witness position was up in 1989 as compared with 1972. Responsibility peace items promoted by Lawrence Burkholder received considerably less support, only one-third, although the larger denominations again were more in favour than smaller ones. If so few supported responsibility in 1989, it is not surprising that in the 1950s when there were fewer still, Burkholder felt rejected, Mennonites being more rural and more conservative then.

Very few support more radical peace action such as protest, refusal to register, non-payment of taxes, and withholding taxes for war purposes, although there seems to be more openness in 1989 than there was in 1972. Peace radicals and liberationists still have much work to do, as support seems to be limited to a few. We conclude that traditional peace attitudes are preferred by a vast majority of Mennonites, especially by MCs and GCs, and that an increasing majority are also willing to extend a peace witness to others. A minority are open to more socially responsible peace ventures, and relatively few are willing to employ radical action. Again, Mennonite diversity and pluralism are quite evident.

Changing Dimensions of Peacemaking

Peace means many things because it is a diverse concept. We used three peace scales to form a continuum, where the Non-resistance scale represents the least active pole, the Activism scale the most active peacemaking pole, and the Witness scale, in the middle, shows modified forms of the other two scales. In table 10.5, we present this passive–active peace continuum: effects of religious involvement, political participation, modernization, denomination, urbanization, education, ethnicity, nationality, and age.

Using the Kauffman and Driedger (1991) North American survey of five denominations of Mennonites, we found that respondents who scored high on Anabaptist beliefs also scored high on all three Non-resistance, Witness, and Activism scales. That is a telling result, suggesting that Anabaptist theology can bridge a diverse range of expression of peace. Those who scored low hardly scored on non-resistance, but did a little better on more activist expressions of peace. The biggest difference was on non-resistance (r .39). Those who were strong on fundamentalist beliefs scored lower on all three peace scales, with negative witness (r –.24), activist (r –.23), and composite peace (r –.19) results. Those who scored high on devotionalism (prayer, Bible reading) followed the Anabaptist pattern more, with generally positive results, especially on non-resistance (r .25). Those highly involved in church participation also followed the Anabaptist pattern, with positive correlations, again especially for non-resistance (r .24). It is clear that respondents who held to Anabaptist beliefs also favoured peace, often in many diverse forms.

On the other hand, those who were strongly individualistic did not favour peace as much as those who were less so; individualists followed the fundamentalist pattern more, with negative correlations (r –.25, –.18, –.15). This negative pattern was strongest with respect to political participation, where the correlation was negative on all four scales (rs ranging from –.58 to –.12). Political participation is negatively correlated with all forms of peace emphasis.

Denominationally, more than a third of the respondents of the Mennonite Church (MC) scored high on the composite peacemaking scale, while only 2 per cent of the Evangelical Mennonite Church members did so. Looking at the passive–active peace continuum, we see that the MCs scored the highest on the Non-resistance scale. About one-third of the MCs scored high on both the Non-resistance and Activism scales. All other four Mennonite denominations did not have nearly as many who scored high on non-resistance. However, 4 out of 10 General Conference (GC) Mennonites scored high on the Activism scale, the highest of the 5 groups.

We also see in table 10.7 that about one-quarter of rural Mennonites

TABLE 10.4
Mennonite Attitudes towards Peace, by Denomination

War and peace items	Percent in 1989					Totals	
	MC	GC	MB	BIC	EMC	1972	1989
Traditional attitudes							
My church sees the principle of peace as mainly conscientious objection	82	80	83	76	64		81
It is wrong to own stocks in companies which produce war goods	81	78	72	64	55	69	77
Previous service programs (I-W, VS, PAX, TAP) are acceptable alternatives to the military	83	74	59	65	54	80	74
Witness attitudes							
Christians should influence government on war, peace, and other issues	64	75	74	68	68	56	70
The Christian should take no part in war	78	65	56	39	11	73	66
We should actively promote the peace position and win others to it	68	75	53	55	42	56	65
Responsibility attitudes							
It is all right to register, but should refuse induction	48	33	21	24	6	29	37
Members of my church would support those who withhold taxes which go for military purposes	41	34	27	32	17		36
It is not right to accept non-combatant service with the military	46	27	14	13	4	36	31

TABLE 10.4
Mennonite Attitudes towards Peace, by Denomination (*concluded*)

War and peace items	Per cent in 1989					Totals	
	MC	GC	MB	BIC	EMC	1972	1989
Radical attitudes							
Members of my church apply peace principle as non-violent acts of protest against militarism	18	20	17	24	36		19
Youth should refuse to register with the draft	12	21	15	8	1	3	15
Should not pay portion of taxes which go for war purposes	11	15	9	6	5	12	11
Withhold part of taxes in lieu of peace service	2	2	1	2	1		2

scored high on three of the scales. Not nearly as many large-city Mennonites scored high on non-resistance (15 per cent), but twice as many (38 per cent) scored high on peace activism. Overall, composite peacemaking shows little difference, but Mennonites living in the city, much prefer active peace to passive non-resistance. While Men-nonites with elementary education opt about equally for both the passive and activist peace poles, those with more education prefer more active peace. We conclude that urbanization and education do not deter general interest in peace, but rather show that city dwellers want a more active expression of peacemaking and are less keen on traditional non-resistance.

Types of peace preferences also vary by ethnicity and nationality. Roughly one-third of the Swiss scored highly on non-resistance, and one-quarter scored high on peace activism. Twice as many Dutch-heritage Mennonites (16 versus 35 per cent) scored high on peace activism as on non-resistance, the reverse of Swiss choices. In the United States, roughly one-quarter scored high on the non-resistance scale, and as many also scored high on peace activism, similar to the Swiss pattern. Canadian Mennonites, however, who are heavily of Dutch heritage, followed the Dutch pattern, with twice as many scoring high on peace activism as on non-resistance.

There are also differences when controlling for age. North American

TABLE 10.5
Percentage High on Peacemaking Dimensions

Factors		Three dimensions			
		Non-resistance (%)	Witness (%)	Activism (%)	Composite peacemaking (%)
Anabaptist beliefs					
High		37*	26	37	44
Low		6	19	22	16
	(r)	(.39)	(.05)	(.14)	(.28)
Fundamentalist beliefs					
High		28	14	25	25
Low		22	40	50	49
	(r)	(.03)	(−.24)	(−.23)	(−.19)
Devotionalism					
High		32	22	31	33
Low		11	24	32	26
	(r)	(.25)	(−.05)	(−.03)	(.10)
Church participation					
High		31	23	29	36
Low		11	17	30	22
	(r)	(.24)	(.10)	(−.04)	(.12)
Political participation					
High		5	33	23	18
Low		56	8	29	38
	(r)	(−.58)	(−.29)	(−.12)	(−.33)
Individualism					
High		11	14	32	23
Low		37	35	35	44
	(r)	(−.25)	(−.18)	(.01)	(−.15)
Denomination					
MC		34	17	30	36
GC		15	26	41	34
MB		10	21	27	20
BIC		9	17	16	12
EMC		1	22	5	2

TABLE 10.5
Percentage High on Peacemaking Dimensions (*concluded*)

	Three dimensions			
Factors	Non-resistance (%)	Witness (%)	Activism (%)	Composite peacemaking (%)
Urbanization				
Large city	15	30	38	34
Rural	25	16	26	27
Education				
Elementary	33	6	37	31
Graduate school	25	38	39	43
Ethnicity				
Swiss	32	21	28	37
Dutch	16	22	35	30
Nationality				
Canada	18	24	48	36
U.S.	23	19	23	27
Age				
–29	16	24	37	28
30–69	23	21	29	30
70–94	25	9	32	30

*Thirty-seven per cent of Anabaptists (High) scored high on non-resistance

Mennonite respondents over fifty years of age divided equally between non-resistance and activism. However, younger Mennonites preferred peace activism, with twice as many under thirty scoring high on activism as on non-resistance. This suggests that the trend is away from non-resistance and towards increased peace activism in the future.

Conclusions

It is clear from the work of Burkholder that Mennonite commitment to peace has taken a variety of forms. Swiss sectarians have followed non-resistance as their guide, being more reluctant to become involved in the marketplace. Mennonites of Dutch–Russian heritage have always been more culturally engaged, willing to become more politically active, where they have tried to express peace in a more culturally responsive way. Each of the two traditions also has its diversity, expressed in a variety of ways, as postmoderns would expect.

Anabaptist theology, developed in a very diverse complex context during the Reformation, was an attempt at holding renewal of spirit and outreach to others together. Those who are currently strongly Anabaptist also support alternatives to military service, and few wish to serve in military-related services. They are involved in evangelism, service to others, MCC work, the welfare of others, justice, and peacemaking. Those who strongly hold to fundamentalist beliefs are also strong on evangelism, but less inclined towards serving others, are more reluctant to serve in MCC, and help those on welfare, working for justice, and peacemaking. Peace clearly separates two theological positions. As Mennonites become more educated and urban, they tend to embrace Anabaptism more, which includes commitment to peace.

Respondents of Swiss origin who belong to the Mennonite Church hold to more traditional expressions of peace in the form of non-resistance, as well as more active peace outreach. General Conference Mennonites are strongest on peace activism – placing much less emphasis on non-resistance. Very few Evangelical Mennonites favour either form of peace, but rather opt heavily for military-related service. Again, there is much denominational diversity. Youth are increasingly opting for peace activism, and such activism is also much more obvious in Canada, where Dutch-origin Mennonites reside, than in the United States.

Most Anabaptists have always understood love to include concern for peace, even non-participation in war. It is clear that in this post-modern information age Mennonites, too, are expressing themselves in diverse ways. Deconstruction as well as reconstruction have taken place, in many forms, in their 500-year history. While leaders such as Harold Bender tried to help mould more unilinear expressions of this multi-theological, multi-ethnic, multinational, multicultural movement, diversity has always been present, depending on where in the world you look. Many of the elements of postmodern Mennonitism were already present in pre-modern Anabaptism. Mennonites have always struggled with the dialectics of orthodoxy–reformation, Church–State, love–hate, rural–urban, sacred–secular, and that struggle is likely to continue.

Notes

1: The Global Challenge

1 Mennonite data in tables 1.1, 1.2, and 1.3 are taken from the 1984 and 1998 *Mennonite and Brethren in Christ World Directory.* These are adult-membership statistics and do not include non-baptised children and youth. Mennonites observe adult baptism, which takes place between ages fifteen and twenty, although this varies by regions, countries, and denominations. The data have been gathered from Mennonite conferences around the world. Conference staff fill out uniform questionnaires, so that 1984 and 1998 statistics and changes are reasonably reliable and comparable.

2: Emerging Mennonite Urban Professionals

1 The Doopsgesinde held a study conference in Amsterdam in August 1992 with the subtitle 'From Martyrs to Muppies,' which was a reference to Emerson L. Lesher's *The Muppie Manual: The Mennonite Professional's Handbook for Humility and Success.* Lesher's 'Muppie,' for 'Mennonite urban professional,' is the term we have adopted to illustrate the profound changes that have occurred among North American Mennonites. See also Driedger 1993. Lesher's subtitle is a tongue-in-cheek reminder that many of the characteristics of professionalism tend to clash with Swiss Mennonite traditions of 'Gelassenheit' and humility. The strong traditions of the more conservative Anabaptists such as the Amish, the Hutterites, and the Old Colony Mennonites stressed non-conformity to the world, where professional individualism and the quest for success were and are taboo. Modern Mennonite 'urban professionals' in North America are indeed embarking on quite a different journey.

2 Two samples were taken, the first in 1972 (Kauffman and Harder 1975) and the second in 1989 (Kauffman and Driedger 1991), of five Mennonite denominations (Mennonite Church, General Conference Mennonite, Mennonite Brethren, Brethren in Christ, and Evangelical Mennonite) which represented roughly three out of four of the adult Mennonites in the United States and Canada. The sample was selected in two phases: (1) random selection of sample congregations and (2) selection of members from within each sample congregation. A total of 174 congregations participated in the 1972 survey, with 3,591 usable returns. In 1989, 153 congregations participated, and 3,083 usuable returns were received. In each case, the total represented 70 per cent of eligible respondents.

Respondents each filled out a 333-item questionnaire at their respective churches, supervised by a training field supervisor. Denominations varied in size, so smaller denominations were oversampled, and a weighting system was employed to correct for oversampling procedures. Generally, there was reason for confidence that the final results did not unreasonably skew the responses in favour of any denominational, regional, community size, or ideological directions. Both samples are as close to a full census result as could be expected when these methodological procedures were used in complex circumstances.

3 Two belief scales were employed to measure religious orthodoxy and Anabaptism, with four or five items from Kauffman and Driedger (1991) included for each scale. Standard beliefs in God, Jesus Christ, Satan, and life after death are included in the orthodoxy scale (Bibby 1987). Mennonite beliefs such as adult baptism, discipleship, discipline, pacifism, and service are used in the Anabaptist scale (Kauffman and Driedger 1991).

4 Two scales are employed to measure moral attitudes and practice. Both scales include items on drinking, smoking, drug use, premartial sex, homosexual acts, gambling, and dancing. Church participation and devotionalism (Bible study, prayer) are used as measures of religious practice. In-group identity was measured by using indicators of communalism (denominational loyalty, close friends in the Church, feeling accepted, loyality to the Church), ethnicity (use of in-group schools, periodicals, language, organizations, friends, endogamy), and separatism (religion–world dualism, avoiding the world, tensions with society). All of these variables are taken together as indicators of 'local village' orientation.

5 Three general dimensions of orientation to the 'global village' are employed, including Church outreach, social concerns, and participation in society, with items from Kauffman and Driedger (1991) again adopted for the construction of scales. Indicators of Church outreach include evangelism and support of

the Mennonite Central Committee (a relief agency with 1,000 workers in 50 countries). Welfare concerns, race-relations measures, and items on the role of women are employed as indicators of support for social concerns, and out-reach. Ecumenicism (cooperation with other church groups), and scales of attitudes towards politics and towards political action, are important mea-sures of the extent to which respondents are engaged with the larger society.

3: Individualism Shaping Community

1 Also see Driedger 1998.
2 Diane Driedger and the author interviewed twenty-three of the top Menno-nite novelists, poets, and creative writers in Winnipeg in 1997, including the ones mentioned. These creative writers were asked about their background, what inspired their writing, why there were so many Mennonite writers in Winnipeg, and the future of Mennonite creative writers.

4: Cultural Changes in the Sacred Village

1 For a good supplementary source see Driedger 1982.
2 The author has 100 letters of correspondence between Johann Driedger and many others, including ministers, bishops, relatives, and government officials. Many interviews were also conducted in 1955 and in 1977, and it is noteworthy that the oral and written traditions match relatively well. Numerous persons were personally involved when some of these incidents occurred, which is important for documentation especially since some occurrences were rather deviant and incredible.

    The boycott was very effective because the store was located in the nearby hamlet of Osler, near the Mennonite block settlement, and the elders were able to enforce the ban through the threat of excommunication. Excommuni-cation meant that the individual was not supposed to sleep with his wife, or eat with his family, relatives, or church members. He was to be shunned socially. This was enforced only in part, depending on the situation and family.
3 At first the bishop insisted that Driedger restore full relations with Hein-richs, which the two accomplished in writing by 20 August 1913 (three years after the first). However, by now the controversy had escalated, so that Bishop Wiens shifted his demands for repentance to other issues.
4 Driedger's letters to his uncle Elias, and correspondence with the ministers, are laden with scriptural quotations and religious language. While both sides accepted the Bible as their authority, it became readily apparent that

they interpreted it very differently, which had been a problem of Anabaptist biblical disputations since the Reformation.

5 Driedger was actually able to communicate with some of the Old Colony ministers (Loeppky and Wall) quite well. It seemed that Bishop Wiens was the most conservative, and correspondence between Driedger and Wiens shows that it seemed to be a test of wills between these two strong personalities. Indeed, many informants volunteered that it had become a personality clash.

6 A gift of $1,000 to the church in those days was a large sum. Presumably, Driedger wanted to demonstrate his sincerity. Reconciliation would cost him something. The content of these letters to the church is interesting. Nowhere does Driedger admit that he was wrong in his vision for the church. However, the letters are filled with references to grief, and pleas for reconciliation and forgiveness. It was very important to appear humble, a virtue that carried a lot of weight. Driedger was accused of being arrogant, a sin in the Old Colony church.

7 The author made an intensive study of the Hague–Osler Old Colony community in 1955 for an MA degree at the University of Chicago by interviewing as many older Mennonites as possible. Many of these were present at the founding of the villages, and had lived in the villages all their lives. This included Mr Friesen, who founded and named Blumenheim; Mr Peters, who played with the wood blocks coming from the Neuanlage church when it was built; Mr Loeppky of Neuhorst; and many others. This was reported in Driedger 1955. A summary of the study was reported in *Mennonite Life* in two articles, in January and April 1958. Most of those interviewed in 1955 are no longer alive.

The author visited the Hague–Osler villages almost every year since 1965. A second survey of all the villages was again made in 1977. Numerous persons were interviewed, including Julius Enns, the Old Colony bishop living in Warman; Jack Quiring, a young Old Colony minister, and *Schultze* of Reinland; Abram Unruh, a *Schultze* of Blumenthal; Jacob Peters, a minister of the Bergthaler church living in Neuanlage; Jacob Driedger (aged eighty-six), who lived most of his life in Blumenheim; Cornelius Driedger and his wife (both in their eighties) who lived most of their lives in Rosenfeld; Jacob Wolff and his wife, in Neuanlage; Jacob Wiebe, young minister of the Gospel Mission church in Osler; Henry Friesen, first convert to the Pentecostal church in Gruenthal; Peter Wiebe, the last remaining village storekeeper in Gruenfeldt; George Guenther, first Guenther resident of the 'Guenther village' in Hochstadt; and others. The author attended church services, interviewed storekeepers, visited farmers, and spoke to retired residents, and so on, again visiting some of the villages in 1977 and many times later.

5: Media Shifts towards the Global Village

1 See also Driedger and Redekop 1998.

6: The Politics of Homemaking and Career

1 See also Driedger and Halli 1997.

Two samples were taken, in 1972 and 1989, of five Mennonite denominations. We reported the details in note 1, chapter 1, collected by Kauffman and Driedger and reported in *The Mennonite Mosaic*.

The dependent variable is attitudes towards abortion. As indicated in table 6.1, six questions have frequently been asked about abortion, given different situations, and usually elicit a range of responses. The question Are you in favour of abortion? was asked relative to the following situations: (1) the woman's health is seriously endangered; (2) the pregnancy is the result of a rape; (3) there is a strong likelihood of a serious birth defect; (4) the family cannot afford another child; (5) the woman is not married and does not wish to be, and (6) the woman does not want the baby. We present responses to all situations, since most studies show that respondents are more pro-choice on the first (1) and least pro-choice on the last (6), after controlling for socio-economic status.

Independent homemaker and career-orientiation scales were developed that included four variables each. The four questions used in the homemaker scale focused on centrality of the wife's role in the household, her dominance in the household, the husband carrying more responsibility outside the home, and the husband's dominance in decision-making. The four questions used for the career-orientation scale focused on the importance of a woman's career, balancing career and children, balancing career and family, and sharing household tasks equally.

The authors constructed these scales and tested them for reliability. The other four independent-variable scales (Anabaptist beliefs, pacifism, socio-economic status, and individualism) were adopted from the Kauffman and Driedger's studies, which were tested for reliability also.

Three religious-beliefs scales (Orthodoxy, Anabaptist, Fundamentalist) were constructed; we used the Anabaptist scale, which focused on importance of adult baptism, importance of non-resistance, balancing evangelism and service, non-swearing of oaths, and separation of Church and State, because it taps special Mennonite beliefs. The Pacifism scale included items related to alternate service to war, taking no part in war, promotion of peace, non-ownership of war stocks, and non-payment of taxes for war. These, too, were tested for reliability.

2 The analysis was performed in two stages. In the first stage, simple bivariate relationships were examined between attitudes towards pro-life or pro-choice and other theoretically important independent variables. These were zero-order relationships, without controlling for other background variables. Hence, the conclusions drawn from these bivariate tables were considered tentative. Variables such as individualism, working outside the home, being a housewife, and salience of anabaptist theology were affected by the socio-economic status of the respondents. Hence, a critical test of the hypotheses could be made only by controlling for socio-ecomonic background variables simultaneously in the form of multivariate analysis. The second stage of analysis involved a method of logistic regression, using as our dichotomous dependent variable pro-life or pro-choice.

We selected background variables based on findings in previous studies and availability of data. Independent variables included attitudes about women involved in careers and those who chose to be homemakers, Anabaptist theology, pacifism, education, income, occupation, individualism, age, and gender. Some of these variables were not measured at interval levels, and had to be manipulated to be included in the logistic regression. For example, variables such as homemaking and women's career included three categories, high, medium, and low. The categories low and high were excluded as reference categories from the equation for homemaking and women's career, respectively. The other variables – Anabaptist theology, individualism, and pacifism – included four categories: low, medium low, medium high, and high. The category high was used as the reference category for pacifism, and low was used for Anabaptist theology and individualism. For the variable gender, the reference category was female, and for occupation, the reference category was farmer.

In our analysis of Mennonite attitudes, we have employed the more conventional logit model to explore the odds of conditional probability of pro-choice or pro-life. The binary dependent variable for the analysis is constructed by assigning the individual a value of one for pro-choice attitudes, and zero for pro-life attitudes.

In table 5.3 we present the results of our logit analyses. The estimated coefficients (including the constant term) are shown after exponentiating them to reflect the odds ratios. Similar to the concept of relative risk, the odds ratio shows the proportional effect on the odds of occurrence of the event (pro-choice attitude) from a one-unit change in the covariate, when the variable is continuous. In the case of a categorical variable, the odds ratio provides the odds associated with the given category, relative to the odds for the reference category. While the odds ratio of greater than one implies a positive effect of the covariate on the occurrence of the event, the odds ratio of less than one is indicative of a negative relationship.

7: Teens Growing Roots and Wings

1 A sample taken in 1989 of five Mennonite denominations (Mennonite Church, General Conference Mennonite, Mennonite Brethren, Brethren in Christ, and Evangelical Mennonite), which represented about 75 per cent of the Mennonites in the United States and Canada, we have used freely in this book. A detailed discussion on methods can be found in Kauffman and Driedger 1991, pp. 273–7.

2 The 1994 Churched Youth Survey was completed by the cooperation of the Josh McDowell Ministry, thirteen denomination leaders, and the Barna Research Group, Ltd. The eight-page survey questionnaire was drafted by the Josh McDowell Ministry Research Center, with input from the participating denominational leaders. The questionnaire was pretested, and was completed anonymously by 3,795 churched youth in late 1993 and early 1994. Each denomination was given the goal of surveying 500 youth from their total church list using a 'multistage stratified random sample probability sample.' Surveys were distributed and completed during a regular youth-group meeting with no prior notice. The thirteen denominations included Assemblies of God, Church of God – Cleveland, Church of God – General Conference, Church of the Nazarene, Foursquare Gospel Church, Free Methodist Church, The Friends Church, International Pentecostal Holiness Church, The Salvation Army, Southern Baptist Convention, The Wesleyan Church, and two Mennonite denominations: the Mennonite Church, and the General Conference Mennonite Church. Findings from this survey of churched youth are more positive than those of general Mennonite youth by Kauffman and Driedger (1991), because churched youth are members and attending church. Also see Driedger and Bergen 1995.

3 Here we are again using Kauffman and Driedger's (1991) data of North American Mennonites, described and used in table 7.1, and described in note 1.

8: Blending Educational Monastery and Marketplace

1 See Driedger 1997. The enrolment data for the seven U.S. Mennonite colleges and the three Mennonite seminaries were gathered from the September, October, and November issues of *The Mennonite Weekly Review* (*MWR*), these data are usually published on page 12, in the 'colleges' section. We also contacted the registrars of all seven U.S. colleges, three seminaries, and the six Canadian colleges, asking them to confirm these data (Canadian College data were not reported in the *MWR*), as well as to supply further information, where it was available. Full-time students, Mennonite students, and full-time-equivalent enrolment figures were obtained from these schools.

2 Total student enrolment (TS) includes all students who have registered for one course or more. Full-time (FT) enrolment includes all students who have registered for four or more courses, or twelve or more hours of classes. Part-time (PT) enrolment includes students who have enrolled in one to three courses, or one to eleven hours of classes. Full-time equivalent (FTE) enrolment includes total number of courses taken, divided by four courses, or 12 hours of registered classwork. Most Mennonite schools follow this formula, except that a few, including the seminaries, count somewhat fewer courses or hours. Conrad Grebel College, located on the campus of the University of Waterloo, is an exception, so we have included all students who are staying in the college dormitories, are registered to take a full academic load, and eat and sleep on the college campus.

3 The two Mennonite Bible colleges in Winnipeg had similar beginnings but have since parted ways. Mennonite Brethren Bible College (MBBC) began in 1944, Canadian Mennonite Bible College (CMBC) in 1947, both the first in a metropolis (Winnipeg). In 1970 their enrolments were similar, CMBC having 122 students and MBBC 109, and their total student counts are very similar in 1993, with MBBC counting 235 and CMBC 220. However, CMBC enrolments have been more steady, with mostly full-time (88 per cent) and a high percentage of Mennonite students (85 per cent), as compared with MBBC. In 1993, MBBC changed its name to Concord. In 1971, 94 per cent of MBBC students were Mennonite, while in 1993 this figure had dropped to 40 per cent. While in 1970, 70 per cent of MBBC students were full-time, in 1993 this figure had dropped to 17 per cent, with only 39 students full-time and 196 part-time at Concord College. Full-time students at Concord dropped below 50 per cent in 1987, when their total numbers rose from 192 to 213, and enrolments dropped to less than half Mennonite in 1990. Many Mennonite Brethren members have moved to British Columbia, so the largest number of MBs are now in that province, supporting Columbia Bible College in Clearbrook. This has made it more difficult for Concord to maintain its Mennonite major-

ity. While total student numbers have remained similar to CMBC totals, Concord has sacrificed both Mennonite student counts and full-time student counts. Whether Concord can maintain an Anabaptist community college in a large metropolis with losses of both Mennonite and full-time students will be the test. Recently the Concord College board has explored relocating in Tuxedo, across the street from CMBC; the move is scheduled to take place in 2000.

4 The *Student Phone Directory* 11/3 (1992–3) lists the names of 28,000 University of Manitoba students. We surveyed the list and identified 1,595 student names of Mennonite origin. Sixteen of the identifiable family names made up half of these students: Friesen occurred 103 times, Dyck/Dueck/Dick 93, Wiebe 74, Penner 72, Peters 59, Klassen 41, Reimer 36, Loewen 34, Thiessen/Tiessen 34, Rempel 33, Hildebrand 32, Enns/Ens 31, Giesbrecht 30, Kroeker 30, Martens 30, and Neufeld 30. The University of Manitoba Telephone Directory (October 1993) listed the names of 1,935 faculty and staff, of which 82 faculty and 97 staff (a total of 179 names) could be identified as having Mennonite family names. Although the author could personally confirm that many of these faculty were active Mennonite church members, we do not know what percentage of the faculty, staff, or students are active Mennonite members. We assume that these numbers are not all that different from Mennonite school figures, where not all students are active Mennonite members either.

9: The Emergence of Women as New Leaders

1 Two surveys of five Mennonite denominations (Mennonite Church, General Conference Mennonite, Mennonite Brethren, Brethren in Christ, and Evangelical Mennonite [For Wayne]) were taken in 1972 ($N = 3,591$) and 1989 ($N = 3,083$). The data for 1989 used here are taken from a questionnaire containing 333 questions, best reported in Kauffman and Driedger 1991, which can be consulted for more methodological details. The 1972 data used are best reported in Kauffman and Harder 1975.

2 An additive scale tapping attitudes about the role of women was created using three survey items shown in table 9.1. The alpha reliability coefficient for the scale was .70, with an N of 6,573, combining the 1972 and 1989 samples. Enormous change has occurred between 1972 and 1989 with regard to attitudes on the roles of women. Support from women in leadership roles has risen 1.17 points; in other words, there has been a 19.5 per cent increase in the six-point scale over seventeen years. The R-square values reflect these relative differences, where 8.6 per cent of the variability was explained by a change in the role of women.

3 The MB conference voted as recently as the 1990s to disallow full ordination of women into the ministry. Since then numerous MB groups, especially in Canada, have formed in cities such as Winnipeg to debate the issue, and agree on plans for further action. See also Coger 1983; Epp 1990; Fischer 1988; Neufeld 1990; and Noren 1991.

4 These data are taken from Carroll, Hargrove, and Lummis 1983, a source that can be consulted for more methodological details. They interviewed samples of clergywomen (N = 739), clergymen (N = 635), lay leaders, and other Church officials in nine denominations, including American Baptist, American Lutheran, Christian Church (Disciples), Episcopal, Lutheran Church of America, Presbyterian (U.S.), United Church of Christ, United Methodist, and United Presbyterian (U.S.) churches in the United States. They included a questionnaire with 94 multidimensional questions in an appendix, from which we drew many of the data on U.S. clergy used here. We also use these data in tables 9.3–9.5.

5 Renee Sauder (1993), a Mennonite minister with pastoral experience in several churches, found 186 Mennonite women who had had pastoral experience in Mennonite churches, and 134 of these completed questionnaires in a survey she conducted for the Mennonite Board of Missions in 1993. Since the questionnaire contained 172 items, many of which were identical to the questions asked by Carroll, Hargrove, and Lummis (1983), these surveys could be compared, even though one was conducted in 1983 and the other ten years later, in 1993. The Sauder survey had a 72 per cent response rate, including 95 U.S. and 38 Canadian Mennonite women with a median age of forty-five and 82 per cent of whom attended seminary. Seventy-seven per cent were married and living with their spouse, 14 per cent were single, and 8 per cent were widowed or divorced. These women originated mostly from the General Conference and Mennonite Church denominations. We use Sauder's sample of Mennonite female clergy in tables 9.3–9.5 and compare trends with Carroll and colleagues' (1983) data. See also Driedger and Nickel Friesen 1995.

10: Peacemaking as Ultimate Extension

1 When I was executive secretary of the Peace and Social Concerns Committee of the General Conference Mennonite Church in Newton (1957–62), our committee on occasion invited Guy Hershberger, then executive secretary of the Peace Problems Committee of the Mennonite Church to speak and actively get involved in the work of our committee. Hershberger spent a lot of time working on alternatives to membership in labour unions. It was

obvious that members of our committee, such as Gordon Kaufman, Robert Kreider, and Don Smucker, held quite different views, which at that time were not as clear to us. We often went to MCC annual meetings, where Harold Bender and Orie Miller were concerned about serving their conservative constituency and where Bender's two-kingdom theology was especially evident. Many of us who were younger could not understand it. At the time John Howard Yoder's theology seemed more relevant.

2 Wuthnow 1981, 1987, 1988a; Dayton and Johnston 1991; Hunter, 1987; Marsden 1984; Rawlyk, 1990.

3 As a student in E.G. Kaufman's 'Basic Christian Convictions' class at Bethel College (1953–4), I found Kaufman's openness to explore all facets of theology very stimulating and challenging. He tried to apply his peace insights as a missionary in China, he had led Bethel through some rough war years in the 1940, and he often talked about sociologists, such as Burgess and Wirth, who had influenced him at the University of Chicago. At the time he had hired a number of Chicago faculty, such as Fretz and R.C. Kaufman, who wrestled with what it meant to be culturally engaged in politics, economics, and theology. It is not surprising that his son, Gordon Kaufman, took a graduate degree in sociology, which has greatly influenced his theological journey as well.

4 For more detail and information, see Dayton and Johnston 1991; and Marsden 1984. Pearson's r correlations are statistically significant when they are a plus or minus .045 or higher. Correlations running between .045 and –.045, which cluster around zero, are considered insignificantly related. In our comparisons we shall consider scores of .10 to –.10 low, scores of plus or minus .10 to .30 moderately correlated, and scores above plus or minus .40 as high. A positive correlation of .48 between Anabaptist theology and peacemaking means that both are high, and one rises as the other does. A negative correlation of –.30 between fundamentalism and peacemaking means that those who score positively on fundamentalism score negatively on questions related to peace. The two go in opposite directions and are negatively associated.

References

Abbott, Andres. 1988. 'Of Time and Space: The Contemporary Relevance of the Chicago School.' *Social Forces* 75: 1149–82

Abbott, Andrew. 1997. 'Transcending General Linear Reality.' *Sociology Theory* 6: 169–86

Ainlay, Stephen C. 1990. 'Communal Commitment and Individualism.' In Leo Driedger and Leland Harder, eds., *Anabaptist–Mennonite Identities in Ferment.* Elkhart, IN: Institute of Mennonite Studies

Anderson, Alan B. 1972. 'Assimilation in the Bloc Settlements of North-Central Saskatchewan: A Comparative Study of Identity Change among Seven Ethno-Religious Groups in a Canadian Prairie Region.' Unpublished PhD dissertation, University of Saskatchewan

Anderson, Cora. 1990. 'Shall Women Preach? Principles and Practices in the Salvation Army and in the Methodist Church in Ontario.' *Conrad Grebel Review* 8: 275–88

Askew, Thomas A. 1987. 'The Shaping of Evangelical Higher Education Since World War II.' In Joel Carpenter and Kenneth Shipps, eds., *Making Higher Education Christian: The History and Mission of Evangelical Colleges in America.* Grand Rapids, MI: Christian University Press

Barnartt, S.N., and R.J. Harris. 1992. 'Recent Predicters of Abortion Attitudes.' *Sociology and Social Research* 66: 320–34

Basran, Guracharn. 1992. 'Change in Agriculture in Canada: Theoretical Perspectives.' In D. Hay and G. Basran, eds., *Rural Sociology in Canada.* Toronto: Oxford University Press

Bellah, Robert N., Richard Madsen, William M. Sullivan, Ann Swidler, and Steven M. Tipton, eds. 1985. *Individualism and Commitment to American Life: Readings on the Themes of Habits of the Heart.* New York: Harper and Row

Bender, Harold S. 1944. 'The Anabaptist Women.' *Church History* 18: 3–24

– 1959. 'Status of Women: Anabaptism.' *Mennonite Encyclopedia*, vol. 5. Scottdale, PA: Mennonite Publishing House

Berger, Peter L. 1967. *The Sacred Canopy: Elements of a Sociological Theory of Religion*. Garden City, NY: Doubleday

– 1977. *Facing Up to Modernity*. New York: Basic Books

Berry, J.W., and J.A. Laponce. 1994. *Ethnicity and Culture in Canada: The Research Landscape*. Toronto: University of Toronto Press

Bibby, Reginald W. 1987a. 'Bilingualism and Multiculturalism: A National Reading.' In Leo Driedger, ed., *Ethnic Canada: Identities and Inequalities*. Toronto: Irwin

– 1987b. *Fragmented Gods: The Poverty and Potential of Religion in Canada*. Toronto: Irwin

Bibby, Reginald W., and Donald C. Posterski. 1985. *The Emerging Generation: An Inside Look at Canada's Teenagers*. Toronto: Irwin

– 1992. *Teen Trends: A Nation in Motion*.Toronto: Stoddart Publishing

Brandt, Di. 1987. *Questions I Asked My Mother*. Stratford, IN: Mercury Press

Brested, James A., and Carl F. Huth. 1961. *European History Atlas: Ancient, Medieval and Modern European History*. Chicago: Denoyer-Geppert

Burkholder, J. Lawrence. 1989. *The Problem of Social Responsibility from the Perspective of the Mennonite Church*. Elkhart, IN: Institute of Mennonite Studies

Burkholder, John Richard. 1991. 'Can We Make Sense of Mennonite Peace Theology?' In John R. Burkholder and Barbara N. Gingerich, eds., *Mennonite Peace Theology: A Panorama of Types*. Akron, PA: Mennonite Central Committee

Burkholder, John R., and Barbara N. Gingerich, eds. 1991. *Mennonite Peace Theology: A Panorama of Types*. Akron, PA: Herald Press

Burkholder, John R., and Calvin Redekop, eds. 1976. *Kingdom, Cross, and Community*. Scottdale, PA: Herald Press

Burnet, Jean R. 1988. *'Coming Canadians': An Introduction to a History of Canada's Peoples*. Toronto: McClelland & Stewart

Cahoone, Lawrence, ed. 1996. *From Modernism to Postmodernism: An Anthology*. Oxford: Blackwell

Carey, James W. 1989. *Communication as Culture: Essays on Media and Society*. Boston: Unwin Hyman

Carroll, Jackson W., Barbara Hargrove, and Adair T. Lummis. 1983. *Women of the Cloth: A New Opportunity for the Churches*. New York: Harper and Row

Clarke, A. 1987. 'Moral Protest, Status Defense, and the Anti-Abortion Campaign.' *British Journal of Sociology* 8: 2–15

Cleghorn, S.J. 1986. 'Research Note on Cardinal Bernadin's "Seamless Garment."' *Review of Religious Research* 28: 129–42

Clement, Wallace. 1988. *The Challenge of Class Analysis*. Ottawa: Carleton University Press

Coenen, W.L.C. 1920. *Bydrage tot de Kennis van de mastshappelijke verhoundingern van de zeitiedeeeniwische Doopera*. Amsterdam: Amsterdam Press

Coger, Marian. 1983. *Women in Parish Ministry: Stress and Support*. Washington, DC: Alban Institute

Coser, Lewis. 1956. *The Functions of Social Conflict*. New York: The Free Press

Cuneo, Carl J. 1990. *Pay Equity: The Labour–Feminist Challenge*. Toronto: Oxford University Press

Dahrendorf, Rolf. 1959. *Class and Class Conflict in Industrial Society*. Palo Alto, CA: Stanford University Press

Dayton, Donald W., and Robert K. Johnston, eds. 1991. *The Variety of American Evangelism*. Downer's Grove, IL: InterVarsity Press

Derrida, Jacques. 1974. 'The End of the Book and the Beginning of Writing.' In Jacques Derrida, *Of Grammatology*. Baltimore: Johns Hopkins University Press

Doerksen, Victor G., George H. Epp, Harry Loewen, Elizabeth Peters, and Al Reimer, eds. 1985–90. *Collected Works of Arnold Dyck*. vols. I–IV. Winnipeg: Manitoba Historical Society

Driedger, Leo. 1955. A Sect in a Modern Society: The Old Colony Mennonites of Saskatchewan. Unpublished MA thesis, University of Chicago

– 1973. 'Impelled Migration: Minority Struggle to Maintain Institutional Completeness.' *International Migration Review* 7: 257–59

– 1977a. 'Mennonite Change: The Old Colony Revisited, 1955–77.' *Mennonite Life* 32: 4–12

– 1977b. 'Research Notes of the 1977 Survey of the Fifteen Old Colony Villages.' Unpublished

– 1982. 'Individual Freedom vs. Community Control: An Adaptation of Erikson's Ontogeny of Ritualization.' *Journal for the Scientific Study of Religion* 21: 226–42

– 1986. 'Community Conflict: The Eldorado Invasion of Warman.' *Canadian Review of Sociology and Anthropology* 23: 247–69

– 1987. *Ethnic Canada: Identity and Inequality*. Toronto: Copp Clark Pitman

– 1988. *Mennonite Identity in Conflict*. Lewiston, NY: Edwin Mellen

– 1989. 'Urbanization of Mennonites in Post-War Canada.' *Journal of Mennonite Studies* 7: 90–100

– 1990. *Mennonites in Winnipeg*. Winnipeg: Kindred Press

– 1991. *The Urban Factor: Sociology of Canadian Cities*. Toronto: Oxford University Press

– 1992. 'The Peace Panorama: A Struggle for the Mennonite Soul.' *Conrad Grebel Review* 10: 289–308

- 1993. 'From Martyrs to Muppies: The Mennonite Urban Professional Revolution.' *Mennonite Quarterly Review* 66: 304–22
- 1994. 'Winnipeg Mennonites in Business: The Family Compact.' In Calvin Redekop, Victor Krahn, and Samuel Steiner, eds., *Anabaptist/Mennonite Faith and Economics*. Lanham, MD: University Press of America
- 1995. 'Alert Opening and Closing: Mennonite Rural–Urban Changes.' *Rural Sociology* 60: 323–32
- 1996. *Multi-Ethnic Canada: Identities and Inequalities*. Toronto: Oxford University Press
- 1997. 'Monastery or Marketplace? Changing Mennonite College/ Seminary Enrollments.' *Journal of Mennonite Studies*: 15: 56–79
- 1998. 'Individualism Shaping Community.' In William Brackney, ed., *The Believer's Church: A Voluntary Church*. Kitchener, ON: Pandora 93

Driedger, Leo and Abe Bergen. 1995. 'Growing Roots and Wings: Emergence of Mennonites Teens.' *Journal of Mennonite Studies* 13: 146–69

Driedger, Leo, and Shiva Halli. 1997. 'Pro-Life and Pro-Choice: Politics of Career and Homemaking.' *Population Studies* 51: 129–37

Driedger, Leo, and Leland Harder. eds. 1990. *Anabaptist–Mennonite Identities in Ferment*. Elkhart, IN: Institute of Mennonite Studies

Driedger, Leo, and J. Howard Kauffman. 1982. 'Urbanization of Mennonites: Canadian and American Comparisons.' *Mennonite Quarterly Review* 55: 269–90

Driedger, Leo, and Donald B. Kraybill. 1994. *Mennonite Peacemaking: From Quietism to Activism*. Scottdale, PA: Herald Press

Driedger, Leo, and Dorothy Nickel Friesen. 1995. 'Mennonite Women in Pastoral Leadership.' *Mennonite Quarterly Review* 68: 487–504

Driedger, Leo, and Paul Redekop. 1998. 'Testing the Innis and McLuhan Theses: Mennonite Media Access and TV Use.' *Canadian Review of Sociology and Anthropology* 35: 43–64

Driedger, Leo, Roy Vogt, and Mavis Reimer. 1983. 'Mennonite Intermarriage: National, Regional and Intergenerational Trends.' *Mennonite Quarterly Review* 57: 132–44

Driedger, Leo, Michael Yoder, and Peter Sawatzky. 1985. 'Divorce Among Mennonites: Evidence of Family Breakdown.' *Mennonite Quarterly Review* 59: 367–82

Dyck, C.J. 1973. *Twelve Becoming: Biographies of Mennonite Disciples*. Newton, KS: Faith and Life Press

Enns, Robert. 1995. '"Community" and the Pacific College Idea: Dilemmas in the Institutionalization of Religion.' In Paul Toews, ed., *Mennonite Idealism and Higher Education: The Story of the Fresno Pacific College Idea*. Fresno, CA: Center for Mennonite Brethren Studies

Epp, Frank H. 1974. *Mennonites in Canada, 1786–1920: A History of Separate People*. Toronto: Macmillan of Canada

– 1982. *Mennonites in Canada, 1920–1940: A People's Struggle for Survival*. Toronto: Macmillan

Epp, Marlene. 1990. 'Carrying the Banner of Nonconformity: Ontario Women and the Dress Questions.' *Conrad Grebel Review* 8: 237–57

Erikson, Erik A. 1977. *Toys and Reasons: Stages in the Ritualization of Experience*. New York: W.W. Norton

Fischer, Kathleen. 1988. *Women at the Well: Feminist Perspectives on Spiritual Direction*. New York: Paulist Press

Fleras, Augie. 1994. 'Media and Minorities in a Post-Multicultural Society: Overview and Apprisal.' In J.W. Berry and J.A. Laponce, eds., *Ethnicity and Culture: The Research Landscape*. Toronto: University of Toronto Press

Francis, E.K. 1955. *In Search of Utopia: The Mennonites in Manitoba*. Altona, MN: D.W. Friesen and Sons

Friedan, Betty. 1965. *The Feminine Mystique*. New York: Dell Publishing

Friesen, Lauren. 1991. 'Culturally Engaged Pacifism.' In John R. Burkholder and Barbara N. Gingerich, eds., *Mennonite Peace Theology: A Panorama of Types*. Akron, PA: Mennonite Central Committee

Friesen, Patrick. 1980. *The Shunning*. Winnipeg: Turnstone

– 1997. *A Broken Bowl*. London, ON: Brick Books

Fuller, Tony, Philip Ehrensaft, and Michael Gertler. 1990. 'Sustainable Rural Communities in Canada: Issues and Prospects.' In M. Gertler and H. Baker, eds., *Sustaining Rural Communities in Canada*. Saskatoon, SK: Canadian Agricultural Restructuring Group

Gans, Herbert. 1962. *The Urban Villagers*. Glencoe, IL: Free Press

Glazer, Nathan, and Daniel P. Moynihan. 1963. *Beyond the Melting Pot*. Cambridge, MA: MIT Press

Glock, Charles Y., B.B. Ringer, and E.R. Babbie. 1967. *To Comfort and to Challenge: Dilemma of the Contemporary Church*. Berkeley: University of California Press

Gordon, Milton M. 1964. *Assimilation in American Life*. New York: Oxford University Press

Granbert, Donald, and Beth W. Granbert. 1986. 'Abortion Attitudes, 1965–1985: Trends and Determinants.' *Family Planning Perspectives* 12: 250–61

Grenz, Stanley J. 1996. *A Primer on Postmodernism*. Grand Rapids, MI: W.B. Eerdmans

Habermas, Jürgen. 1996. 'An Alternative Way Out of the Philosophy of the Subject: Communicative Versus Subject-Centered Reason.' In Jürgen Habermas, *The Philosophical Discourse of Modernity*. Cambridge, MA: MIT Press

Hall, David. 1991. 'Modern China and the Postmodern West.' In Eliot Deutsch, ed., *Culture and Modernity: East–West Philosophic Pespectives*. Honolulu: University of Hawaii Press

Hanson, P., and A. Muszynaki. 1990. 'Crisis in Rural Life and Crisis in Thinking: Directions for Critical Research.' *Canadian Review of Sociology and Anthropology* 27: 1–22

Hay, David A. 1992. 'Rural Canada in Transition: Trends and Developments.' In D. Hay and G. Basran, eds., *Rural Sociology in Canada*. Toronto: Oxford University Press

Hay, David A., and Guracharn S. Basran, eds. 1992. *Rural Sociology in Canada*. Toronto: Oxford University Press

Herberg, Will. 1955. *Protestant, Catholic, Jew*. New York: Doubleday

Hershberger, Guy F. 1944. *War, Peace and Nonresistance*. Scottdale, PA: Herald Press

Hess, E.M. 1977. 'A Study of the Influence of Mennonite Schools on Their Students in the Lancaster (Pennsylvania) Conference of the Mennonite Church.' *Mennonite Quarterly Review* 51: 78–9

Holland, Scott. 1995. 'Communal Hermeneutics as Body Politics or Disembodied Theology?' *Brethren Life and Thought* 40: 94–110

Hollander, E.P. 1960. 'Competence and Conformity in the Acceptance of Influence.' *Journal of Abnormal and Social Psychology* 61: 365–9

Hoover, Stewart M. 1995. 'Media and the Moral Order in Postpositivist Approaches to Media Studies.' *Journal of Communications* 45: 136–46

Hornaday, John A. 1982. 'Research about Living Entrepreneurs.' In *Encyclopedia of Entrepreneurship*, ed. Calvin Kent et al. Engelwood Cliffs, NJ: Prentice-Hall

Innis, Harold A. 1951. *The Bias of Communication*. Toronto: University of Toronto Press

– 1952. *Changing Concepts of Time*. Toronto: University of Toronto Press

– 1954. 'Concepts of Monopoly and Civilization.' *Explorations* No. 3: 7–16

Jaggar, Alison W., and Paula Rothenberg Struhl. 1978. *Feminist Frameworks: Alternative Theoretical Accounts of the Relations between Men and Women*. New York: McGraw-Hill

Juhnke, James C. 1992. 'A Historical Look at the Development of Mennonite Higher Education in the United States.' Paper presented at the Symposium 'Mennonite Higher Education Experience and Vision,' 26–8 June 1992, Bluffton, OH

Juhnke, James C. 1989. *Vision, Doctrine, War: Mennonite Identity and Organization in America, 1890–1930*. Scottdale, PA: Herald Press

Kanagy, Conrad L. 1996. 'Changing Mennonite Values: Attitudes on Women, Politics and Peace, 1972–1989.' *Review of Religious Research* 37: 143–61

Kant, Immanuel. 1970. 'An Answer to the Question: What is the Enlightenment?' In H.B. Nisbet and Hans Reiss, eds., *Kant's Political Writings*. Cambridge: Cambridge University Press

Karim, H. Karim, and Gareth Sansom. 1990. *Ethnicity and the Mass Media in Canada: An Annotated Bibliography*. Ottawa: Multiculturalism and Citizenship

Kauffman, J. Howard, and Leo Driedger. 1991. *The Mennonite Mosaic: Identity and Modernization*. Scottdale, PA: Herald Press

Kaufman, Gordon D. 1985. *Theology for a Nuclear Age*. Philadelphia: Westminster University Press

Kauffman, J. Howard. 1989. 'Dilemmas of Christian Pacifism Within a Historic Peace Church.' *Sociology Analysis* 49: 368–85

Kauffman, J. Howard, and Leland Harder. 1975. *Anabaptists Four Centuries Later: A Profile of Five Mennonite and Brethren in Christ Denominations*. Scottdale, PA: Herald Press

Keim, Albert N. 1990. *The CPS Story: An Illustrated History of Civilian Public Service*. Intercourse, PA: Good Books

Keohane, Nannerl O., Michelle Z. Rosaldo, and Barbara C. Gelpi, eds. 1982. *Feminist Theory: A Critique of Ideology*. Chicago: University of Chicago Press

Keyfitz, N. 1995. 'What Happened in Cairo? A View From the Internet.' *Canadian Journal of Sociology* 20: 81–9

Klassen, Peter J. 1989. *A Homeland for Strangers: An Introduction to Mennonites in Poland and Prussia*. Fresno, CA: Center for Mennonite Brethren Studies

Klippenstein, Lawrence, ed. 1979. *That There Be Peace: Mennonites in Canada and World War II*. Winnipeg: Manitoba CO Reunion Committee

Krahn, Cornelius. 1959. 'Status of Women: Prussian–Russian Background.' *Mennonite Encyclopedia*, vol. 4. Scottdale, PA: Mennonite Publishing House

– 1980. 'Dutch Mennonites Prospered in "Golden Age."' *Mennonite Weekly Review* 58: 6–8

– 1981. *Dutch Anabaptism: Origin, Spread, Life, and Thought*. Scottdale, PA: Herald Press

Kraybill, Donald B. 1977a. 'A Content and Structural Analysis of Mennonite High School Songs.' *Mennonite Quarterly Review* 51: 52–66

– 1977b. 'Religious and Ethnic Socialization in a Mennonite High School.' *Mennonite Quarterly Review* 51: 329–51

– 1978. *Mennonite Education: Issues, Facts and Changes*. Scottdale, PA: Herald Press

Kraybill, Donald B., and Phyllis Pellman Good, eds. 1982. *Perils of Professionalism*. Scottdale, PA: Herald Press

Kreider, Robert, and Rachel Waltner Goossen. 1988. *Hungry, Thirsty, a Stranger: The MCC Experience*. Scottdale, PA: Herald Press

Kuhn, Thomas. 1962. 'The Nature and Necessity of Scientific Revolutions.' In Thomas Kuhn, *The Structure of Scientific Revolutions*. Chicago: University of Chicago Press

Lam, Lawrence. 1980. 'The Role of Ethnic Media on Immigrants: A Case Study of Chinese Immigrants and Their Media in Toronto.' *Canadian Ethnic Studies* 12: 74–90

Lesher, Emerson L. 1985. *The Muppie Manual: The Mennonite Professional's Handbook for Humility and Success*. Intercourse, PA: Good Books

Levine, N., Ellwood B. Carter, and Eleanor Miller Gorman. 1976. 'Simmel's Influence on American Sociology.' *American Journal of Sociology* 81: 813–45

Levinson, Paul. 1990. 'What If He Is Right?' *Canadian Psychology* 35: 355–7

Lewis, Oscar. 1960. *Tepoztlan: A Village in Mexico*. New York: Holt, Rinehart and Winston

Lichdi, Diether Goertz, ed. 1990. *Mennonite World Handbook: Mennonites in Global Witness*. Carol Stream, IL: Mennonite World Conference

Loewen, Harry, ed. 1988. *Why I Am a Mennonite: Essays on Mennonite Identity*. Scottdale, PA: Herald Press

Luker, K. 1984. *Abortion and the Politics of Motherhood*. Berkeley: University of California Press

Luxton, Meg. 1980. *More Than a Labour of Love*. Toronto: Women's Press

Lynd, Robert S., and Helen Merrill Lynd. 1929. *Middletown*. New York: Harcourt, Brace and Company

Lynd, Robert S., and Helen Merrill Lynd. 1937. *Middletown in Transition*. New York: Harcourt, Brace and Company

Lyon, David. 1994. *Postmodernity*. Minneapolis: University of Minnesota Press

Lyotard, Jean-François. 1984. *The Postmodern Condition: A Report on Knowledge*. Minneapolis: University of Minnesota Press

MacMaster, Richard K. 1985. *Land, Piety, Peoplehood: The Establishment of Mennonite Communities in America, 1683–1790*. Scottdale, PA: Harold Press

Marsden, George M. 1991. *Understanding Fundamentalism and Evangelicalism*. Grand Rapids, MI: W.B. Eerdmans

Marsden, George M., ed. 1984. *Evangelicalism and the Modern American*. Grand Rapids, MI: W.B. Eerdmans

Martens, Katherine, and Heidi Harms, eds. 1997. *In Her Own Voice: Childbirth Stories from Mennonite Women*. Winnipeg: University of Manitoba Press

Mauss, Armand L. 1994. *The Angel and the Beehive: The Mormon Struggle with Assimilation*. Urbana, IL: University of Illinois Press

McIlwraith, Robert D. 1994. 'Marshall McLuhan and the Psychology of Television.' *Canadian Psychology* 35: 331–50

McLeod, J.R. 1991. 'The Seamless Web: Media and Power in the Post-Modern Global Village.' *Journal of Popular Culture* 25: 2–9

McLuhan, Marshall. 1964. *Understanding Media: The Extensions of Man.* New York: McGraw-Hill

McNeill, William H. 1986. *Poly-Ethnicity and National Unity in World History.* Toronto: University of Toronto Press

Mennonite World Conference. 1984. *Mennonite World Handbook and Mennonite World Conference Map.* Kitchener, ON: Mennonite World Conference

– 1998. *Mennonite and Brethren in Christ World Directory, 1998.* Strasbourg, France: Mennonite World Conference

Moore, John Allen. 1984. *Anabaptist Portraits.* Scottdale, PA: Herald Press

Mowlana, Hamid. 1983. 'Mass Media and Culture: Toward an Integrated Theory.' In William B. Gudykunst, ed., *Intercultural Communication Theory.* Beverly Hills: Sage

Nagel, Joan. 1984. 'The Ethnic Revolution Emergence of Ethnic Nationalism.' *Sociology and Social Research* 69: 417–34

National Geographic Society. 1998. *Population: Millennium in Maps.* Washington, DC: National Geographic Society

Nett, Emily. 1988. *Canadian Families: Past and Present.* Toronto: Butterworths

Neufeld, Tom Yoder. 1990. 'Paul, Women and Ministry in the Church.' *Conrad Grebel Review* 8: 289–99

Newman, William M. 1973. *American Pluralism: A Study of Minority Groups and Social Theory.* New York: Harper and Row

Niebuhr, H. Richard. 1951. *Christ and Culture.* New York: Harper and Row

Noren, Carol M. 1991. *The Women in the Pulpit.* Nashville: Abingdon Press

Nuechterlein, Anne Marie, and Celia Hahn. 1990. *The Male-Female Church Staff: Celebrating the Gifts, Confronting the Challenge.* New York: Alban Institute

O'Neil, John. 1996. *The Poverty of Postmodernism.* London: Routledge

Park, Robert. 1950. *Race and Culture.* Ed. by Everett C. Hughes. Glencoe, IL: The Free Press

Peachey, Paul. 1954. *Die soziale Herkunft der schweizerishen Täufer in der Reformationszeit.* Karlsruhe: Mennonite Central Committee

Penner, Horst. 1978. *Die ost- und westpreussischen Mennoniten in ihrem religioesen and socialen Leben in ihren Kulturellen und wirtschaftlichen Leistungen.* Weierhof: Mennonitischer Geschichtsverein

Peters, Marilyn, Anneke Welcker, and M.M. Mattijssen-Berkman Doorwert. 1990. 'Mennonite Women in the Netherlands.' *Mennonite Encyclopedia*, vol. 5. Scottdale, PA: Herald Press

Pigades, L. 1991. 'Language Change and Language Stability of the Ethnic Press in Canada during the Twentieth Century.' *Canadian Ethnic Studies* 13: 3–11

Preheim, Rich. 1995. 'Bluffton College Enrollment Rises 75 Percent in 10 Years.' *Mennonite Weekly Review* 73: 1–2

Rawlyk, George A., ed. 1990. *The Canadian Protestant Experience, 1760–1990.* Burlington, ON: Welsh

Redekop, Calvin W. 1969. *The Old Colony Mennonites: Dilemmas of Minority Life.* Baltimore, MD: Johns Hopkins University Press

Redekop, Calvin W., Stephen C. Ainlay, and Robert Siemens. 1995. *Mennonite Entrepreneurs.* Baltimore: Johns Hopkins University Press

Redekop, Calvin W., and Samuel J. Steiner. 1988. *Mennonite Identity: Historical and Contemporary Perspectives.* Lanham, MD: University Press of America

Redekop, Gloria Neufeld. 1990. 'The Understanding of Woman's Place among Mennonite Brethren in Canada: A Question of Biblical Interpretation.' *Conrad Grebel Review* 8: 259–74

Redekop, John H. 1991. 'A Perspective on Anabaptism in Canada.' In John R. Burkholder and Barbara N. Gingerich, eds., *Mennonite Peace Theology: A Panorama of Types.* Akron, PA: Mennonite Central Committee

Redfield, Robert. 1956. *Peasant Society and Culture.* Chicago: University of Chicago Press

Reid, Angus. 1996. *Shakedown: How the New Economy Is Changing Our Lives.* Toronto: Doubleday

Reimer, Priscilla B. 1990. *Mennonite Artist: Insider as Outsider.* Winnipeg: Main Access Gallery

Reisman, David. 1950. *The Lonely Crowd.* New Haven, CT: Yale University Press

Rokeach, M. 1973. *The Nature of Human Values.* New York: The Free Press

Sauder, Renee. 1993. 'Women in Pastoral Ministry: Survey and Reports.' Elkhart, IN: Mennonite Board of Missions

Sawatsky, Harry Leonard. 1971. *They Sought a Country.* Berkeley: University of California Press

Schlabach, Theron F. 1988. *Peace, Faith, Nation: Mennonites and Amish in Nineteenth-Century America.* Scottdale, PA: Herald Press

Schipani, Daniel. 1991. 'An Emerging Neo-Sectarian Pacifism.' In John R. Burkholder, and Barbara N. Gingerich, eds., *Mennonite Peace Theology: A Panorama of Types.* Akron, PA: Mennonite Central Committee

Schludermann, Shirin, and Eduard Schludermann. 1990. 'Beliefs and Practices of Students in Mennonite and Catholic Schools.' *Journal of Mennonite Studies* 8: 173–88

– 1994. 'Values of Winnipeg Adolescents in Mennonite and Catholic Schools.' *Journal of Mennonite Studies* 13: 130–45

Scott, J., and H. Schuman. 1988. 'Attitude Strength and Social Action in the Abortion Dispute.' *American Sociological Review* 53: 85–101

Seidman, Steven. 1994. *Contested Knowledge: Social Theory in the Postmodern Era.* Oxford: Blackwell

Shore, Marlene. 1987. *The Science of Social Redemption: McGill, the Chicago School, and the Origins of Social Research in Canada.* Toronto: University of Toronto Press

Sider, Ronald J. 1987. *Completely Pro-Life: Abortion, the Family, Nuclear War, the Poor.* Downers, IL: InterVarsity Press

Simmel, Georg. 1950. *The Sociology of Georg Simmel.* Edited by Kurt Wolff. Glencoe, IL: The Free Press

– 1955. *Conflict and the Web of Group Affiliations.* Glencoe, IL: The Free Press

Smith, Michael Peter. 1992. 'Postmodernism, Urban Ethnography, and the New Social Space of Ethnic Identity.' *Theory and Society* 21: 493–531

Snyder, C. Arnold. 1995. *Anabaptist History and Thought: An Introduction.* Kitchener, ON: Pandora Press

Stachniak, Eva. 1991. 'Canadian Reflections: The Images of Canada and Poland in the Polish Ethnic Press (1908–89).' *Canadian Ethnic Studies* 23: 1–10

Stayer, James M. 1991. *The German Peasant's War and Anabaptist Community of Goods.* Montreal: McGill-Queen's University Press

Suderman, Robert J. 1981. 'Liberation Pacifism.' In John R. Burkholder and Barbara N. Gingerich, eds., *Mennonite Peace Theology: A Panorama of Types.* Akron, PA: Mennonite Central Committee

Swanson, Louis E. 1989. 'The Rural Development Dilemmas.' *Resources for the Future* 96: 14–16

Tamney, J.B., S.D. Johnson, and R. Burrton. 1992. 'The Abortion Controversy: Conflicting Beliefs and Values in American Society.' *Journal for the Scientific Study of Religion* 31: 32–46

Tapscott, Don. 1998. *Growing Up Digital: The Rise of the Net Generation.* New York: McGraw-Hill

Taylor, Mark C. 1984. 'Erring: A Postmodern A/Theology.' In Mark C. Taylor, *Erring: A Postmodern A/Theology.* Chicago: University of Chicago Press

Tiessen, Hildi. 1995. *Conrad Grebel College, Undergraduate Calendar, 1995–97.* Waterloo, ON: Conrad Grebel College

Tocqueville, Alexis de. 1969. *Democracy in America.* Trans. by George Lawrence. New York: Doubleday

Toews, John B. 1981. 'The Emergence of German Industry in the South German Colonies.' *Mennonite Quarterly Review* 55: 289–371

Toews, John E., Valerie Rempel, and Katie Funk Wiebe. 1992. *Your Daughters Shall Prophesy: Women in Ministry in the Church.* Hillsboro, KS: Kindred Press

Toews, Paul. 1995. *Mennonite Idealism and Higher Education: The Story of the Fresno Pacific College Idea.* Fresno, CA: Center for Mennonite Brethren Studies

Toynbee, Arnold J. 1954. *A Study of History.* London: Oxford University Press

Tribe, L.H. 1990. *Abortion: The Clash of Absolutes.* New York: W.W. Norton

Unruh, C.P. 1913. Certification of Henry W. Fisher as constable for the Neuanlage Mennonite Church by C.P. Unruh, 26 April 1913

Urry, James. 1989. *None But Saints: The Transformation of Mennonite Life in Russia, 1789–1889.* Winnipeg: Hyperion

van den Berghe, Pierre L. 1981. *The Ethnic Phenomenon.* New York: Elsevier

van der Zijpp, N. 1959. 'Status of Women: Netherlands.' *Mennonite Encyclopedia*, vol. 4. Scottdale, PA: Mennonite Publishing House

Vankooten, G.C. 1987. 'A Socioeconomic Model of Agriculture: A Proposal for Dealing with Environmental Problems in Rural Economy.' *Prairie Forum* 12: 157–68

Warman Commission of Inquiry. 1908. Proceedings of the Commission of Inquiry by the Deputy Attorney General and Deputy Commissioner of Education into Mennonite Private Schools, held at Warman, Saskatchewan, 28 and 29 December 1908

Weber, Max. 1956. *The Protestant Ethic and the Spirit of Capitalism.* New York: Scribner

Wiebe, Armin. 1984. *The Salvation of Yasch Siemens.* Winnipeg: Turnstone

Wiebe, Joel. 1994. *Remembering ... Reaching: A Vision for Service.* Fresno, CA: Fresno Pacific College

Wiebe, Katie Funk. 1992. 'Women in the Mennonite Brethren Church.' In John E. Toews, Valerie Rempel and Katie Funk Wiebe, eds., *Your Daughters Shall Prophesy.* Hillsboro, KS: Kindred Press

Wiebe, Rudy H. 1962. *Peace Shall Destroy Many.* Toronto: McClelland & Stewart

Wittgenstein, Ludwig. 1965. 'Lecture on Ethnics.' *The Philosophical Review* 74: 3–12

Wuthnow, Robert. 1981. 'Two Traditions in the Study of Religion.' *Journal for the Scientific Study of Religion* 20: 16–22

– 1987. *Meaning and Moral Order.* Berkeley: University of California Press

– 1988a. *The Restructuring of American Religion.* Princeton, NJ: Princeton University Press

– 1988b. *The Struggle for America's Soul: Evangelicals, Liberals, and Secularism.* Grand Rapids, MI: Eerdmans

Yoder, John. 1995. 'From Monastery to Marketplace: Idea and Mission in Graduate and Professional Programs at Fresno Pacific College.' In Paul Toews, ed., *Mennonite Idealism and Higher Education: The Story of the Fresno Pacific College Idea.* Fresno, CA: Center for Mennonite Brethren Studies

Yoder, John Howard. 1964. *The Christian Witness to the State.* Newton, KS: Faith and Life Press

- 1972a. *The Original Revolution*. Scottdale, PA: Herald Press
- 1972b. *The Politics of Jesus*. Grand Rapids, MI: Eerdmans
- 1984. *The Priestly Kingdom: Social Ethics as Gospel*. Notre Dame, IN: Notre Dame University Press

Zolf, Dorothy. 1989. 'Comparisons of Multicultural Broadcasting in Canada and Four Other Countries.' *Canadian Ethnic Studies* 21: 13–26

Zorrilla, Hugo. 1988. *The Good News of Justice*. Scottdale, PA: Herald Press

Index